Children in Adult Prisons

Children in Adult Prisons
An International Perspective

Edited by
Katarina Tomasevski

 Frances Pinter (Publishers), London

© Defence for Children International 1986

First published in Great Britain in 1986 by
Frances Pinter (Publishers) Limited
25 Floral Street, London WC2E 9DS

British Library Cataloguing in Publication Data
Children in adult prisons: an international perspective.
  1. Child prisoners
  I. Defence For Children International
  II. Tomasevski, Katarina
  365   HV9069

ISBN 0-86187-617-2

Typeset by Folio Photosetting, Bristol
Printed by SRP Ltd, Exeter

Contents

List of tables

viii   *List of tables*

---

* These tables are based on data collected in the DCI Exploratory Study. Since it has not been possible to check the reliability of information for all the countries surveyed against other sources, the DCI will welcome all corrections and additions to the information given herein.

Foreword

The plight of imprisoned children everywhere represents a dramatic human problem which demands the urgent attention of a caring world. In the past, newspaper and other media reports have evoked widespread pity for the suffering of these young people, but have fallen short of provoking concrete action which would improve the quality of their lives.

While the great majority of these children are really victims of severe poverty, many of them street children forced to violate laws in order to survive, they are incarcerated as criminals. The desperation which drove them to unlawful acts and the social marginalization which they already suffer are reinforced by imprisonment. Often cast out by the communities and even their families, these boys and girls are in profound need of care, protection and understanding — not further alienation and stigmatization as delinquents. These young survivors demand our support rather than our punishment, respect and re-integration into society rather than jail and further deprivation.

Children of the poor, and particularly street children, often lack both the skills and the opportunity to make possible the survival in dignity of themselves and their families. Long hours of work frequently deprive them of precisely the education and training they require for regular employment and the possibility of becoming useful and proud members of their communities. Prison seldom affords any such preparedness, condemning them instead to a lifetime of marginalization and even criminality. All too frequently, young people imprisoned with the idea of reforming their behaviour leave the jail even less able to cope with the outside world than before.

Clearly, new alternatives to the incarceration of children must be found — alternatives rooted in the community and designed to prevent the crime rather than to punishing the offender. It must also be recognized that all children have undeniable rights — in the home and community, in city streets and workplaces, and even in prison if they suffer that misfortune. They are first and foremost children, and the shortcomings of their special situation should not deprive them of their childhoods.

In expressing, with other agencies of the United Nations, its concern for the all-too-often deplorable situation of children in prison, UNICEF does not forget that the first priority for children is to physically survive their earliest years. This chronological priority would have little point, however, without a commitment to the idea that the young life saved must also be a life worth living.

We are pleased to have been able to help finance the study which has led to the writing of this book, and we sincerely hope the results will stimulate positive action by governments and non-governmental organizations towards help for those young people who are, or could be, behind barred windows and locked doors.

James P. Grant
Executive Director
United Nations Children's Fund

Acknowledgements

The contents of this book constitute one of the basic documents resulting from the Exploratory Study on Children in Adult Prisons. Alongside it are national surveys undertaken by researchers in the twenty-seven countries encompassed by the first phase of the Study; a study on alternatives to imprisonment written by Daniel O'Donnell; and the Final Report on the Exploratory Study on Children in Adult Prisons prepared by Sanford Fox. They are being made available as documents in their own right.

The number of persons who assisted in the carrying out of research and in the writing of the findings and reports is well above a hundred. First and foremost, we are indebted to Professor Sanford Fox who had developed the questionnaire for national surveys and co-ordinated the research aspect of the Exploratory Study. Since some of the national researchers requested anonymity, and several national reports were co-authored by individuals and/or independent bodies, we are not identifying them by name here but expressing our great appreciation to all. We are also grateful to the members of the Advisory Panel set up for the Exploratory Study for their on-going guidance and assistance, in particular to Martin Ennals, Yvonne Tolman-Guillard, Alan Grounds, and representatives of the International Commission of Jurists, Rädda Barnen, Terre des Hommes-FGR, UNSDRI and UNICEF-Geneva. The International Secretariat of Amnesty International provided invaluable assistance in collecting information on political repression against children. Moreover, Alan Grounds of the AI British Section Working Group on Children was indispensable in obtaining the most elusive data and we thank him for his commitment to this project. Tina Dolgopol, Martin Ennals, Daniel O'Donnell and Per Tegmo assisted in the structuring, editing and presentation of the reports of the Exploratory Study, and Francis Parakatil took care of the administrative co-ordination of the Study. Mrs. Carry Dikshoorn kindly assisted with editing and corrections of the manuscript. Finally, we express our gratitude to the various bodies that provided financial support for the Children in Prison Project: Joseph Rowntree Social Service Trust (UK), Rädda Barnen (Sweden), Terre des Hommes (FRG), Dutch Inter-Church Aid, Central Union for Child Welfare (Finland), '1% for Development'

(UN Staff Fund, Geneva), Council of Europe, Ministry of Foreign Affairs of Norway and Denmark, UNICEF, European Human Rights Foundation, Commune of Florence and Migros Foundation (Switzerland). This is not an exhaustive list of the individuals and organizations who contributed to carrying out the Study: we are also thankful to all those who have not been, or did not wish to be, mentioned.

Defence for Children International
Geneva, August 1985

1 Introduction: the Defence for Children International Exploratory Study on children in adult prisons

The following extracts are from material collected by the Defence for Children International Exploratory Study. Throughout the book quotations from this material will be printed in italics and the source indicated only by the name of the country referred to. The material is kept at DCI, Geneva, and is available on request.

These places should not be permitted to allow kids into them because they don't really have a chance in this society. The ones that don't get hurt or molested usually end up twice as tough as when they came in. When a kid starts in this system at a young age, you can be sure that they will be returning.
> Response from a Canadian adult prisoners' association
> to the DCI questionnaire on children in adult prisons

The threatening physical implications of jailing a juvenile in an adult facility are no better illustrated than by reviewing the number of juvenile suicides in jails.
> United States

During a period of depression the minor procures a sharp object (razor blade, broken glass) and tries to cut veins on one or both of his hands . . . The self-mutilations have a contagious nature to the effect that an establishment can well be without a single case of self-mutilation for weeks in a row and then find itself, all at once, in the midst of a series of cases over a few days, without anybody being able to state the exact reason.
> France

No welfare officer or social worker ever visited the prisoners. The prisoners felt alienated from society. Desperation, a horror of their situation, and total helplessness was apparent in the younger inmates, between eleven and fourteen. Hopelessness about the future was felt by most of them.
> Pakistan

During my stay at the District Prison I ascertained that the human dignity of prisoners was intentionally and systematically violated, that prisoners were beaten and flogged, that prisoners' labour was rigorously exploited, that prisoners did not have the health protection needed, that disciplinary sanctions

1

were being executed in violation of the law, that the penal institution was not immune to corruption, that outside supervision was inadequate.
Testimony of a criminologist, Yugoslavia

He did not like the 'boss' of the cell and when he refused their sexual advances, he was told 'they would make a woman of me'. He was regularly assaulted by the other inmates, and the last thing he remembers was being hit over the head several times with a broom. He was apparently raped and later found himself in hospital. He is now physically and mentally disabled.
South Africa

When young prisoners are accommodated in the cells, they are in continuous communication with adult prisoners. Indeed, there is a recognized system of hierarchy and the young prisoners are at the lowest rung of the ladder. They are, therefore, subject to maltreatment both from older inmates and from the wardens. When, as sometimes happens, they are beaten up by adult prisoners, they must not report to the authorities. They are exposed to other, more criminal tendencies, e.g. robbery and smoking of Indian hemp, as well as being subjected to homosexual practices.

Adult prisoners make the young prisoners do all the dirty work, which they detest, like clearing out toilet pails and washing clothes and blankets. Sometimes, the young prisoner's clothes are seized by an adult. Many times the young prisoners are forced by threats of physical violence to carry out instructions from adult prisoners which may be violating prison regulations. Indeed, observations and interviews revealed that young prisoners were more anxious to abide by rules and regulations set up in their cells by adult prisoners than by those of the prison authorities.
Nigeria

The DCI Exploratory Study on Children in Adult Prisons has been the first attempt at systematic analysis of the fate of children imprisoned with adults world-wide. The study started from the assumption that imprisonment of children with adults — for whatever reason, for whatever length of time, in whatever facilities — does occur everywhere. Research and information-gathering activities confirmed the initial assumption: imprisonment of children with adults is a universal phenomenon.

At this early stage of the study it was not possible to conduct surveys in all countries, neither was it possible to have a representative sample of the countries of the world. Irrespective of the country surveyed, however, it was revealed that children were incarcerated with adults.

The exploratory study included empirical surveys carried out in a number of selected countries, analyses of responses from governments to requests for information on children imprisoned with adults, and a number of inter-governmental and non-governmental sources of information on the implementation of obligations concerning the rights of children. While the data gathered are fragmentary, the use of different sources of information has ascertained the scope of the existing information. As had been presumed at the initiation of the exploratory study, the subject of children in prison has been neglected by the relevant inter-governmental and non-governmental organizations. There is no consistent information-gathering or international action. Gaps in legislative protection of imprisoned children and similar gaps in statistical coverage of the youngest inmates testify to the urgency of the protection of rights of children in this area where they are jeopardized most.

The lack of data dictated the narrowing of the exploratory study to areas and issues where at least fragmentary information was available. Consequently, this book has a message to convey by what it excludes as much as by what it includes — its purpose is to alert the world to the necessity of becoming informed about imprisoned children. Experiences during the research carried out so far show that the lack of information about imprisoned children does not mean that there are no children in this category. Surveys of countries varying from Denmark to Colombia, from Zaire to Yugoslavia, have demonstrated that children do get imprisoned with adults in every country: as suspects of alleged crimes, as illegal immigrants, as truants, as beggars, as 'uncontrollable', as witnesses to adults' crimes or as hostages in states of siege.

The purpose of this book is to shed some light on the nature and scope of the problem of children imprisoned with adults. Neither all the issues envisaged in the original research outline nor all the countries selected for empirical surveys could be included. Faced with the dilemma of using incomplete data or waiting until information gaps could be closed, we opted for presenting the problem and illustrating our findings with as much information as we could obtain. The underlying reasoning is simple: the problem of lack of information on imprisoned children will be overcome solely by continuation of information-gathering and international action. Inability to collect all the information needed would have been a weak justification for not publishing the information available.

The DCI policy has been to endorse the principle that children should never be imprisoned, least of all with adults. That approach requires challenging laws and practices which demand or at least tolerate imprisonment of children with adults. Existing conditions require the inclusion of analyses of the treatment of imprisoned children and advocacy of palliative measures to offset some of the worst effects of imprisonment. This does not mean the betrayal of the principle that children should not be imprisoned at all, but pragmatic recognition that plenty of time and effort have to be devoted to the realization of that objective, and that imprisoned children have to be helped in the meantime.

The book focuses on the nature and scope of the problem of imprisonment of children as a global phenomenon. It was not possible to include all the findings from the empirical part of the study — prison conditions, treatment of children in adult prisons, statements from the imprisoned children themselves. National surveys resulted in a wealth of factual information which requires further analysis. This book only summarizes some of the findings relating to those topics which have been identified as being of universal concern from the viewpoint of rights and interests of children.

The exploratory study was initiated in December 1982 and its investigatory phase encompassed 1983 and 1984. The study originated from concern about the fate of children incarcerated in adult penal facilities. Information reaching the DCI was both disquieting and fragmentary; it was therefore decided to make an effort to investigate the problem in depth and on a world-wide basis.

The initial research outline, developed in December 1982 and January 1983, emphasized the DCI concern

about both the principle of such detention and actual and alleged consequences for the children involved such as: physical and sexual abuse by other inmates or staff, physical and emotional neglect, severe malnutrition, physical and mental illness left without treatment, suicide, psychological trauma, integration into a criminal way of life. In addition, of course, children who are incarcerated tend to be relatively disadvantaged, and their incarceration simply serves to reinforce this disadvantage.

The goal of the exploratory study was defined in the following terms: *to shed light on the nature and scope of the problem of children detained in facilities where adults are incarcerated, and to advance proposals for action to promote and defend the interests of children in this respect.*

The study was based on the assumption that there are always better alternatives to the imprisonment of children, children being defined as persons up to the age of eighteen years. The basic philosophy has been expressed as:

> *the belief that it should never be necessary to place children in custodial facilities with adults as a result of their alleged or actual criminal behaviour, and the conviction that the state's treatment of children explicitly or implicitly in its care should be judged on the same criteria as those used to assess whether or not parents are fit to care for their children.*

The problem of defining 'children' is one not likely ever to be solved. Any age-categorization is fundamentally arbitrary. Any universally applicable age-classifications neglect differences in age structure of the population in various parts of the world and changes in the process of reaching adulthood. Yet, arbitrary as they may be, age-categorizations are necessary to determine the framework within which children are entitled to special protection.

The determination of age-limits for children to be exempted from the adult system of criminal justice has been a controversial issue throughout the exploratory study. However, the study was based on the definition of *the child as any person up to the age of eighteen years*. The initial research design for the investigation of children in adult prisons adopted eighteen as the demarcation line between childhood and adulthood. While basic international instruments on the rights of the child endorse that definition, the research team was aware of differences existing in penal legislation and in statistics both between and within countries. The case of the right of children to special protection *as children* requires consistency. There is none in practice. The interests of children demand the analysis of inconsistent practices from the viewpoint of their rights; international standards on the rights of children entitle them to special procedures and treatment, outside the adult system of criminal justice.

The results of the investigation carried out within the exploratory study show an enormous diversity of laws and practices with respect to age-categorizations within the system of criminal justice. Promising signs of an emerging system of juvenile justice can be discerned, but there is as yet no 'case' for a change of the age-determination on the international level. Therefore, eighteen as the dividing line between childhood and adulthood remains the basic definition of the study.

The original research outline specified that all children incarcerated in adult penal facilities should be included in the investigation:

> *The scope of the research is not limited by any reason why children are held in adult facilities: it includes children who are there solely because a parent is an inmate, because a child is destitute, abandoned, or a 'status offender' (a child who violates a law applicable only to children's conduct, e.g. truancy), or because the child is in the care, or is the responsibility of, the state and there is 'no other place' to keep him or her, as well as because the child has been charged or convicted of criminal conduct.*

Incarceration of children in specialized (children's or juvenile) custodial facilities has been excluded from the exploratory study. It was decided that an investigation into the problem of children in adult facilities should be the exclusive topic for this first study. Still, the narrowing of the scope of the study to adult facilities did not exclude prisons termed otherwise. Basic terms for that part of the investigation were defined as follows:

> *'Prison' does not necessarily mean the incarceration of juveniles convicted of an offence in institutions bearing the name 'prison' or 'jail' . . . many other establishments are called by names ('rehabilitation centres', 'training units', 'camps', etc.) which may mask the reality of their purposes and the conditions of detention, and which can be assimilated with the prisons as such.*

> *Facilities where adults are incarcerated are defined as any facility in which adults are housed who are deprived of their liberty because they are suspected of, charged with, or convicted of a criminal offence. . . . children are considered to be detained in facilities where adults are incarcerated when they are or may be kept overnight in such facilities under conditions which permit at least visual or auditory communication between children and adult inmates.*

Information available indicated that the problem of incarceration of children in adult facilities was universal:

> *It seemed that the phenomenon was, in different forms and for different reasons, apparently universal in incidence: children were in prison in countries on all continents and with very different socio-political and economic realities.*
> *. . . despite the universality of the problem and the seriousness of its effects, there is little or no research into its many facets from an international standpoint, and there are few conclusive investigations even at the national level.*

One of the aims of the study has been to initiate consistent information-gathering on children in prison. The first study carried out could not fill such a large information gap. Results obtained within the exploratory study are far from representative either by the criterion of the seriousness of problems or of countries where children suffer most. The dissemination of results of the exploratory study is coupled with an invitation to correct and supplement the data the DCI could collect.

The exploratory study did, however, confirm the initial assumptions: the problem of children in adult prisons is both serious and universal. Results obtained so far provide sufficient grounds to affirm the accuracy of the initial assumption: there always is a better alternative to the imprisonment of children with adults. A great deal of effort will be needed to make such alternatives workable. Still, the DCI's principal orientation is to assess the problem and advocate alternatives from the viewpoint of the rights and interests of children. The aim of the study was formulated in the following manner:

The aims of the study are to determine the incidence, by sex and age, of the incarceration of children in adult prisons, to identify risk situations, specifying effects on children, and to define required action at all levels to combat the practice, with special reference to existing or needed international and national legal texts and declarations. The importance to be attached to such an action is clearly demonstrated by the fact that the act of putting children in prison can be the first step towards the violation of a vast range of their fundamental rights, from health and protection from violence, to family life and harmonious development.

8 Rights of the child approach to child delinquency

The International Seminar on Children in Prison with Adults was convened in Florence in December 1984 to bring together participants in the DCI Exploratory Study and examine possibilities of a follow-up based on general conclusions of the empirical part of the study. One of the major conclusions of the seminar addressed the issue of obligations of the state towards children in the following terms: *'States must recognize their responsibility for the development of children in such a way that children are neither victimized nor criminalized.'*

National surveys in a number of countries identified children exposed to conditions and circumstances conducive to crime. Some of them subsequently commit crimes themselves. But all children who are brought into adult prisons are victimized in some way. If children are put into a situation where they ought not to be they cannot be held responsible for the way they act in such circumstances. This assertion suggests a chain of responsibilities for *preventing* children from exposure to conditions generating crime: the principal responsibility for securing the rights of the child rests with the family. However, states have reserved for themselves the right to intervene if the interests of the child so require. Also, the recognition of child rights put states into the position of acting *in loco parentis*: the absence or inadequacy of family care and custody does not mean quenching the rights of the child — states undertook an obligation to provide special protection for all children.

International law spells out the rights of children and the obligations of states to recognize and realize those rights. The fundamental provision states that all children are, without any discrimination, entitled to special protection from the family, from society and from the state. Moreover, by the ratification of relevant international instruments[1] and by national laws states specified their obligations towards children. The recognition of child rights provides a legal basis for *requiring* states to implement their obligations but it has to be emphasized that *what* states say does not mean that their living up to their words can be taken for granted.

Some quotations from states' reports on their implementation of their obligations toward children are given here to show that, at least in principle, states accept the obligation to act *in loco parentis*:[2]

Bulgaria: 'As children [all the children within the jurisdiction of the government] are entitled to the same care and protection from the State.' (E/1980/6/Add.29, p. 10);

Canada: 'All provinces and territories make statutory provisions for the intervention of the public authority or its delegated representative when children under a specified age (16, 17 or 18) appear to be neglected or in need of protection ... In turn, the federal government contributes to the cost of services to these children and their families under cost-sharing arrangement with the provinces.' (E/1980/6/Add.32, p. 33);

Chile: 'In the area of assistance, the country has numerous institutions, both state and private, for protecting infants and adolescents, and for several decades has had extensive legislation on the subject ... It established the National Service for Minors (Servicio Nacional de Menores), a body subordinate to the Ministry of Justice and "responsible for carrying out any measures necessary to assist and protect young people ..."' (E/1980/6/Add.4, p. 3);

Denmark: 'It is the duty of the social welfare committee to look into the conditions under which children are living and to support parents in the upbringing and care of their children. Where a child is assumed to be in need of support, the social welfare committee shall offer special guidance and support ... It is the duty of the local authorities to provide adequate accommodation for children and young persons in institutions.' (E/1980/6/Add.15, pp. 3–4);

Federal Republic of Germany: 'Under the Youth Welfare Act every German child has the right to an adequate education so that he can develop his physical, emotional, and social abilities and capacities. It is primarily up to the parents to safeguard this right. The state intervenes in the framework of youth assistance programmes only where the child's right to education is not guaranteed by his family.' (E/1980/6/Add.10, p. 15);

India: 'The National Policy for Children, adopted on 22 August 1974, envisaged that adequate services be provided to children both before and after birth and through the period of growth to ensure full physical, mental, and social development. This policy also envisages the increase in the scope of such services, so that all children in the

country will enjoy optimal conditions within a reasonable time.' (E/
1980/6/Add.34, p. 8);

Italy: '[the constitutional principle is equality of all citizens]
whatever may be their condition, including personal and social
conditions, and the consequent task of the state to remove the
obstacles of an economic and social nature which *de facto* hinder the
full development of the human being.' (E/1980/6/Add.31, p. 30);

Spain: 'Direct action by the state takes the form of maintaining and
supporting centres for children lacking a home environment . . . a
public investment programme for the construction of day-care
centres . . . lastly, the National Social Welfare Fund has a budgetary
appropriation for helping non-profit agencies or institutions that
care for neglected infants and disadvantaged children.' (E/1980/6/
Add.28, p. 12);

United Kingdom: 'Statutory responsibility for the protection of
children and young persons is vested in the local authorities . . . a
local authority may seek from the courts an order either placing a
child in the local authority's care, or making the authority
responsible for the supervision of his welfare, where it is considered
that his proper development is being prevented or neglected, his
health is being impaired or neglected, or he is being ill-treated . . .' (E/
1980/6/Add.16, p. 13).

It is a truism that not all children enjoy equal conditions for
development, some of them do not even have conditions sufficient
for survival. On the other hand, it would be utterly incorrect to blame
child delinquency entirely on inadequate living conditions of
children. The balance between two extremes is found in applying
results of vast numbers of criminological studies concerning the
youngest strata of offenders; there are economic, social and political
conditions which influence, sometimes even drive certain categories
of the young to delinquency. As the most vulnerable stratum of
society, children suffer most in any economic, social or political
turmoil. Least capable of supporting themselves, the youngest are
often found within those groups recognized as marginalized in
specific communities. The lack of life-supporting and income-
generating options for the youngest drive them to survive as they can.
They are often in conflict with the law. Being in conflict with the law
places the child in a controversial situation: the child is treated as if it

were an adult because actually it behaved as if it were an adult. Legally and morally, the child should not have been forced into adult-type behaviour in the first place. However, this 'should not' does not help thousands of children caught stealing to survive.

One of the tasks of this book is to raise some of the issues illustrating why certain categories of children are driven to delinquency; to identify those economic, social and political conditions which seem to be most conducive to child delinquency, and to determine to what extent such conditions can be attributed to states, i.e. how much child delinquency can be traced to the non-implementation of govenmental obligations toward children.

The DCI Exploratory Study did not envisage inquiries into motives and underlying causes of delinquency leading to the imprisonment of children. However, some of the findings of the national surveys indicated the need to take into account economic, social, and political conditions as conducive to delinquency, ultimately leading to imprisonment of children.

> *The national survey of Morocco states that the largest number of offences committed is attributed to boys aged fourteen to sixteen. Most of those boys do not have access to education, nor do they have employment. Also, most of those boys are found in towns (only 19 per cent of child delinquents are of rural origin). Rapid urbanization and massive rural exodus are identified as underlying causes of child delinquency.*
>
> *In India, 77 per cent of the imprisoned boys interviewed were too poor to go to school, or to hire a lawyer to defend them.*
>
> *In Pakistan only 16 per cent of the imprisoned children are literate. Most of them either belonged to very poor families or had no family at all.*
>
> *The survey for Costa Rica notes, for example, 'a recent increase in the Dickensian phenomenon of parents who depend on criminally generated income of their children'.*
>
> *In Chile, since the military coup, juvenile delinquency, drug abuse, prostitution and vagabondism are consequences of a social system in crisis and of economic policies adopted by the regime which reduced large sections of the population to poverty.*
>
> *While political, economic, and social circumstances remain unchanged, rehabilitation of delinquent minors will not attain its objectives. Once the rehabilitation is finished, the minor is confronted with a society which denies him any opportunity to study or to work, which denies him all the basic rights. The minor remains in a disadvantaged position, with every possibility of renewed delinquency.*

We have learned that existing research into problems of imprisoned children starts too late and ends too soon: it begins at the entry of a child into a police cell, detention camp or prison, and finishes upon the release of the child from custody. The results of the research thus demonstrate the 'how', but do not even tackle the 'why'. The results of the national surveys more often than not included descriptions of particular conditions in the country affecting the delinquency and imprisonment of children. Thus, the survey of Chile has been divided into two parts, the first dealing with political imprisonment of children and the second dealing with delinquents of children; the survey of Yugoslavia showed the lack of even statistical data for recent years on imprisonment for offences against public security; the survey of Colombia revealed the release of children from prison being dependent on repayment of the value of the goods stolen by the child; the survey of Morocco could not be carried out in its empirical phase because of the denial of access to prisons.

Every piece of research indicated a set of problems specific for the particular country. In such conditions, drawing generalizations is difficult. Yet, the results of the research revealed identical or similar patterns which can be identified as common features. For example:

— the insufficiency of the resources allocated to facilities and treatment for imprisoned children is a major obstacle to their adequate treatment in custody;
— the majority of child inmates come from socially disadvantaged strata;
— the objective of rehabilitation of delinquents, particularly of the youngest ones, is not being achieved by the present penal systems;
— the chronic overcrowding of prisons is a universal feature.

It had not been the intention of the study to analyse *reasons* for the imprisonment of children, whether for delinquency, vagrancy, illegal entry into a country, or matters of security. The study focused on the conditions and treatment of imprisoned children, whatever the reason for imprisonment might have been. The national surveys revealed a range of types of incarceration of children which national researchers emphasized as being unacceptable from the viewpoint of the rights of the child. The Florence seminar brought together information and experiences were exchanged. The discussion of reasons for the incarceration of children resulted in the following assessment:

Concern for the underlying causes that bring children into conflict with the law, or in some countries with an under-trained or under-accountable police force, tended to overshadow the question of mere law-breaking in many of the examples given.

The fact that the majority of children detained have been charged with offences against property, or the person, or with drug, public order or political offences, contrasted with a number of cases cited where children are imprisoned for what is seen to be 'their own good' or in preference to something that is seen to be 'worse'.

In Zaire, the children of a convicted thief may be put in prison because the judge wishes to protect them from the aggrieved families whose goods were stolen.

In Tanzania, children may commit crimes so as to be put in prison, where they are better fed than outside.

In Costa Rica, the authorities practise rehabilitation, and children are held in prison only for 'practical' or 'humane' reasons, e.g. when considered dangerous or, in the case of pregnant teenage girls, because a children's home is considered unsuitable.

Other reasons discussed were court backlogs (Belgium), homelessness or abandonment (practised on a daily basis by Yugoslav emigré *parents in France), internal migration (Africa) and discriminatory immigration law (England).*

General prevention of child delinquency: the obligation of states to provide special protection for all children

The general postulate of criminology that prevention is always better than repression applies fully to child delinquency. Prevention of child delinquency has commonly been classified on three levels:

(1) primary prevention — policies aimed at raising living standards of the population and at satisfying basic needs;
(2) secondary prevention — policies and measures specifically targeted at children exposed to conditions which might lead to delinquency;
(3) tertiary prevention — treatment and rehabilitation of delinquent children.

The prevention of child delinquency requires the consideration of the interrelationship between welfare policies and the increase or decrease of delinquency at the lowest possible level of observation —

in a city, a local community, etc. The general postulate of modern criminology is that the improvement of living conditions on an equitable basis is the best method of crime prevention.

That criminological truism has been fully supported by the international law on the rights of the child. The International Covenant on Economic, Social and Cultural Rights, which spells out the obligations of the state towards children, established a procedure whereby states submit periodic reports on the degree of the realization of the guaranteed rights. It is worth noting that the subject of child delinquency is found in the section on the protection of children and young persons, entitled as follows: 'special measures for the care and education of children separated from their mothers or deprived of a family; physically, mentally or socially handicapped children; and delinquent minors.'[3]

It is important to note that United Nations' policy proposals for the treatment of juvenile delinquents refer usually to the fifteen to twenty-five age group and emphasize primary and secondary prevention.

The interregional preparatory meeting for the Seventh UN Congress on the Prevention of Crime and Treatment of Offenders agreed on a set of recommendations on the topic 'Youth, Crime, and Justice'. The first four recommendations are the following:

(1) Every effort should be made to ensure that youth have the right to and facilities for full participation in national development, in particular with respect to work, education, political participation, legal facilities, and cultural activities.
(2) The family should be supported and strengthened because of its role in the socialization of the young and in the prevention of juvenile delinquency.
(3) Educational systems should be evaluated to ascertain whether they were relevant for the emotional and social needs of youth and prepared the young for work and leisure activities.
(4) Special attention should be given to the needs of the young and the prevention of delinquency in the urban setting. In particular, *attention should be given to homeless and street children in the urban setting*.[4]

The latest draft of the Standard Minimum Rules for the Administration of Juvenile Justice gives the following explanation of the approach adopted: '. . . fundamental perspectives refer to social policy in general and aim at promoting juvenile welfare to the greatest possible extent, which will minimize the necessity of intervention by the juvenile justice system. This in turn will minimize the harm which may be caused by such intervention.'[5]

That approach has not only been favoured by the relevant international instruments, but accepted by states, as reflected in their reports on implementation.

In its report on policies and services for children in need of care and protection, India refers to Children's Acts which specify the obligations of the state with respect to children in need of care and assistance:

> These legislations [Children's Acts] deal with the treatment and rehabilitation of the socially neglected children, such as the neglected, destitute, victimized, delinquent and exploited. The basic objective underlying the Children's Acts is *the recognition by the State of its obligation to provide general protection for children*. The preamble of the central government's Children's Act of 1960 . . . lays down that the purpose of the legislation, *inter alia*, is to provide for the care, protection, maintenance, welfare, training, education and rehabilitation of neglected or delinquent children. [E/1980/6/Add.34, 15 November, 1983, para. 23, p. 10.]

On the other hand, national legislation often specifies acts or omissions which directly jeopardize rights and interests of children and defines the most serious of those as criminal offences. The Study had adopted the view that States should be evaluated as to their care of children in their custody by the same criteria as parents or guardians. One could draw an analogy between criminal law provisions concerning the care and custody of children by parents and similar duties and obligations of public officials. The example of the legislation of the Federal Republic of Germany can be quoted:

> Section 170b of the Criminal Code provides for the punishment of persons who fail to comply with their duty to pay maintenance, so that the living of the dependent child is jeopardized. . . . According to this section, it is also punishable for a person to grossly neglect his duty to look after a child under 16, thus putting him at risk of leading a criminal life . . .' [E/1980/6/Add. 10, 4 February 1980, p. 17.]

Such an analogy, that is, an evaluation of the governmental policies needed for the prevention of the delinquency of children in contradistinction to their obligations towards children, puts child delinquency into a different perspective. A *rights of the child*

Table 1 Proportion of total central government expenditure on defence, education, health, social and economic services (in percentages)

Country	Public services	Defence	Education	Health	Social welfare	Housing	Community services	Economic services	Agricult./ forestry	Roads	Transport communications	Other purposes
Austria	7.3	2.9	9.6	12.2	45.6	3.2	1.4	12.2	2.4	3.7	3.4	5.7
Bangladesh	...	8.4	10.6	8.5	2.2	n.a.	n.a.	31.7	10.0	n.a.	4.0	...
Bulgaria					*no information*							
Canada	8.2	7.8	3.2	5.2	34.9	2.3	0.7	18.3	2.1	0.2	4.7	20.3
Chile					*no information*							
Colombia					*no information*							
Costa Rica	10.3	2.9	22.6	32.8	11.2	2.9	1.7	14.9	5.2	8.3	0.4	11.6
Denmark					*no information*							
Finland	7.2	5.2	14.0	10.9	28.0	2.7	1.5	26.2	11.8	4.3	4.3	4.3
France					*no information*							
Germany, F.R.	4.2	9.1	0.8	19.3	49.7	0.3	0.1	7.4	0.3	1.4	3.6	9.1
India	6.2	20.2	1.9	2.2	...	4.3	n.a.	24.3	6.6	...	n.a.	40.1
Italy	8.0	3.5	8.9	10.6	33.0	0.6	0.8	10.4	1.6	1.3	4.9	24.9
Jamaica	12.4	2.7	18.4	7.8	3.3	5.8	2.9	22.8	6.7	3.7	2.5	23.8
Japan					*no information*							
Morocco	16.5	16.6	16.2	2.8	5.6	1.0	1.6	30.5	5.6	2.2	9.3	8.9
Netherlands	6.3	5.4	11.9	11.6	37.9	3.0	0.9	11.0	0.9	1.0	2.2	11.9
Nigeria	11.7	23.5	4.5	2.5	2.5	4.1	2.6	32.3	1.7	11.5	10.5	16.4
Pakistan	8.2	33.5	2.2	1.1	5.0	1.8	2.3	31.0	1.4	1.8	8.1	14.9
Romania	0.8	4.6	3.2	0.9	20.3	n.a.	0.3	54.3	6.1	1.1	4.6	15.4
South Africa					*no information*							
Spain	4.2	3.9	7.1	0.6	60.9	1.4	0.9	11.3	3.2	0.7	1.8	9.7
Switzerland	4.7	10.5	3.1	12.8	49.5	0.7	0.3	12.4	4.1	3.7	3.8	6.3
Thailand	9.4	19.9	20.8	5.1	3.2	1.4	0.4	21.2	9.9	6.4	1.2	18.6
United Kingdom					*no information*							
United States	4.9	23.7	1.9	10.7	34.0	2.3	0.3	8.8	3.0	3 1.1	1.2	13.7
Yugoslavia	7.6	50.4	n.a.	n.a.	7.2	n.a.	0.3	16.6	n.a.	...	...	17.9
Zaire	22.6	...	...	...	...	...	2.2	...	...	...	...	26.6

Source: International Monetary Fund – *Government Finance Statistics Yearbook*, vol. VIII, 1984, pp. 28–9.
Note: the figures have been rounded; therefore the total expenditure may not be 100.0%

approach to child delinquency makes it possible to raise issues which are clearly outside the subject of imprisonment of children. One such question is the priority of the needs of children within the resource allocation scheme of a particular state.

It has not been possible to find exact data (absolute or relative figures) on investment in the welfare and development of children as compared with investment in the treatment of child and juvenile delinquency. Instead, some data on resource utilization will be used to show the overall priorities and proportions within governmental expenditure.

Table 1 shows the data for the countries covered by the DCI Exploratory Study according to the major expenditure items used by the International Monetary Fund. The table hardly needs any comment: the figures speak for themselves. Moreover, the topic of this study is far more specific than general resource utilization for the benefit of children. It has been included in this book for the sole purpose of giving the reader an idea of the differences between the countries surveyed, and should be analysed in connection with Table 3. The latter presents UNICEF-selected development indicators relevant to the condition of children in a particular country. The message is the following: the welfare state of the children is not only connected with the present state of economic and social development of the country, but also with the policy adopted. Cutting down expenditure on education or social welfare or housing will be reflected in the condition of children. The use of resources for military expenditure or for the repayment of foreign debt will also have an effect on the state of children. Perhaps the link is not obvious at first sight, but it can be analysed within the framework of competition for investment between various items of expenditure — between civilian and military expenditure, between welfare and economic services.

It seems that the low priority of the needs of children within the state's resource utilization has been determined both by independent researchers and by the United Nations' bodies. Two assessments may be mentioned here. Joan Brown, in her study *Children in Social Security*, concludes: 'Only rarely have the needs of children been the predominant factor in decision-making. Instead, child support has been manipulated to serve other goals, of which the most important have been the maintenance of a wage/benefit gap and the restraint of public expenditure.'[6]

In its latest annual report on the state of the world's children,

UNICEF analyses the effects of the world-wide economic crisis on children. The relative increase of the proportion of children who live below the poverty line has been attributed to the sluggish rates of economic growth and to the cutting down of social and child welfare investments. UNICEF concludes: 'by both hard-headed economic calculation and by the most elementary tenets of human welfare, investment into the health and skills and well-being of children is the most essential investment of all.'[7]

There is another aspect of the lack of investment in the welfare and development of children: if children are not provided for, they have to provide for themselves. Therefore, at a very early age they might be forced into premature adulthood by having to provide for their own needs.

Child labour — whatever else one might say about it — is competitive with education. The ILO prohibitions or discouragement of child labour are based on the idea of labour being allowed after the school-leaving age. Compulsory education generally lasts up to the age of fifteen and employment of children should in principle be prohibited or at least restricted before they reach that age. Yet, one consequence of the prohibition is the lack of data on the work of children under the age of fifteen. Though incomplete, some data are available, as shown in Table 2.

Yet another aspect of such a situation has to be stressed: it is a form of discrimination against children. Children might have to work full time to earn their living, and frequently to support the family, but they do not acquire rights as adults. For most purposes they are treated as children.

Ruth Leger Sivard emphasizes two instances of discrimination against children: 'In 25 countries young men are eligible to go to war at an earlier age than they are eligible to vote. Every minute 30 children die for want of food and inexpensive vaccines and every minute the world's military budget absorbs $1.3 million of the public treasure.'[8] Perhaps those different facets of the position of children could be summarized in the following way: although children have no say in decisions having an impact on their lives, they are the most vulnerable segment of the population. The quotation from Ruth Leger Sivard is a part of her introduction to her surveys of world military and social expenditure, which she calls a report on world priorities.

Table 3 illustrates what its author, Ruth Leger Sivard, calls 'the opportunity cost of military expenditure'. This notion implies that

Table 2 Participation of children in the economically active population by age group (by percentage)

Country	Age group 10–14	Age group 15–19
Austria	—	49.7
Bangladesh	52.0	46.1
Canada	—	46.6
Chile	—	20.6
Costa Rica	13.7	43.5
Denmark	—	48.5
Finland	—	39.3
France	—	18.2
Germany, F.R.	—	42.5
India	5.2	40.7
Italy	—	29.7 (age group 14–19)
Jamaica	—	50.2 (age group 14–19)
Japan	—	18.9
Netherlands	—	26.6
Pakistan	21.5	40.3
Romania	0.4	34.8
Spain	—	41.2 (age group 16–19)
Switzerland	—	54.0
United States	—	49.1 (age range 16–19)
Yugoslavia	—	22.2

Source: ILO 1984 Year Book of Labour Statistics, Geneva, 1985, pp. 13–44.
Note: Data on child labour are scarce and basic data do not exist for many countries. Usually, the legal prohibition of child labour below the age of 15 results in the elimination of the category of working children under 15 from the official statistics. Therefore, data are incomplete and their reliability cannot be presumed. However, the existing information used by the ILO has been given above to illustrate differences in the status of children in different countries — in some, the majority of children will be employed, in others the majority will be full time at school.

security-keeping and human-needs-satisfying demands are competitors for public resources. The outcome of competition for funds can be summarized as a zero-sum-game. The table illustrates to what extent security-keeping demands gain over human needs. Opportunity costs are unmet social, human, developmental needs.

If countries with a significant proportion of the GNP used for military purposes are listed, those whose military expenditure is above 5 per cent, are the following: Chile, Morocco, Pakistan, the United Kingdom and the United States. The burden it imposes on

Table 3   World military and social expenditure, 1983

Country	Military data		Civilian data	
	Public expenditure per capita in US$	*Public expenditure per soldier in US$*	*Economic–social standing*	*Public expenditure per capita in US$*
Austria	118	17,860	17	561
Bangladesh	2	2,167	136	2
Bulgaria	133	7,919	31	176
Canada	195	59,519	11	784
Chile	132	16,545	49	113
Colombia	12	4,575	68	24
Costa Rica	n.a.	none	52	117
Denmark	314	46,000	3	868
Finland	170	20,325	8	585
France	492	53,467	4	599
Germany, F.R.	434	54,018	6	616
India	6	4,032	117	7
Italy	171	26,224	21	321
Jamaica	9	5,000	56	76
Japan	85	41,079	20	524
Morocco	53	9,655	102	53
Netherlands	373	45,887	13	947
Nigeria	30	15,671	104	39
Pakistan	15	2,895	123	5
Romania	61	7,337	35	117
South Africa	81	26,977	64	103
Spain	107	11,708	28	117
Switzerland	331	117,389	12	831
Thailand	26	5,368	85	23
United Kingdom	478	81,386	14	494
United States	632	70,231	9	571
Yugoslavia	113	9,534	46	124
Zaire	7	10,000	118	12

Note: the two columns on the left represent military expenditures in the particular country (current and capital expenditure to meet the needs of the armed forces) expressed in expenditures per capita and per soldier respectively; the two columns on the right consist of 'civilian' measurements, the first one is economic–social rank of the country among all the countries consisting of three factors: GNP per capita, education, and health) on the scale, where rank 1 is held by Sweden, and rank 142 by Chad. The last column represents 'civilian' expenditures per capita, comparable to military expenditures per capita given in the first column.
Source: Sivard, R.L., *World Military and Social Expenditures 1983. An Annual Report on World Priorities.* World Priorities, Washington, 1983, pp. 36–41.
Explanations of the terms used: National *military expenditures* are current and capital expenditures to meet the needs of the armed forces. They include military assistance of the foreign countries and the military components of nuclear and space research and development programmes.

Table 3 (*continued*)

Armed forces represent manpower in the regular forces, including conscripts. Paramilitary forces and reservists are not included.

Economic–social rank is a single figure for each nation to summarize its rank among all nations in economic and social indicators. Three factors are combined: GNP per capita, education, and health. The method of averaging gives equal importance to each of the three elements.

'Civilian' expenditures include public expenditures for education and health care. Public education expenditures represent current and capital expenditures by governments for public education and subsidized private education for pre-school through university levels. Public health expenditures represent current and capital expenditures by governemnts for medical care and health services.

their public expenditure, especially in the case of the developing countries, can be seen — *inter alia* — from the data on educational attainment given in Table 4.

A glimpse of the actual meaning of the opportunity cost of military expenditure can be obtained from a comparison between the left-hand and right-hand columns of Table 3: military expenditure per capita is as a rule higher than civilian expenditure. This is reflected, though in a fragmentary manner, in the ranking of countries by socio-economic standing. One might speculate endlessly on the development needs which could have been met, were it not for the military expenditure.

Children are, in principle, entitled to the best any country can give them; to assert that the rights of children have to be made an actual priority in resource allocation requires analyses of the actual priorities in resource use and how they affect the realization of the child rights. The DCI surveys, not only in developing countries, raised the issues of poverty of child prisoners, lack of education and of educational opportunities, the obligation of children to assist in family support at too early an age. Those issues come within the purview of resource allocation of a country. The perspective of the rights of children enables the crossing of disciplinary boundaries and the discussion of governmental expenditure within the project on children in prison. The underlying assumption is that imprisoned children represent one of the issues of economic and social policies which have to be tackled within the overall framework.

The results of the children in prison study are corroborated by conclusions of the UNRISD comparative study of the legal status of children. It is worth citing some of the conclusions for the countries also included in the DCI project.

The analysis of the treatment of child delinquents in the United States sets forth the principal assumptions of the juvenile justice

Table 4   Development indicators relevant to the condition of children

Country	GNP per capita US$ 1980	Population in millions of the population 1980	Age structure Under 15 %	Under 5 %	Life expectancy 1980	Infant mortality 1975–82	Child death rate 1980	Primary school enrolment Male %	Female %	Adult illiteracy Male %	Female %	Calorie supply as % of requirement	Average index of food production 1969–70 = 100 (for 1978–82)
Austria	10,230	7.5	20	6	72	17	1	99	98	–	–	135	110
Bangladesh	130	90.0	46	18	46	140	20	79	49	50	81	–	94
Bulgaria	4,150	8.9	33	8	73	22	1	97	95	3	7	143	114
Canada	10,130	24.0	23	8	74	12	..	100	100	–	–	127	109
Chile	2,150	11.3	33	11	67	46	2	100	100	6	9	110	93
Colombia	1,180	29.0	40	15	63	59	4	100	100	14	16	98	122
Costa Rica	1,730	2.3	38	13	70	29	1	100	100	8	9	113	112
Denmark	12,950	5.1	21	6	75	9	..	–	–	–	–	127	111
Finland	9,720	4.8	21	7	73	9	..	85	85	–	–	116	105
France	11,730	54.0	22	7	74	11	1	100	100	–	–	136	115
Germany, F.R.	13,590	62.0	19	5	73	15	1	–	–	–	–	127	110
India	240	684.0	41	15	52	129	17	92	63	44	72	89	101
Italy	6,480	57.0	22	6	73	18	1	100	100	3	5	136	111
Jamaica	1,040	2.2	41	13	71	30	..	99	100	10	7	118	96
Japan	9,890	118.0	24	7	76	9	..	100	100	1	1	126	93
Morocco	900	21.0	46	18	56	114	15	93	56	59	83	107	87
Netherlands	14,470	14.2	22	6	75	10	..	100	100	–	–	125	127
Nigeria	1,010	80.0	47	20	49	141	28	–	–	54	86	83	87
Pakistan	300	85.0	47	19	50	131	18	81	31	61	82	99	101
Romania	2,340	23.0	27	9	71	31	2	98	98	2	5	130	145
South Africa	2,300	30.0	42	16	61	101	13	–	–	–	–	116	102
Spain	5,400	38.0	26	8	73	15	..	100	100	4	9	127	102
Switzerland	16,440	65.0	20	6	75	10	..	86	87	–	–	127	127
Thailand	670	48.0	43	16	63	59	4	85	78	7	17	97	115
United Kingdom	7,920	56.0	21	6	73	14	1	100	100	–	–	133	128
United States	11,360	230.0	23	7	74	14	1	–	–	–	–	133	118
Yugoslavia	2,620	23.0	24	8	70	35	2	99	98	6	19	136	115
Zaire	220	26.0	45	18	47	117	22	100	77	23	61	102	88

Source: UNICEF. *The State of the World's Children 1982–83*. 'Annexe: Statistics about children and world development'. pp. 131–6.

system: 'that children are inherently good and, therefore, delinquency and other misbehaviours of children are *preventable*; that the *state should use* its authority and *resources* to combat those conditions that cause or contribute to juvenile delinquency'.[9]

The study of the treatment of children by the law in Colombia concludes as follows: 'In a developing society such as Colombia, the problems of poverty, unemployment, malnutrition, and illiteracy affect the child most directly. Whereas it is the minor that is most entitled to enjoy all the benefits of society, it is precisely he or she that most suffers from its malfunction and negative aspects.' The conclusion refers to the earlier finding of the study with respect to the obligation of the state to provide for 'minors in a state of abandonment', that is, those who have no sustenance. It is asserted therein that '. . . bearing in mind the prevalence of serious social problems in the country, the vast majority of Colombian children are in a state of abandonment in the full sense of the term'.[10]

The study of the United Kingdom points out the widespread policy of over-emphasizing child delinquency at the expense of its underlying causes: 'As in most countries, the state in Britain is more concerned about juvenile delinquency than it is about other aspects of children and their welfare.'[11] It reiterates the universally accepted thesis that prevention is always better than cure. Most government policies follow exactly the opposite approach: repression instead of prevention, the treatment of delinquent children as if they were adults, and imprisonment with adults.

Multiple role of the state

Basic country profiles are given in Table 4 from UNICEF selection of development indicators that are relevant to the condition of children. The data are presented for the countries surveyed, and even a cursory glance shows enormous discrepancies: GNP per capita ten times higher or lower certainly determines the quality of life of the population; the age structure of the population definitely makes minimum-age legislation substantially different for a country in which 45 per cent of the populace are younger than fifteen as compared to one which has only 19 per cent of the population under fifteen. A food supply below the estimated requirements for the country indicates the existence of malnutrition, and the victims are always children. School enrolment ratios show that the postulate of all-encompassing, compulsory, and free-of-charge education has not yet been realized in quite a few countries.

Even the data relating to countries as units of measurement and hiding internal inequalities indicate that the fate of children varies depending on the country in which a child lives. Those data do not reveal anything about internal inequalities within countries.

Data on school enrolment and child labour illustrate some aspects of the life of children in a particular state. Those percentages hide the fact that school is often not available for the destitute, socially disadvantaged children. Rates of employment of children demonstrate that children are bread-winners, sometimes even for whole families. Sometimes, such data are used to advocate different rules for children in different countries. Such a step would violate the essential rights and the equality of children. In other words, it is a fact that not even minimum international guarantees can be implemented for all children world-wide; states which cannot implement them are required to make an effort to improve existing conditions. The realization of economic, social and cultural rights is always conceptualized as 'progressive'. Acquiescence with 'existing conditions' as an excuse for the neglect of children amounts to complicity with violations of the rights of children. Progressive implementation means that states have to make an effort, to the utmost of available resources, to improve the enjoyment of basic rights by all children.

Ideally, children under fifteen should be at school full time. As can be seen from Table 5 on compulsory education and school attendance, countries which do not have regulations on compulsory education are becoming an exception. However, mere existence of compulsory education as a norm does not mean that the conditions for its implementation really enable all the children to take part in primary education.

In the introduction to its data on compulsory education UNESCO states: 'However, in many countries and territories where the urgent problem is to provide sufficient schools for all children, the existence of compulsory school laws may be only of academic interest since almost all such regulations exempt a child from attending if there is no suitable school within reasonable distance from his home.'[12] The table itself shows that in spite of the existence of compulsory education, many countries do not show a school enrolment ratio close to 100 per cent. If data for regular school attendance were available, the picture would undoubtedly show a much lower proportion of children actually at school.

Table 5 Compulsory education and school enrolment ratios

Country	Compulsory education		School enrolment ratios			
	Duration (in years)	Age range	Primary education		Secondary education	
			%	Age group	%	Age group
Austria	9	6–15	86	6–9	68	10–17
Bangladesh	none	none	63	5–9	25	10–14
Bulgaria	8	7–15	95	7–14	69	15–17
Canada	8–10	6–16	[102]	6–11	89	12–17
Chile	8	6–14	[119]	6–13	[55]	14–17
Colombia	5	7–12	[128]	6–10	[46]	11–16
Costa Rica	9	6–15	[107]	6–11	[48]	12–16
Denmark	9	7–16	[98]	6–11	[83]	12–17
Finland	9	6–16	[85]	7–12	[90]	13–18
France	10	6–16	[100]	6–10	78	11–17
Germany. F.R.	9	6–15			79	6–18
India	5	6–11	78	5–9	27	10–15
Italy	8	6–14	[102]	6–10	[73]	11–18
Jamaica	9	6–15	92	6–11	57	12–18
Japan	9	6–15	98	6–11	78	12–17
Morocco	no data available		56	7–11	[22]	12–18
Netherlands	10	6–16	94	6–11	82	12–17
Nigeria	6	6–12	no data available			
Pakistan	none	none	[56]	5–9	[16]	10–16
Romania	10	6–16	[98]	6–13	[83]	14–17
South Africa	7–9	7–16	no data available			
Spain	10	6–16	98	6–10	67	11–17
Switzerland	9	6–15	data on enrolment incomparable			
Thailand	7	7–15	no data available		[29]	14–18
United Kingdom	11	5–16	97	5–10	77	11–17
United States	10	7–17	no data available			
Yugoslavia	8	7–15	[99]	7–10	[82]	12–18
Zaire	6	6–12	no data available			

Note: school enrolment ratios have been expressed as net enrolment ratios wherever available; where the net ratio was not available, the gross enrolment ratio has been given instead and marked by square brackets.
Source: Education Statistics – Latest Year Available. Current surveys and research in statistics. Doc. CSR-E-41, UNESCO. Division of Statistics on Education. Office of Statistics. Paris. November 1981.

Most analyses of child delinquents focus on school drop-outs and early school leavers. The great discrepancy between the enrolment ratio of primary and secondary schools demonstrates that large numbers of children cease their education at a very early age. The obvious question is: where do they go from there? Unfortunately, there are no comprehensive studies on the fate of such children. But an awareness of the problem has emerged, as is evident from the ILO-coined term 'disadvantaged youth in the developing countries'. It refers to 'persons of both sexes, aged between 15 and 24, who have not managed to complete their compulsory education, who are seeking work for the first time or are unemployed or seriously underemployed, and who are members of low-income families'.[13]

United Nations estimates of the number of children under fifteen who work varies between 55 million and 145 million.[14] Even the latter figure is presented as an underestimate. The problem of exact data is the same as in the case of children in adult prisons: such practices are illegal according to both international and national legislation, and numbers are therefore not officially reported.

Analyses of child labour indicate that a significant proportion is a result of economic necessity — children have to provide for their own livelihood because both the family and the state have failed in their protective functions. Children do not have a wide option with regard to income generation: survival dictates acceptance of whatever is available. Sometimes, the only available mode of securing survival is delinquency. Quite a few states imprison children for begging, wandering without means of livelihood, travelling on trains without a ticket.

The DCI Exploratory Study has focused on the imprisonment of children with adults for whatever reasons as an observable pheno-menon whose causes were not being explored. Research results revealed imprisonment of children for non-offences, or non-criminal offences, or offences which could be justified if those obliged to pro-vide for children were held accountable for their failure to do so.

Table 6 compares the implementation of two obligations: the protection of children in need and the handling of delinquent children, and the manner of the exercise of those obligations. The principal question thus raised is the separation, or non-separation, of the function of the state as *protector* of children in need and that of *prosecutor* of delinquent children.

Numerous national practices revealed by the DCI surveys show a mixture of two *separate* and *different* roles of the state: its role of

Table 6 Two roles of the state: custody of children in need and imprisonment of delinquent children

Country	Children in need of care and protection: legislation, procedures, institutions	Separation of children in need of care from delinquent children
Austria	Legislation providing for social assistance to children and on the protection of minors Obligations of the State to provide social assistance needed for the development of minors	Non-separation Youth homes (open institutions) for children in need of care and delinquent children up to age 14
Canada	Jurisdiction over children is divided between the federation and federal units Children in need of care: committal to foster homes, children's aid societies of child welfare institutions	Separation in principle Exception: conversion of penal proceedings into child welfare proceedings up to 16/ 18 years of age
Chile	The National Juvenile Council: duty of assistance to and protection of children in irregular situations	Non-separation: both children in need of care and delinquent children in custody at Houses of Minors
Colombia	Constitutional provision: every child is entitled to conditions needed for development, well-being, and education The Colombian Institute for Family Welfare: duty of care for children in need of protection up to age 18	Non-separation: abandoned children, children in moral or physical danger and delinquent children at Houses of Minors
Costa Rica	Constitutional provision: children have the right to protection by the state The National Board for Children: duty of protection of mothers and children	Mixed jurisdiction of juvenile courts: minors under 16 in a state of social danger (penal, juvenile, civil and family jurisdiction)
Denmark	Local social welfare committees: duty to supervise and support children up to the age of 20	Mixed jurisdiction: social welfare authorities administer institutions both for social problems and delinquent children
France	Constitutional provision: children have the right to protection Children's and/or guardianship courts: duty of judicial protection of minors	Non-separation: protective measures (educational assistance, supervised education, tutelage measures) for all endangered minors

Table 6 (*continued*)

Country	Children in need of care and protection: legislation, procedures, institutions	Separation of children in need of care from delinquent children
Germany, F.R.	Children have the right to protection primarily by parents, secondly by the state Guardianship courts: neglected children under age 17 can be placed in welfare homes	Penal detention of children possible for the need of education Penal custody can be converted into an educational measure
India	Children have the right to protection, especially socially handicapped children Child Welfare Boards: duty of care of neglected, destitute, delinquent and victimized children	Non-separation Children's homes, borstals, and reformatories both for children in need of care and for delinquent children
Jamaica	No information	Non-separation: approved schools and children's homes for both categories Penal detention of children for the purpose of education and welfare up to the age of 21
Japan	Duty to provide custody and education of children vested in parents	Custody of delinquent children (up to age 14) in communal welfare centres
Morocco	Public and private services and associations for the protection of children	Non-separation Penal detention of children by virtue of parental punishment
Netherlands	Special branch of law: children's and youth protection The National Council for Child/Youth Protection: duty of protection and care of children/youth in need	Separation: civil law measures against children up to age 16 Conversion: child protection measures can be used instead of punishment up to the age of 20
South Africa	The scope of rights determined by race Children in need of care: placement in children's homes by a decision of children's courts	Separation in principle Conversion: criminal proceedings can be transformed into children's court inquiry

Table 6 (*continued*)

Country	Children in need of care and protection: legislation, procedures, institutions	Separation of children in need of care from delinquent children
Spain	Constitutional provision: children have the right to protection and all the rights provided in international agreements The Social Assistance Commission: duty to assure care and custody for children in need of care	Mixed jurisdiction: the Tribunal Guardianship for Minors – legal protection and corrective measures for minors up to age 16
United Kingdom (England and Wales only)	Children are entitled to measures of protection specified by domestic law Local authorities have to receive orphans and deserted children into their care	Local authorities have custody of both children in their care and offenders on remand
Yugoslavia	Children are entitled to protection, primarily within the family Social guardianship organs: duty to secure care and custody for children in need	Non-separation: both children in ned of care and delinquent children in children's homes

securing protection for needy children, and its role of prevention and punishment of delinquency. While in theory those two should be and are separated, the practice ignores the difference between them.

Some examples of 'crimes' leading to the imprisonment of children illustrate one aspect of the problem:

A seventeen-year-old boy told the interviewer in Nigeria: 'the important reason why the magistrate sent me here was because she believed I didn't have a place of abode'.

The researcher from Colombia wrote what he experienced during visits to prisons: 'I was approached by several children who begged for money. Some needed only two or three hundred pesos (two or three $US) to regain their freedom . . . possibilities [normally available] range from stealing the money from a fellow-inmate to saving money from making brooms. [The length of stay] usually depends on how soon the young inmate can secure the few hundred pesos needed to pay for the goods that they have been charged with stealing.'

The report from India includes the following conclusion: 'For the destitute, poverty is their only crime. Chased from their villages by the spectre of hunger, these children flock to towns to look for a means of survival: rag-picking, polishing shoes, cleaning cars, pickpocketing.'

The phenomenon is not confined to the developing countries. *The report from the United Kingdom (England and Wales) includes an interview with a seventeen-year-old boy: 'I also had very little money, so I tried to break into a house to steal some food. That was when I was caught.' The boy was sentenced to two months in a detention centre. He has no fixed abode. 'I have been in care and in and out of institutions since I was two years old, when my parents separated.' His property at the time of the offence was threepence.*

Another aspect — the imprisonment of children who did not even perform an act which would be an offence for an adult — was discussed at the Florence seminar, and the following conclusion was reached after the general debate: 'The use of prisons instead of child welfare institutions was denounced by the seminar as unacceptable under any conditions. The frequent justification used for the imprisonment of children — that they are better off in prison than at liberty — was carefully analysed during the seminar.' One of the working groups expressed its conclusion in the following terms:

> *The Group examined the wider issue of imprisonment of children from the viewpoint of the rights of the child. Such an approach necessitates the interest of the child to be adopted as the guiding criterion, and its application always requires examination of alternatives first. It was concluded that in any circumstances (whether cases of children in conflict with the law, or those of dependent children whose mothers are to be imprisoned) there is an alternative to imprisonment.*

One of the major conclusions of the Florence seminar reads as follows:

> *The use of prisons as a substitute for social assistance facilities is a deplorable practice of states, which violates the essential rights of the child; imprisonment of homeless children, child immigrants, child refugees is unjustifiable; such practices can only be eliminated if states devote more resources to the solution of social problems, instead of resorting to criminal justice procedures because of the lack of social welfare facilities and measures.*

Some conditions identified as conducive to widespread criminalization of children

Economic, social and political conditions conducive to delinquency have been illustrated best by both project research work and United Nations' sources for Chile:

Criminality today is of a different nature than previously, when it had been practised mostly by habitual criminals. Today's criminals are generally coming from a non-criminal background and are young people, aged between 10 and 25 years, without much education, and without a chance to find any employment. . . . In such a situation, the borderline between what is and what is not a crime becomes blurred. Stealing electricity and drinking water, stealing from shops or from vans transporting food, which nowadays takes place frequently, is not seen by most of the poor as a crime, but as a desperate strategy for survival.

The United Nations Special Rapporteur on the situation of human rights in Chile states in his 1983 report — *inter alia* — the following:

> The real unemployment rate today exceeds 30 per cent, which is three times the traditional figure. Furthermore, 85 per cent of the unemployed draw no unemployment benefits, and real wages have fallen by 16 per cent in the last twelve months. For these reasons, consumption in the poorest families has diminished significantly. At the same time, the social action by the government has also decreased. . . . social spending per capita on education, health, work, housing, and other services decreased by 20 per cent between 1974 and 1982.[15]

While we are able to quote only sources relating to Chile, such conditions and policies by no means exist solely in Chile. The pattern is recognizable enough to be applicable to many other countries.

An ILO study on child labour includes an account of the relationship between street work of children and their subsequent conflict with the law: 'The degree of moral danger involved in child labour is reflected in the fact that most of the children who find themselves in remand homes tend to come from the class of children who are exposed to the vicissitudes of urban life through working on the street.'[16]

Another explicit link is found in the UN study on the situation of black children under apartheid; it describes

> Children who have to spend more and more hours working as news-vendors, garden boys, carrying parcels for white women shoppers, in order to earn extra to supplement the meagre wages of their parents, to buy school books or to pay school fees. As eventual drop-outs, they join the army of the illiterate, unskilled and unemployed. They are forced by society to become juvenile delinquents.[17]

Living conditions in Western Europe, however different they might be on the average, do not secure income-generating opportunities for those in need of work. The latest UN Report on the World Social Situation stresses that 'unemployment is a disproportionate burden on the very young'; job-seekers aged fifteen to twenty have three to four times less chance of getting employment than adults.[18]

The piece of conventional wisdom '*il faut manger pour vivre . . . et voler pour manger*' is not only a convenient slogan, but also a part of the law in some parts of the world. The state of necessity has been recognised by quite a few national legislative bodies as an exculpating factor: some offences, though indictable under normal circumstances, can be justified if the perpetrator had no choice and confined himself to the saving of his own life. Chilean law expressly recognizes the drive of hunger justifying theft of food if there were no other means of saving life: '*Traditionally, the Chilean courts have accepted as extenuating circumstances the situation of a 'state of necessity' for the cause of the 'drive of famine'* (hurto famélico) *to the effect that a person was obliged to steal food not to die of hunger.*'

An additional factor has to be added with respect to children: the essential legal principle is that children are to be provided for — by no legislation in the world are they supposed to provide for their own needs. The obligation to care for children is divided between the parents and the state, the state acting *in loco parentis* for the benefit of children. The survey in Table 6 shows that most, if not all, national laws include principles and provisions on the rights of children to protection by the state.

The failure of parents, primarily, and of the state, secondly, to discharge their obligations towards children leads to their destitution. The need to survive can lead to acquiring means for survival by any method available. And there are not many means available to children. Breaches of the prohibition to steal lead first to the establishment of the responsibility and second, to punishment of the child. The chain of events which led ultimately to punishment, often imprisonment of the child, is left out of the penal system. Responsibilities *towards* children are not brought up, merely responsibilities *of* children.

The DCI Exploratory Study has not resulted in a large number of common methods of dealing with child delinquency being identified because of the diversity of the countries surveyed. Nevertheless, there is one universal feature in all national reports: the major crime leading towards the imprisonment of children is theft.

Some of the national surveys carried out within the framework of the DCI Exploratory Study identified the proportion of theft among offences leading to the imprisonment of children:

> *The survey of Germany, F.R. found theft to be the reason for imprisonment of children in 52 per cent of the cases; in the survey of Morocco it is stated that theft was the offence in 66.8 per cent; in South Africa theft is the most frequent offence leading to imprisonment, for white children in 71 per cent of the cases, for black children in 94 per cent of the cases; in Nigeria theft and related offences lead to the imprisonment of children in 95 per cent of the cases, the remaining 5 per cent is imprisoned because of wandering without means of livelihood; in India theft and other property-related offences account for 98 per cent of imprisonment of children, while in 23 per cent of the cases all the belongings of the child are taken away by the police upon imprisonment. While no quantitative data are given for other countries surveyed, in the survey for Pakistan the researcher concludes that the majority of inmates are 'street children', while the researcher for Costa Rica emphasizes that theft constitutes the single most important cause of the imprisonment of children.*

The issue of children facing or experiencing imprisonment because of offences against property draws the attention of any observer to the economic conditions which might be the driving force behind children's delinquency. They often are. Yet, the economic status of the child, that is of his or her family, is also the factor determining whether the child will be imprisoned while awaiting trial or not. Bail has been instituted as an economically determined measure of avoiding deprivation of liberty; its discrimination against the poor therefore is obvious. It has been stressed in the survey of India: *'The procedure for granting bail, whether in bailable or non-bailable offences is, however, difficult and weighs heavily against the poor and helpless accused, as they remain unable to meet the basic requirements of furnishing personal bonds and/or sureties for the amount specified by the bail-granting authority.'*

Besides bail, probation is also influenced by the socio-economic status of the child's family. Release of the child is determined by an estimate of his or her family circumstances, and an unfavourable evaluation victimizes the child by keeping him/her imprisoned because of factors clearly outside the accountability of the child. It has been vividly described in the survey of Jamaica:

> *. . . the young person himself plays no part in the decision-making process. His parent(s) do, however . . . The primary role they play is to convince the court that*

they are in sufficient control of their child as to ensure that he will not be in further trouble. In this regard the social circumstances of the parent(s) become important. The better, financially, the parent(s)' circumstances, the more likely it is that the child will not be incarcerated. A consequence of such a situation is that young persons who end up so incarcerated are predominantly from the low-income sector of society. Additionally, family circumstances might prevent the child from being released on probation; one case has been described as indicative of the policy followed: 'the position was that the offender was not considered a fit subject for probation only because of the home to which he had to return, as there was nowhere else for him to go'.

The Guiding Principles for Crime Prevention and Control[19] attach importance to 'structural causes of injustice, of which criminality is often but a symptom'. They include the following provision: 'In view of the staggering dimensions of social, political, cultural and economic marginality of many segments of the population, criminal policies should avoid transforming such deprivation into likely conditions for the application of criminal sanctions'.

The DCI Exploratory Study did not investigate the proportion of expenditure for the system of criminal justice in relation to the over-all governmental budget and to related items of expenditure. Therefore, we have no data to compare investment in welfare with those in criminal justice, or investment in the welfare of children with those for dealing with child delinquents. However, there is a conclusion of the study which has to be mentioned here: it is not advocated that governments invest more in prisons or other institutions for custodial treatment of offenders. As the chapter on alternatives to imprisonment shows, the DCI policy and conclusions of the research within the framework of the exploratory study both advocate alternatives to imprisonment, not more prisons, not even better prisons.

A research project of the Hubert H. Humphrey Institute of Public Affairs entitled 'Youth in Confinement: Justice by Geography', focusing on juveniles in custodial institutions in the United States attempted to identify correlations between the incidence of confine-ment of juveniles and factors influencing sentencing policies. Research results obtained so far show the strongest correlation between the number of juveniles sentenced to custody and the capacity of custodial institutions (i.e. the available 'detention beds' in correctional institutions for juveniles). That conclusion suggests that the establishment of new institutions might in practice develop into an additional incentive for sentences involving deprivation of liberty.

Notes

1 The International Covenant on Economic, Social and Cultural Rights, adopted in 1966 and entered into force in 1976, ratified by eighty states, spells out states' obligations towards children — *inter alia* — in Article 10, paragraph 3:

> Special measures of protection and assistance should be taken on behalf of all children and young persons without any discrimination for reasons of parentage or other conditions. Children and young persons should be protected from economic and social exploitation. Their employment in work harmful to their morals or health or dangerous to life or likely to hamper their normal development should be punishable by law. States should also set age limits below which the paid employment of child labour should be prohibited and punishable by law.

2 Reports from states which ratified the International Covenant on Economic, Social and Cultural Rights encompassed by the exploratory study on their implementation of obligations towards children have been used to ascertain whether states recognize the rights of children to special protection. The following reports have been used for this book: *Austria* E/1980/6/Add.19 of 15 October 1980; *Bulgaria* E/1980/6/Add.29 of 8 March 1982; *Canada* E/1980/6/Add.32 of 13 December 1983; *Chile* E/1980/6/Add.4 of 21 December 1979; *Denmark* E/1980/6/Add.15 of 7 April 1980; *Germany, F.R.* E/1980/6/Add.10 of 4 February 1980; *India* E/1980/6/Add.34 of 15 November 1983; *Italy* E/1980/6/Add.31 of 21 April 1983; *Netherlands* E/1980/6/Add.33 of 8 November 1983; *Spain* E/1980/6/Add.28 of 16 February 1982; *United Kingdom* E/1980/6/Add.16 of 3 September 1980; *Yugoslavia* E/1980/6/Add.30 of 3 January 1983.

3 General Guidelines for Reports on Articles 10–12 of the International Covenant on Economic, Social and Cultural Rights, prepared in accordance with resolution 1988 (LX) of the Economic and Social Council.

4 *Report of the interregional preparatory meeting for the Seventh United Nations Congress on the Prevention of Crime and the Treatment of Offenders* on topic IV: 'Youth, Crime, and Justice', Beijing, 14–18 May 1984, U.N. Doc A/CONF.121/IPM/1, 27 June 1984, para. 57.

5 Committee on Crime Prevention and Control — *Standard minimum rules for the administration of juvenile justice*. Report of the Secretary-General, U.N. Doc E/AC.57/1984/2/Rev.1, 3 January 1984, para. 12, p. 5.

6 Brown, J., *Children in Social Security*, Institute for Policy Studies, London, 1984.

7 UNICEF, *The State of the World's Children 1984*, Oxford University Press, Oxford, 1984.

8 Sivard, R.L., *World Military and Social Expenditures 1983, An Annual Report on World Priorities*, Washington, 1983, p. 5.

9 Soler, M. *et al.*, 'Legal rights of children in the United States of America' in Mamalakis, Pappas, *Law and the Status of the Child*, pp. 675ff.

10 Martinez De Duran, S., 'Child legislation in Colombia' in Mamalakis, Pappas, *Law and the Status of the Child*, pp. 182 and 168.

11 Freeman, M., 'The rights of the child in England' in Mamalakis, Pappas, *Law and the Status of the Child*, p. 666.

12 UNESCO, *Education Statistics — Latest Year Available*, Paris, November 1981, p. 10.

13 *Cf.* Corvalan-Vasquez, O., 'Vocational training of disadvantaged youth in the developing countries', *International Labour Review*, **122**, No. 3, May–June, 1983, p. 367.

14 *Cf. Children at Work*, International Labour Office, Geneva, 1979, and Bouhdiba, A., *Exploitation of Child Labour*, U.N. Doc. E/CN.4/Sub.2/479/Rev.1, New York, 1982.

15 *Report of the Special Rapporteur on the situation of human rights in Chile*, U.N. Doc. A/38/385, 17 October 1983, para. 265.

16 *Children at Work*, Elias Mendelievich (ed.), International Labour Office, Geneva, 1979, Part II, 'Some aspects of child labour in ten countries: Nigeria', p. 118.

17 Commission on Human Rights, *Violations of Human Rights in Southern Africa*, 'Situation of black children under apartheid', Report of the Ad Hoc Group of Experts, U.N. Doc. E/CN.4/1983/38, 20 January 1983, para. 69.

18 *United Nations Report on the World Social Situation 1982*, U.N. Doc. E/CN.5/1983/3 and ST/ESA/125, United Nations, New York, 1982, p. 54.

19 *Guiding principles for crime prevention and criminal justice in the context of development and a new international economic order*, U.N. Doc. A/CONF.87/14 (1980).

3 Victimization of children by political repression

Occasional references to children in the information on victims of torture, 'disappearances' and political trials indicate that children have not been spared any of the types of persecution inflicted on adults. Nobody would argue that political persecution of adults is acceptable, but that of children is deplorable. However, it has rarely been argued that children have a right to protection which goes beyond human rights of adults. Children's right to protection is based on their vulnerability and inability to secure their own rights and interests. The first section of the study argued in favour of the protection of children *by* the state. The present section raises the problem of the protection of children *from* the state.

When sifting the existing documentation on political repression, one finds frequent references to direct victimization of children. However, information on children as victims of political repression has not been consistently gathered by any organization. Moreover, children suffer through victimization of their parents. Indirect victimization of children has received insufficient attention as well. Children frequently witness arrests, abductions or torture of their parents. Many of them are left on their own, without any material or emotional support. Many children are subjected to forced adoption or are registered under false names as orphans. The suffering of children under such conditions has not been sufficiently documented and the fate of children whose parents are objects of repression is seldom considered as an issue of violation of child rights.

There is a general lack of documentation on the victimization of children by political repression. It is a self-perpetuating information gap because children seem to be in-between terms of reference of the existing information-gathering bodies and the focus of inquiry for none. Nevertheless, the problem is too important to be left out, though it cannot be extensively documented. What follows is a list of examples gathered from the United Nations and Amnesty International documentation; it is intended to shed some light on what children have been exposed to in recent years. There is no purposeful selection of types of victimization or countries — the study had to confine itself to the documentation available. The national surveys carried out within the DCI Exploratory Study included accounts of victimization of children by political repression for only two countries — Chile and South Africa. Those are discussed first.

The survey of Chile includes descriptions of children, detained for political reasons, becoming victims of torture:

> *A two-year-old girl was detained together with her mother in Valparaiso in 1975. The child had been transferred to a police station and later to a hospital, from which she was eventually released because of her serious health condition. After a two-month detention, she had grave bruises on arms and legs.*

> *A three-year-old boy was detained at an air-force base at Colonia in 1975. His mother was tortured and raped in his presence. The child was beaten and left without food and water for four days.*

> *A minor of sixteen was, in August 1983, detained by* carabineros *for sixteen hours on the street near his house. The minor had later been taken to a police station where he was beaten by eight* carabineros, *stripped of his clothes and locked up in a cell. At four a.m. he was taken from his cell by civilians and beaten and tortured with electricity for one hour. One day later the minor was released without any charges having been made against him. A medical examination revealed multiple bruises and a dislocated right shoulder. Since then the minor suffers from nervous fears.*

> *A student of sixteen had been arrested in February 1984 while watching a street demonstration. The minor was transferred to San Rafael, but owing to beatings and torture he had to be taken to Sotero del Rio hospital. He was later handed over to a court, the 11th Juvenile Court of Santiago where his case was dismissed after forty-eight hours.*

An excerpt from the survey of South Africa:

> *By March 1982, approximately fifty people (including one sixteen-year-old) had died in detention while held under terms of security legislation. In 1982, the Detainee Parents' Support Committee sent a memorandum to the Minister of Law and Order alleging the torture of detainees. Affidavits claimed various torture methods were used on detainees such as sleep deprivation for long periods, electric shocks, suffocation, assaults with batons, hosepipes and gun butts, mid-air suspensions, assault on genitals, interrogation sessions while naked, hooding, death threats and threats against family and friends. Children are not granted any special protection in terms of security legislation.*

Those two reports deal with countries which are the most

frequently discussed 'violators' of human rights. However, they alerted the author to the problem of the possible existence of victimization of children by political repression in the countries covered by the exploratory study.

It has not been possible to repeat the empirical surveys. But neither was it possible to ignore the issue of victimization of children by torture, ill-treatment, police brutality, internal banishments, detention while incommunicado, 'disappearances' and mass killings in rural areas. The documentation available has therefore been sifted to single out the problems referred to in relation to children.

The main conclusion of this part of the study is: children are seldom referred to as victims of political repression. It is evident from such divergent practices as omitting to note the age of victims (references are generally made to 'young persons') or describing the 'disappearance' of a father of six children without noting that those six children are victims who are also, maybe even more, in need of assistance.

The following pages contain examples of victimization of children through major forms of political repression which could be substantiated by reliable data. While inter-governmental, primarily United Nations documentation, has been dealt with first, the documentation of Amnesty International provided a much more exhaustive source of information. An attempt has been made to focus primarily on the countries covered by the DCI Exploratory Study. In some instances, the practices of widespread victimization of children in other countries have been noted as well.

The international human rights' law and United Nations' policy documents always emphasize the necessity for special protection of children from any type of repression, especially from violence. However, details received by inter-governmental organizations by far exceed subsequent action undertaken. The UN summary of data on 'grave and persistent violations of the rights of detained persons in the form of such practices as torture and other cruel, inhuman or degrading treatment, arrests and detentions on vague grounds or no grounds at all, detention incommunicado, forced disappearances, unfair trial procedures, abuse of executive and preventive detention, death during detention, extrajudicial and summary executions', provided by non-governmental organizations (NGOs), bears out the names of countries where violations occurred.

Children are not spared any of the violations reported. The evidence includes testimony from children who survived torture, and

information on those who did not. 'Testimonies by twelve former
detainees included that of a fifteen-year-old schoolboy who claimed
that he had been whipped and that his interrogator had threatened to
gouge out his eyes if he did not reveal his father's whereabouts.'[1]

The Report on Colombia of the Inter-American Commission
includes Case No. 3470 on mistreatment and torture of '. . .
approximately 150 individuals, among them students and their
immediate family members. Their homes were also raided and they
were taken away for no reason. In violation of the rights of the family,
even minors were detained. Jorge Bernal, sixteen years of age, was
detained, blindfolded, mistreated and not fed for eight days.'[2] The
students were tried by court martial for alleged membership of a
subversive movement; nobody was tried for the alleged torture.

Mass killings

Mass executions of children have been reported to take place in Iran.
According to the NGO documentation collected by the United
Nations, proceedings leading towards execution can hardly be
considered judicial because the whole process lasts only a few
minutes. Among hundreds of those executed there are many
children. The International Federation of Human Rights claims that
at least nineteen young girls were executed in August 1983.[3] Reports
in the Iranian press referred to the execution of children as young as
thirteen. Amnesty International submitted a statement referring to
'extrajudicial executions which are believed to have taken place all
over Iran, but particularly in Kurdish areas. . . . in some instances
unarmed villagers of all ages, including old people and children, are
believed to have been the victims.[4]

Mass killings in rural areas have been reported from Latin
America and Africa as well. Victims in Colombia, in January 1984,
include Beatriz Urrego, who was fifteen at the time of her death.
Another account of victims in Colombia includes four dead and
eighteen wounded, among them three children, of the Paez Indian
Community. Amnesty International documentation includes a
description of the event:

> Some 300 Paez peasants from the *resguardo* [the land surrounding an
> Indian community which legally belongs to them] had been occupying
> farmland on the *hacienda* 'Lopez Adentro', claiming it was part of the
> *resguardo*'s ancestral lands and maintaining that they were forced to seek

to occupy and work the land because, if not, they would die of hunger. Reports received by Amnesty International outline the following sequence of events: the peasant occupiers had left the land on 23 January after the arrival of an army patrol and a meeting with an army officer who informed them that a meeting with officials of the government's agrarian reform agency, INCORA, [Instituto Colombiano de Reforma Agraria] and the governor of the department would be arranged at the *hacienda* on 25 January for arbitration of the dispute over the land. The occupiers returned on 25 January and awaited the arrival of the INCORA commission: no commission arrived, however, and the area was surrounded by armed police, who informed the community that they had five minutes in which to leave the area. The occupiers refused to leave and were fired upon first with tear-gas canisters, some of which were reportedly thrown back at the police; the police then fired into the group of occupiers, wounding or killing them indiscriminately. Those with gunshot wounds reportedly included Jaime Conda, aged 13, Efacio Torres, aged 13, and Aureliano Tulio, aged 14. Occupiers reportedly sought to defend themselves with sticks and rocks after the tear-gas had been thrown at them and the shooting began, and some police personnel were reportedly injured.[5]

The Inter-American Commission on Human Rights dealt with cases of mass killings on many occasions, declaring the government responsible for violations of fundamental human rights and requesting an official investigation to be carried out. Among them were the following two cases:

Case 6717 (El Salvador):
At 6.30 a.m. on February 26, 1980, a military force occupied the rural villages of El Rosario, Plan de Ojos de Agua, La Laguna, ElTerrero, El Común y Caserío La Lomona, Dulce Nombre de María, Chalatenango (70 kilometers to the north of the capital), burned the homes of the peasants, and assassinated Antonia Guardado and her daughter María Guardado (7 years old); Rafael Navarro (20 years old), whose throat was cut and his body cut into two pieces after he was killed; Berta Lidia Landaverde, who was found burned; and Luisa Abrego, together with her six-month old daughter.

Case 7481 (Bolivia):
The Max Toledo regiment of Viacha, a part of the Tarapaca and the Camacho de Oruro regiments, attacked Caracoles with guns, mortars, tanks and light warplanes. The miners defended themselves

with stones, sticks and some dynamite charges. By Monday afternoon, most of the miners were killed.

They beat the children with cables and made them eat gunpowder. They made the young men lie down on broken glass and made the mothers walk over them, later the soldiers walked on top of them.

The soldiers acted like savage beasts because they were drugged; and they did not hesitate to rape the women and also the young girls and even little girls.

Widespread violence against the Sikh community in India, in November 1984, did not spare children either. A visit to the relief camp at Shakurpur (Rani Bagh) by the Indian People's Union for Democratic Rights (PURD) and the People's Union for Civil Liberties (PUCL) provided the following description:

> In a large hall of the Shakurpur Camp housing the Sultanpuri victims of the carnage sit a row of women and children huddled together with shock and grief inscribed on every part of their being. There is not a single boy of over ten years in the group and boys are rare. Each group consists of a woman of the older generation, three or four young widows, a few adolescent girls, and the rest are children, ranging from ten years to nursing infants. One such household consists of eighteen people rendered absolutely destitute with not a single earning member left; all four adult males have been murdered. Two of the younger women have new-born babies, one six days old (it was born a day before the killings) and another ten days old. They stared blankly, holding the babies in their arms, too dazed to speak or even to mourn. But the older woman who lost her husband and three sons gave vent to her grief bitterly: 'it would be better to give us all poison, how will we live and for whom?' She was voicing the sentiment of many of the women present, all of whom had watched their men folk being attacked and cut down, then doused with kerosene and set ablaze. Not one of these were willing to consider returning to their original homes after the brutal massacre they had lived through. How can they even think of it unless the guilty are identified and punished?[6]

'Disappearances'

Children are also victims of forced or involuntary disappearances. The UN Working Group referred to the information on the disappearance of babies and children in the following terms:

> There is no doubt that while practices resulting in enforced or involuntary

disappearances can under no circumstances be justified or excused, those situations affecting or involving children are particularly grave and warrant every attention and concern from the international community. Instances of the enforced or involuntary disappearance of children may not only deny or infringe some or all of [human rights], but in addition they may entail breaches of specific principles on children's rights set forth in a number of international instruments . . .[7]

'Disappearances' are a misnomer for abductions, unacknowledged detention, detention incommunicado, and frequently for killings in secret. People do not disappear, but they are taken away by force, and often with their children. Worse, children are made to 'disappear' to be used as hostages against their parents and they are often tortured to reveal their parents' whereabouts.

An extreme of the 'disappearance' of children are dozens of cases of the 'missing children' of Argentina. Many of them were born in secret detention centres and taken away from their mothers. Some of those were subsequently 'adopted' by persons taking part in the process of torture against the parents: newly born babies 'disappeared', birth certificates were falsified, adoption procedures were often illegal. Cases of 'disappearances' often end up with the discovery of dead bodies. There are widely reported 'disappearances' of children in Ayacucho (Peru) as well:

Amnesty International has received information that on 9 December 1983 the bodies of six teenagers — three boys and three girls — between the ages of fourteen and eighteen were uncovered ten miles outside the city of Ayacucho, near the main road, Ayacucho to Cusco. The bodies showed signs of torture. It is believed that the teenagers were first killed and their bodies then taken and dumped into an isolated ravine where they were intended to remain hidden. The bodies were found stripped naked, apparently a measure to make their identification more difficult. Amnesty International has received no information as to the identity of these teenagers, but it is believed that they may be among the many young people reported detained by Peruvian security forces, who have 'disappeared'. Although Sendero Luminoso guerrillas have also carried out execution-style killings of young people, there is reportedly no evidence in this case to suggest guerrilla responsibility.[8]

Ten children, aged fourteen to seventeen, 'disappeared' at the end of 1983 and were believed to be held in unacknowledged detention by the Peruvian military, possibly subjected to torture, or maybe executed. Summarizing, it has been stated: in Ayacucho, to be young is to be suspect.

Torture and ill-treatment

A person who experienced torture in Guatemala describes torture against children:

> ... I also saw them pull a boy of about seventeen by his testicles and an officer slashed his jaw in two with his knife; and he cut his wrists to the bone; but I suppose, although the boy screamed at first, he stopped later because he'd fainted. I also saw another boy they had handcuffed with his hands behind his back; they also locked his feet together then lifted him up between the two of them and dropped him. I saw his teeth drop out and gushes of blood — that's how they break your ribs — from the way you fall — and that's when they give you the worst kicks.[9]

The Amnesty International Report on Human Rights Violations in Zaire states: 'The most frequently reported forms of ill-treatment are the most crude: beatings and starvation.' The documentation includes information on the torture of two young men:

> *They were apparently ill-treated in many different ways at Mulimbi military camp in Uvira and at the 'B2' detention centre in Kinshasa from March to June 1981. In Uvira their wrists and ankles were tied tightly together behind their backs, so that they were in a position known as* sur commande. *They were kept tied up like this for hours on end. They were also badly beaten, they were shot at by their interrogators — evidently to frighten them. At the 'B2' detention centre they were also severely beaten and ill-treated in other ways. One of them was put in a hole in the ground; a panel was put on top and a fire lit. He had to stay there while the fire was burning. He was also hit on the feet — a form of ill-treatment the guards call 'haut talons'. And he was forced to lie on the ground and be trampled on by the guards. Both detainees were also tied up and burned with candles and had electric shocks administered to their genitals.[10]*

The Inter-American Commission on Human Rights dealt with communication alleging torture of children on numerous occasions. This case involved torture of mothers and their small children:

Case 2029 (Paraguay):

i.   A communication dated March 1, 1976 denounced to this Commission a number of deaths, disappearances, illegal detentions and torture, especially of women;

ii. According to the claimant, Oflda Recalde, the mother of four children, has spent nine years in prison; Gilberta Verdd, 65 years of age, who spent 'almost ten years in prison for having attempted to defend her husband who was decapitated in her presence,' has again been arrested and is being held incommunicado in the Department of Investigations; Agripina Portillo has spent more than one year incommunicado in the Investigations Department; Teresa Asilvera entered 'prison with a two-year-old child and left prison when the child was six years old, and throughout this period her child was subjected to the same treatment as that given adult prisoners;' Rosa Goiburd 'was arrested in an advanced stage of pregnancy, had her child in jail, alone, and before leaving spent approximately three years there with her small child;' Gladys de Mancuello, 'arrested in 1974 very late in her pregnancy, had her child in prison and is still there with her child;' Marfa Candelaria Ramirez 'lost her unborn child under torture, did not receive medical attention, and was released only when she was near death.'

Punishment by flogging has been reported in Pakistan:

> Women have also been flogged, as have old men and minors who, even by martial law regulations, are not liable to such punishment. In one case, a pregnant woman was sentenced to be flogged, and her sentence was suspended only till her delivery. Many victims of flogging lose consciousness, but the lashing continues after they have been revived. Cases of people who have required hospitalization after flogging are frequent ... A number of victims have died and some have been paralysed as a result of these brutal floggings.[11]

The regulations on the execution of the punishment of flogging mention as an extenuating circumstance old age, but not youth. The Execution of the Punishment of Whipping Ordinance of 1979 specifies: 'If the convict is too old or too weak, having regard to the sentence of whipping awarded, the number of stripes shall be applied in such a manner and with such intervals that the execution of punishment does not cause his death.' The law prohibits the flogging of minors, regulations and the practice ignore that prohibition, leaving children totally unprotected.

In Bangladesh Mostafa, an eleven-year-old servant, was arrested and, according to the information in the Bangladeshi press, tortured to death in Kamalapur. In November 1983 the Bangladesh Society for the Enforcement of Human Rights decided to provide legal assistance to the father of the boy to initiate the investigation of the case. The outcome is not known.

Kudimu Katanga, a young man reportedly a deaf-mute, died in custody of the South African security forces in Namibia in November

1982. Four security officers were brought to trial a year after his death. The evidence presented to the court included a description of their forcing Kudimu Katanga to run for several kilometers in front of their car, beating him as he was running. He collapsed and died. Two security officers were convicted of the offence of assault and the other two were acquitted.

Douraidi Moulay Boubaker died after almost two months of hunger-strike in August 1984 in Morocco. He was imprisoned in January following widespread food riots together with tens of other students and schoolchildren. He was eighteen when he died. Earlier, at the end of 1982 and the beginning of 1983, a large number of students and secondary school pupils were arrested in connection with demonstrations against a change in the examination system. Some of them were held incommunicado, detained without charge or trial and tortured. Some of them went on a hunger-strike, protesting — among other things — against the denial of access to a medical doctor for injuries suffered in police detention. No information is available of any investigation being undertaken into the reasons for and conditions of their detention.

Kampan, an eighteen-year-old fisherman, and Stephan, his sixteen-year-old friend, were freed from detention at Kanyakumari police station in India in March 1984 by a group of 300 fishermen. Their ordeal began when Kampan found a camera and returned it to its owner. He was subsequently taken to the police station and accused of stealing the camera and money. He was tortured and in semi-consciousness mentioned the name of his friend Stephan. Stephan was then brought to the police station and tortured. After days of torture he mentioned a third name. The ordeal finished only when they were released from the police station by the 300 fishermen.

In Romania the prison guards are reported to beat prisoners with rubber truncheons even for minor infringements of prison discipline, such as inability of the prisoner to fulfil the work-norm. In Yugoslavia the beating of prisoners — again, minors do not seem to be excluded — is not only practised, but it is represented as 'legal'. An account from the Yugoslav press describes it:

> It is not an exaggeration to state that order and discipline in prison are based on fear of beatings. Prisoners are often beaten, and threatened to be beaten every day and on every occasion. They are told that the beating of prisoners is provided for by law. . . . At least one prison guard I talked to

was genuinely convinced that corporal punishment existed as a legal sanction for prisoners, while the majority of inmates in the female ward believed the same, some of them quoting twenty-five strokes with a rubber truncheon as a 'legal' sanction.

Political arrests, detention, trials and imprisonment

Children are victims of political arrests, detention, and imprisonment. The collection of information concerning detainees in the Occupied Arab Territories, including Palestine, includes an account of large-scale arrests 'directed essentially against males over twelve or thirteen, in particular Palestinians, but also many Lebanese; there are also a number of women among the persons arrested.'[12]

Large numbers of children are brought to political trial in South Africa.

> A review of juveniles in political trials, published by the International Defence and Aid Fund, states that between 1977 and mid-1981 over 700 were detained under various security laws, and that of these around 230 were charged and 100 appeared as state witnesses.... Witnesses may be kept incommunicado and are allowed only one visit a week by a visiting magistrate. Those who refuse to give evidence against colleagues or friends, or those who make statements in court which differ from those made to the police during detention, face prison sentences.[13]

In Yugoslavia many children have been tried for offences of 'Albanian nationalism', 'irredentism', or 'hostile propaganda'. Reports on trials make children distinguishable because they are referred to by initials. Otherwise, they do not seem to enjoy any special protection as minors. The offences consist of membership in a 'hostile' organization, writing of slogans, pamphlets or poems with 'hostile' contents, or participation in hostile demonstrations. Sentences range from one year to three years of imprisonment. While minors are sentenced to 'juvenile imprisonment', during the police custody and pre-trial detention they are held with adults. There has also been a case of the 'disappearance' of a sixteen-year-old schoolboy. Fatmir Bytyqi was arrested by the police on 31 August 1981 in the morning. His father came to the police station to inquire about his son and was informed that the boy had been released. The boy has not been seen since.

Mass arrests of students and secondary-school children have been reported from Morocco, Zaïre, Bangladesh, Pakistan and the West Bank. Allegations of torture and ill-treatment often follow the reports on arrests. Recently, evidence of torture of large numbers of students and pupils has been provided by Amnesty International for all those countries. While it is difficult to ascertain which ones are under eighteen years of age and therefore children by the definition adopted for the exploratory study, sufficient grounds exist to believe that children are not spared because of their 'tender age'.

In Morocco, the practice of mass arrests is followed by long-term detention incommunicado (*garde à vue*). Legally, such detention can last only for eight days, with a possible extension for an additional four days. In practice, extensions are indefinitely renewable. Detainees have no access to family, to a lawyer, not even to a medical doctor. They often require assistance for injuries sustained during the detention. The response from detainees is frequently a hunger-strike. The result of hunger-strikes is the death of inmates, but the authorities do not often respond by ameliorating the conditions of detention. A description is contained in a letter from a prisoner published by Amnesty International:

> We made our first attempt to go on a hunger-strike for eight days. It was met by total indifference from the officials and, to tell the truth, it was convenient for the jailers, who only came in once a day, in the morning, to discharge an already not too heavy task. In fact, the only result we got was the reduction of the already insufficient food rations.[14]

Notes

1   The administration of justice and human rights of detainees: *Question of human rights of persons subjected to any form of detention and imprisonment*, synopsis of material received from non-governmental organizations in consultative status with the Economic and Social Council, prepared by the Secretariat. E/CN.4/Sub.2/1984/13, 5 June 1984, p. 3.

2   Inter-American Commission on Human Rights, *Report on the Situation of Human Rights in the Republic of Colombia*, OEA/Ser.L/V/II.53, 30 June 1981, pp. 120–1.

3   Report of the Secretary-General, prepared pursuant to paragraph 4 of Commission on Human Rights Resolution 1983/34, 8 March 1983, UN Doc. E/CN.4/1984/28, 29 February 1984, paras 36 and 38.

4   UN Doc. E/CN.4/1984/NGO/1, 2 February 1984, pp. 2 and 3.

5   'Colombian Peasants Shot Dead — Paez Indian Community', Amnesty International document AMR 23/05/84, 15 February 1984.

6   *Who Are the Guilty?* Report of a Joint Inquiry into the Causes and Impact of the Riots in Delhi from 31 October to 10 November 1984, People's Union for Democratic Rights and People's Union for Civil Liberties, Delhi, November 1984, p. 18.

7   *Report of the Working Group on Enforced or Involuntary Disappearances.* E/CN.4/ 1492. 31 December 1981. p. 67.
8   'Disappearance' of Minors Reported in Peru. Amnesty International. AMR 46/ 02/84. 16 January 1984.
9   *Disappeared.* Amnesty International (British Section). London. December 1981. p. 16.
10 *Human Rights Violation in Zaïre.* An Amnesty International Report. London. 1981. p. 19: and *Political Imprisonment in Zaïre.* An Amnesty International Special Briefing. Doc. AFR 62/01/83. 9 March 1983. p. 15.
11 Written statement of the World Peace Council. UN Doc. E/CN.4/1984/NGO/9. 9 February 1984. p. 3.
12 *Question of the violations of human rights in the Occupied Arab Territories, including Palestine.* Note by the Secretary-General. E/CN.4/1983/5. 2 February 1983. p. 3.
13 *Violations of human rights in South Africa.* Report of the *Ad Hoc* Working Group of Experts prepared in accordance with Commission of Human Rights Resolution 5 (XXXVII) and Economic and Social Council Resolution 1981/41: additional information on the effects of the policy of apartheid on black women and children in South Africa. E/CN.4/1983/38. 20 January. 1983. p. 17.
14 Report of an Amnesty International Mission to the Kingdom of Morocco. 10–13 February 1981. p. 69.

4 Protection of children from treatment as if they were adults: minimum-age legislation

The issue of minimum-age legislation is one of the crucial aspects of the protection of children. The current inconsistency between age limits for specific areas of rights and obligations of children has undoubtedly discriminatory effects: children are not permitted to vote, while they can be drafted into the armed forces and fight a war. The minimum age for electoral rights is set at eighteen or twenty-one years, while international humanitarian law appeals to states not to draft children below fifteen into armed forces and to refrain from involving children directly in armed conflicts.[1] In other words, children are not considered to be mature enough to have a say in governing a country, including its involvement in hostilities, but they are considered to be mature enough to fight wars decided upon by adults.

With respect to the subject-matter of penal responsibility, the discriminatory effect of the existing legislation is even more obvious: children aged seven or ten are considered to be 'adults' for the purpose of prosecution and penal sanctions, while they have to wait another ten years to be granted adult status for most other purposes.[2]

Minimum-age legislation has been developing in various fields for the protection of children. It is increasingly forced to take account of the need to dispose of arbitrariness in setting age-limits. The minimum age for beginning employment endorsed by the ILO has been related to the school-leaving age. The general rule is that children should not be allowed to start full-time employment before completion of compulsory primary education. The obvious motive is making primary education compulsory and available to all children, while regulating child labour so that it does not prejudice school attendance.

Minimum age for marriage has been set at the same age as minimum age for employment, fifteen, and it follows a similar reasoning: children should not be allowed to marry before at least completing primary school.

The exception to the emerging process of synchronization of

50

minimum-age determination are political rights. Children acquire the full scope of their political rights at eighteen or even after twenty. Objectively, it is difficult to justify differences in minimum-age legislation. Some of the existing discrepancies are illustrated in Table 7.

Analyses of minimum-age legislation today show that the component of arbitrariness has to diminish. In various domains the age-limits relating to important events in the life cycle are being set objectively and identically. The objective of minimum-age legislation is to protect children from being abused, harmed and exploited. It is based on the ability of children of various ages to comprehend and control the consequences of their own acts, to control their own lives. Such a reasoning exposes the inconsistency of holding a child accountable for a criminal offence at the age of twelve, whilst prohibiting him from casting a vote in a national election before the age of twenty-one.

Minimum-age determination protecting children from the death penalty

The International Covenant on Civil and Political Rights (ICCPR) sets the rule which has been accepted without exception as an international standard: 'Sentence of death shall not be imposed for crimes committed by persons below eighteen years of age and shall not be carried out on pregnant women.' This minimum age of eighteen (at the time of the commission of the offence) corresponds to the demarcation line between children and adults made by the DCI Exploratory Study.

Movements against the death penalty, based on the protection of the inherent human right to life, have developed into lobbies for the abolition of the death penalty both internationally and internally. Within the United Nations, the death penalty has been a constant item on the agenda from 1959. Besides recommendations for restricted use of the death penalty and interpretations of safeguards for the persons sentenced to death, the United Nations passed numerous resolutions condemning the use of the death penalty. One example is the Security Council Resolution 473 (1980) of 13 June 1980, expressing 'grave concern' about killings of school-children who protested against apartheid in South Africa.

An investigation into the use of the death penalty against children was not envisaged by this project. However, an analysis of the

Table 7   Differing criteria of adulthood: age determination for various rights of children

Country	Compulsory school age	Minimum age for employment	Minimum age for imprisonment	Minimum age to marry men	women	Minimum age for political rights To vote	To be elected	Legal determination of full age
Austria	6–15	15	14	19	16	19	21	19
Bangladesh	not compulsory							18
Bulgaria	7–14	16	14	18	18	18	18	21
Canada	6–15	15	14/16	14	12	21	21	21
Chile	6–15	15	16	21	21	18	18	18
Colombia	7–11	14	16	18	18	18	18	18
Costa Rica	6–14	12/15	16			18	21	18
Denmark	7–16	15	15	18	18	18	18	18
Finland	7–16	15	15	18	17	18	18	18
France	6–16	16	13					18
Germany, F.R.	6–15	15	14					18
India	6–11	12/15	16	21	18	21	21	21
Italy	6–14	14/15	14	18/16	18/16	18	18/25	18
Jamaica	6–17	12/15	14			18	18	18
Japan	6–15	15	15					
Morocco	not compulsory	12	12/16	18	15	18	25	18/21
Netherlands	6–16	15	16	18	18	18	18	18
Nigeria	6–11	12	12					
Pakistan	not compulsory	12/10						
Romania	6–16	16	14	18	16/15	18	23	18
South Africa	7–14	none	7/10					
Spain	6–15	16	16			18	18	18
Switzerland	6–15	15	15					
Thailand	7–15	none	16					
United Kingdom	5–16	16	14	16	16	18	21	21
United States	7–16	16						
Yugoslavia	7–15	15	16	18	18	18	18	18
Zaire	6–11	16	16					

Source: ... data are taken from UNESCO Yearbooks, information supplied to the ILO on the implementation of its conventions and recom-

imprisonment of children cannot ignore the issue of the death penalty which is — *inter alia* — an irreversible violation of the right to life.

In the countries covered by the DCI Exploratory Study a great many children, persons under eighteen, have been sentenced to death or executed. Two countries often reported for this have been Nigeria and the United States.

Some seventy people were publicly executed in Nigeria in the first half of 1984. Public executions are attended by the general public, including children. The exact number of persons who were under eighteen at the time of the commission of the offence is not known from the reports available. Some cases have been documented by Amnesty International:

— Bayo Adelumola was sentenced to death for murder, having committed the crime in 1982 at the age of seventeen;
— four people were sentenced to death for murder of a guard during an armed robbery; two of them, Danjuma Umoru and Dejo Olatunji, were seventeen at the time of the robbery;
— Kingsley Iloapuesi was condemned to death for an armed robbery committed when he was sixteen;
— Toyin Ogundipe was sentenced to death for stealing a bus; he was seventeen at the time of the offence.

There are more issues to be raised against the use of the death penalty in Nigeria apart from its application to persons under eighteen. The judicial procedure is handled by the so-called Armed Robbery and Firearms Tribunals (composed of military officers, except for the chairman who is a civilian judge) and there is no right of appeal against the sentence. Mistakes cannot be corrected — the death penalty is irreversible. However, apart from armed robberies, legislative changes enacted in the second half of 1984 introduced the death penalty for seventeen other offences, and the decrees are to be applied retroactively! One of the justifications given for the increase in the number of offences for which the death sentence can be applied was 'easing congestion in state prisons'.

The practice of the use of the death penalty in the United States is different from the one in Nigeria. While in Nigeria the whole judicial procedure takes approximately one year (severely restricting safe-guards for persons facing a death sentence), in the United States the process can last ten years. Therefore, it is difficult to estimate the number of persons who have been sentenced for crimes committed when they were under eighteen. However, the available data indicate that the number of people on 'death row' who were children at the time of offence is over 50. Some cases have become well known:

— George Stinney is still remembered as the youngest child executed; forty years ago he was electrocuted at the age of fourteen; according to the media reports at that time the guards had difficulties in electrocuting the boy — he was too small: 'young Stinney was such a small boy that it was difficult to attach the electrode to his right leg';
— Jessie de la Rosa was executed on 15 May 1985 by lethal injection; he was convicted of robbery and murder committed in 1979, when he was seventeen;
— Monty Lee Eddings was sixteen when he shot a highway patrol officer; the death sentence was modified to life imprisonment after the US Supreme Court had ruled that the decision had not taken into account the violent and abusive childhood of Monty Lee Eddings as a mitigating factor.

According to the United States' statistics, there have been 288 executions altogether of persons under eighteen sentenced to death. Recent accounts of sentencing policies and assertions of the unwillingness of the American judiciary to prohibit sentencing children to death alert us to the risk of increased numbers of executions of children. Moreover, some of the children were fourteen or fifteen at the time of the offence. In practice, when a child or a juvenile is transferred from a juvenile into (adult) criminal court, he or she could be sentenced to death. Therefore, in at least one state (South Dakota) children as young as ten could be sentenced to death.

The necessity of treating offences committed by children by separate procedures and specialized bodies has been recognized, in one form or another, by most countries. The underlying assumption is the same: children cannot be held responsible for offences which would have been crimes if performed by adults. If a child-offender is brought before a court, a juvenile or a children's court, he or she is not declared 'guilty'. The delinquent child is variously declared to be in need of control, assistance, care, intensified supervision. If a custodial measure is applied, it is not punishment, but an educational or a re-educational measure.

The prohibition of imposition of the death penalty on children, persons under eighteen, has been adopted in the national laws of most countries. The United States and Nigeria are not the sole exceptions. Execution of children has recently been noted in Iran and Somalia. Such practices are perhaps a strong argument in favour of keeping children outside the adult system of criminal justice.

Protection of children from imprisonment by minimum-age determinations

There is a practically universal consensus that child delinquency should not be dealt with by the adult system of criminal justice. Legally, in most countries children up to a determined age are considered not to be penally responsible. However, while there is an agreement on principle. national laws vary in the definition of the age-range for the determination of 'children'. The minimum age of penal responsibility is set as low as seven (Canada, India, Thailand, South Africa) or as high as fourteen (Austria, Italy, Yugoslavia) and sixteen (Chile, Spain). One can obtain little guidance from comparative studies of age determinations by national laws. The second possible source of uniformity in age determination is statistics. That does not help either — the lack of international standards in age classifications in penal statistics is explained by differences in legal determinations:

> Since the minimum age of legal responsibility varies from country to country, age classifications for this topic should provide for utmost flexibility among the younger population. Because legal responsibility for persons under the age of ten is rare, and possibly non-existent, the highest level of detail [of data to be examined] calls for single years from age ten to twenty-four, and for five-year groups for those aged twenty-five to sixty-four. Single year data are extended *[from age ten] to age twenty-four, because it appears that most crimes are committed by the population aged fifteen to twenty-four.*[3] (emphasis added)

Statistically, this might be correct. Children might be perpetrators of acts technically defined as criminal. Legally, children should be protected from exposure to criminality by (1) preventing them from having to provide for their own needs by legal or illegal means, and (2) assisting children who performed adult-type illegal acts so as not to be exposed to opportunities to repeat them.

Efforts to establish some internationally accepted standards with respect to the minimum age of children who could be imprisoned with adults are impeded by the fact that both international and national laws explicitly prohibit or at least implicitly disfavour such a practice. The laws and regulations allowing the imprisonment of children are therefore formulated in such a way as to recognize the possibility as *exceptional*. Reasons for condoning such exceptions vary from declaring a child to be 'unruly' to the recognition of insufficiency of specialized institutions to deal with children. National laws follow the general principle of imprisonment being the ultimate measure to be applied against adults, and applied with even more restraint against juveniles and children. The legislation usually stipulates the deprivation of liberty to be used only if the adjudicating authority deems that no alternative measure would do.

Research into national laws and their application commonly followed the same pattern: in principle, imprisonment of children was expressly prohibited, or at least provided with the safeguard of specialized institutions or separate wards within adult institutions. At the level of penal legislation, it was usually determined that imprisonment of children might exist as a legally envisaged exception. At the level of the application of the legislation, it was found that imprisonment of children does exist, but since those practices are violations of the spirit or the letter of the law consistent data-gathering has been restricted.

Table 8 gives some indication of the legal regulation of age classification of children within the meaning of the DCI Exploratory Study (*i.e.* persons under eighteen). It has not been possible to conduct a thorough investigation into national laws, but the data available are given in the table. The purpose is to show the average age classifications of the youngest stratum of persons charged with or sentenced for delinquency. It is obvious that no country applies the rule of defining as children all persons up to eighteen for the purpose of penal proceedings and sanctions. Our categorization of children as persons up to eighteen cuts across the usual category of 'children' (persons up to ten, fourteen, or fifteen) and 'juveniles' (the age category between children and adults called 'adolescents', 'youthful offenders', 'growing-up youth', etc.).

One conclusion can be safely stated: all countries do recognize the necessity of separation of children from adults. There are variations in age ranges and procedures envisaged to deal with the youngest, but the separation in principle seems to exist without exception.

Otherwise, there are no commonly accepted age classifications in the national laws of countries covered by the study. Perhaps the only encouraging sign from the viewpoint of protection of children is the widespread introduction of the category of 'juveniles', which — if consistently applied — would separate children completely from the adult-type system of criminal justice. The development of separate legislation and institutions for juvenile justice generally covers an age range higher than our upper limit for chidren (for example, the UN definition of youth recommends the age range of fifteen to twenty-five). If separate proceedings, institutions and treatment are demanded for juveniles, it is somewhat easier to argue the case for children.

The DCI Exploratory Study has paid little attention to the existing laws. It focused primarily on the matter of practice. National laws were therefore analysed only as the general framework, to establish parameters within which the practice could be analysed. More often than not, empirical research provided evidence of the practice being a substantive departure from the legislation. Moreover, the legislation was analysed by the principal criterion of safeguards provided for children. Declarations of principle and general rules were, therefore, ignored if exceptions possibly detrimental to children could be found in the laws themselves. If the general rules were as quoted in Table 8, restrictions on the imprisonment of children would have given a different picture: possibilities for the imprisonment of children would seem to be practically non-existent. Empirical surveys ascertained that there were children in adult prisons in every country surveyed. The analysis of the legislation was therefore inspired by searching for those rules which allow such practices.

However, any age classification raises the issue of principle and can be challenged as being arbitrary. Moreover, differences between the age structure of the population of developed and developing countries make it necessary to question the acceptability of universal age classifications. Finally, legal age determinations have no relevance for the protection of children if the age as provided by law is not ascertained by the officials dealing with children. Those three issues were frequently raised by the national surveys, and a brief account of them is given below.

In the report on children in adult prisons in Costa Rica the problem of the age limit of seventeen as representing the division between children and adults has been analysed in a wider context of the determination of maximum age for the right to separate treatment.

Table 8   Comparison of age range determining the right of children to separation from adults in criminal justice systems

Country	Age range for the jurisdiction of specialized bodies for children	Age range for the jurisdiction of juvenile courts	Minimum age at which children can be placed in an adult prison	Maximum age for the separation of juveniles from adults
Austria	up to 14	14–18	14	24/25
Canada	7–14/16	14/16–20/21	14	20/21
Chile	up to 16	16–18	16	20/21
Colombia	12–16	16–18	16	18/21
Costa Rica	12–16	16–17	16	21
Denmark	up to 15	15–18/21	15	21
France	up to 13	13–18	13	21
Germany. F.R.	up to 14	14–18	14	14/25
India	7–16	16–21	16	21
Italy	up to 14	14–18	14	25
Jamaica	10–14	14–17	14	20
Morocco	12–16	16–18	16	18
Netherlands	12–16	12–20	16/17	21
Nigeria	4–12	14–17	12	23
Pakistan	7–12	15–18	10	21
Romania	up to 14	14–18	14	18
South Africa	7–14	10–21	7/10	21
Spain	up to 16	16–21	16	25
Switzerland	up to 15/18	15–18	15	21/25
Thailand	7–14	14–18	16	18
UK: Scotland	up to 14/16	14–21	14/16	20/21
UK: England & Wales	10–14	14–16	14	21
Yugoslavia	up to 14	14–18	16	27
Zaïre	up to 16	up to 16	16	16

Notes: the data have been gathered from states' reports on the implementation of the principle of separation of children from adults in custody (ICCPR. article 10) and from DCI surveys. The Table is given for the purpose of illustration only. because national laws recognize numerous exceptions to the age classifications or allow discretion to deciding bodies as to treatment as 'child', 'juvenile' or 'adult'. However, some approximation of the existing age classification had to be included and the above are *average* age determinations envisaged by national laws as they could be found in the sources of information available.

Explanation of the terms used: (1) age range of the jurisdiction of specialized bodies for children, whether children's courts. child welfare institutions, guardianship or other entities established for decision-making in respect of children-delinquents gives – where available – the lower and upper age limit of children coming within their jurisdiction. The variety of existing bodies and the lack of data on their work in this phase of the project prevented in-depth research. therefore, the data given are those which were available at the time of writing.

Table 8 (*continued*)
(2) age range of the jurisdiction of juvenile courts includes information on age classification related to the jurisdiction of specialized juvenile courts, where they exist, juvenile judges within ordinary criminal courts, or other institutionalized arrangements for the separation of juveniles within penal proceedings.
(3) minimum age at which children can be placed in an adult prison represents the age which could be determined by an analysis of the legislation of the respective country. The age cited above refers to the legal minimum age at which a child can be put into an adult prison for the execution of a sentence or while awaiting trial. Most national laws determine a higher minimum age for the sentence of imprisonment than the one given above. We included the references to minimum age principally requiring placement in a specialized institution if such a requirement was followed by a provision allowing the placement of children in adult institutions 'for a temporary purpose' or 'if circumstances so require' or 'if there is no other secure accommodation available', i.e. where the law allows departure from the principle of separation.
(4) the maximum age for separation of juveniles from adults in custody refers to the upper age limit determined for the separation of the youngest category of inmates ('children', 'juvenile', 'youthful offenders') from adults, either in specialized institutions or in separate departments of adult institutions.

The correctional authorities interviewed also emphasized that when abuse of young adult prisoners does occur, it is not limited to seventeen-year-olds but may also affect eighteen, nineteen and twenty year olds, for example. Chronological age, in other words, is inevitably a somewhat arbitrary criterion for determining whether or not detention as an adult is likely to be harmful for a given individual. Raising the age of majority by one year would not solve the problem of abuse, or even eliminate the arbitrariness of the age-limit. . . . The decision to establish seventeen as the age of majority for penal purposes is difficult to evaluate objectively. . . . It may well be that recognizing penal responsibility at age seventeen is consistent with the assumption of adult responsibility and a somewhat accelerated pace of psychological maturing, which responds to both objective social conditions and prevailing social expectations. . . . On the other hand, it could be argued that it is an anomaly to impose adult penal responsibility on those denied the legal status of adult for most other purposes.

The actual determination of minimum age for the imprisonment of children is obviously influenced by numerous factors and different conditions in the respective countries. However, there are examples of states lowering the minimum age for the penalty of imprisonment: in Colombia the minimum age used to be eighteen according to the legislation of 1946, but changed to sixteen in 1968. In Zaïre the minimum age was set at eighteen in 1950 and lowered to sixteen in 1978. The underlying reasoning is not a change in the process by which children acquire maturity sufficient to expose them to prison conditions, but an increase in juvenile delinquency, which tempts states to lower the limits for the penalty of imprisonment and apply the ancient 'medicine' of deprivation of liberty to isolate the delinquent juveniles from society.

Such a reasoning is explained in the report from Zaïre:

> *On the other hand children between sixteen and twenty-five years of age are treated as adults, for the judiciary statistics show that most of the offences committed in our country (armed robberies, murders, blackmail, etc.) are perpetrated by young people between sixteen and twenty-five years of age. These young people must be treated as adults, for if they are placed in a 'State Establishment for Custody and Education', they will corrupt younger offenders.*

The reasoning is acceptable from the viewpoint of the protection of society from crime, but — at least — doubtful from the viewpoint of the rights and interests of children. Analyses of increases in juvenile delinquency show its relationship with changing socio-economic conditions, with the rate of school enrolment, with the rate of youth unemployment; it is often stated that significant increases in juvenile delinquency are an urban problem; consequently, temporary deprivation of liberty cannot solve it.

The lowering of the minimum age for imprisonment of young delinquents does not solve the problem. It does not even address the problem — it just tackles the consequences and postpones dealing with the same problem again after the release of juveniles from imprisonment. The lowering of minimum age for imprisonment vividly shows the predominance of the interests of the state at the expense of the interests of children and juveniles.

The usefulness of the legal determination of the minimum age for imprisonment of children depends on the verification of age in practice. Cases of the actual non-verification of age are evidenced by research results: access to prisons enabled researchers to find out that children apparently under the legally determined minimum age are imprisoned. The limitations of the coverage of the exploratory study and obstacles to access to prisons do not make a complete survey possible. However, some examples can be given to demonstrate the necessity of granting access to prisons for the purpose of verifying the implementation of protective legislation relating to children. The minimum age for imprisonment set in Pakistan is sixteen, with complementary regulations on the separate of children under sixteen even from juveniles between sixteen and eighteen. Yet, juvenile wards in prisons house persons between the ages of ten and twenty-one. In Nigeria the minimum age is sixteen, but children of twelve can be found imprisoned. The minimum age is also set at sixteen in Morocco, but children between nine and fifteen can be found in prisons.

The actual determination of age has been singled out by many researchers as an obstacle to the implementation of the principle of protection of children. An exhaustive account of the verification of age comes from India.

> *[Age,] though an essential constituent of the admission [to prison], in practice is mostly not mentioned. It seems that the age of the prisoner is mostly recorded as given in the detention order. . . . It seems that the age of the apprehended boy is mostly the guess work of the arresting authority. . . . This seems to be so because of administrative and judicial convenience.*

Cases of imprisoned children came to the attention of the Indian Supreme Court, which ordered the immediate release of children under fifteen from prison in the Tihar jail case.

Another problem is the false reporting of age by children themselves. While some children report a lower age in order to be entitled to treatment as children or juveniles, an example from Costa Rica shows the opposite: children sometimes report a higher age, one of the reasons being that as an adult the child will only be fined; if he admits being under the legal age, he will get a custodial sentence.

In Colombia, the actual verification of age is carried out with the assistance of medical personnel. However, it does not seem to be faultless: 'some children have no identity papers. In such cases, the doctor will determine the age, but this method does not prevent children under sixteen from being mistakenly imprisoned'.

Notes

1   *The First Additional Protocol to the Geneva Conventions of 1949* requires States Parties to 'take all feasible measures in order that children who have not attained the age of fifteen years do not take a direct part in hostilities and, in particular, they shall refrain from recruiting them into their armed forces'.
2   A lengthy comparative study into the right of the child in various municipal laws conducted under the auspices of UNITAR singled out the inconsistencies in minimum-age determination for different rights and obligations of children as an area where changes are necessary. It is stated therein that 'there is a growing realization that there should be some congruity among the legal age limits for children with regard to different activities or responsibilities, and that there should be some reasonable relationship between a particular age limit and the

purpose it is supposed to serve'. Mamalakis Pappas, A., *Law and the Status of the Child*, UNITAR, New York, 1983, p. xxxvi.

3   *Provisional Guidelines on Standard International Age Classifications*. United Nations Department of International Economic and Social Affairs, Statistical Office, Statistical Papers, Series M, No. 74, UN Doc. ST/ESA/STAT/SER.M/74, New York, 1982, Chapter X: 'Public order and safety: characteristics of offenders and dispositions', p. 11.

5 International minimum standards for the treatment of children deprived of liberty

The right of everyone to be free from arbitrary arrest, detention, and exile, as specified in the ECOSOC Resolution 624 B (XXII), can be violated by a range of types of deprivation of liberty, not necessarily connected with a suspicion of or charge with a criminal offence or with political arrests, detention or exile.

A United Nations study[1] has formulated the basic principle as follows: 'No one shall be subjected to arbitrary arrest or detention. Arrest or detention is arbitrary if it is (a) on grounds of or in accordance with procedures other than those established by law or (b) under the provisions of a law the purpose of which is incompatible with respect for the right to liberty and security of person.' That principle and others remained in the form of a draft, but they provide a good criterion for the evaluation of state practices against desirable human rights' standards.

The following pages consist, first of excerpts from national surveys which show the range of grounds for the deprivation of liberty of children. Their inclusion is to emphasize the necessity for developing regulations and proceedings for children, often unaccompanied by their family, who find themselves deprived of liberty — again, often together with adults — with meagre chances to protect their rights and interests. An analysis of the relevant international law relating to the protection from arbitrary arrest or detention and to the protection of rights of detainees would go beyond the objectives of this study. Our aim has been far more limited: only those provisions which are directly relevant to children are mentioned, together with calling attention to the lack of those provisions which seem indispensable for the protection of children deprived of liberty.

DCI surveys on children imprisoned with adults included accounts of detention, internment or imprisonment of children who were not suspected of or charged with an offence. The survey of the West Bank includes the following description:

But for a very large number of minors detention does not necessarily stem from or lead to a trial. Existing military orders permit the authorities to hold a person up to eighteen days without trying him or even charging him. Eighty-five per cent of the cases in our sample were persons simply detained and not tried, and about half of them were held for eighteen days or less. . . . It was even revealed that written orders by the Commander of the Israeli Army instructed local commanders to employ this method to harass minors by arresting them, releasing them on he eighteenth day for a day or two, then re-arresting them — and so on without any charges or trials.

Another description is given in the national survey of Chile:

The list of children who passed as hostages through Villa Grimaldi and other secret detention centres is long. In these centres they had to be present while their parents were tortured, or they were tortured themselves. Today they are still paying the psychological cost, whether in exile or not, for having been considered dangerous to the security of the state.

Then there is the dramatic situation of children born in prison. Still in the womb, they suffered from the effects of beatings, electrical shocks and psychological tensions which were inflicted upon their mothers in secret prisons. Later, in public detention centres, they lacked the most elementary things necessary for normal physical and psychological development.

Equally painful has been the experience of adolescents who had been deprived of liberty for up to three years and who were condemned to exile before coming of age.

Detention in Chile and the West Bank is based on the application of security and military regulations and fits within the framework of political repression. However, instances of the detention of children which is not 'political' in the ordinary meaning of the word have also been identified within the DCI project.

A large number of children are incarcerated on the basis of immigration legislation, for offences such as illegal entry into a country or over-staying the permission to remain in a country. Often, children are incarcerated together with their families, but there are exceptions.

Within the DCI Exploratory Study, the only information obtained on the scope of that problem relates to England:

The figures for children detained on entry to this country include children of any age, normally but not always incarcerated with a friend or a relative. In Harmondsworth specific provision is made for unaccompanied children to be placed in the care of a selected female detainee. . . . [From the observation data on the Harmondsworth Detention Centre] it has been alleged by inmates that children have been bullied by the guards, shouted at and given orders which they do not understand (as they speak no English).

In Thailand children are detained together with their families in the Suan Phly Detention Centre in Bangkok. Some 400 illegal immigrants and refugees are kept there in four cells. Children who were born in the Detention Centre are likely never to have left the cell.

In Bulgaria and Romania children can be imprisoned for violations of emigration regulations. The Penal Code of Bulgaria defines the crossing of the border without permission as a crime: 'Article 279, para 1: Whoever crosses the borders of the country without permission from the competent authority, or, even with permission, does not cross at the points designated for this purpose, shall be punished with deprivation of liberty for up to five years and a fine of up to 3,000 leva. The court may also order forced residence.'

Apart from violations of emigration regulations, in Romania 'parasitism' is an offence leading to imprisonment for up to six months. Trials determining such imprisonment are summary, without any provisions for legal defence. Also, administrative decrees on the implementation of the obligation to work provide grounds for forced employment and residence of any person above the age of sixteen. The decree 25/1976 on 'the assignment of able-bodied persons to useful employment' states that all persons above sixteen ot engaged in full-time education have to register for employment. Any person refusing to accept a job, whether in his or her place of residence or not, will be obliged to do so by a court order under the threat of police enforcement.

In Zaïre 'irregulars, vagabonds and beggars' can be subjected to detention in re-education camps, officially called 'social rehabilitation centres'. Amnesty International has reported on several campaigns which consisted of the rounding up of hundreds of *balados* (unemployed youth in cities) and 'relegating' them to re-education camps in remote parts of the country. The removal of juveniles without education and employment from cities might sound reasonable, were it not for reports of deaths from starvation and ill-treatment in such 're-education camps'.

Due process of law: procedural safeguards against arbitrary deprivation of liberty

Results of the DCI surveys revealed that children are incarcerated with adults on many different grounds: they are detained while investigations are made as to whether to start criminal proceedings against them as suspects or witnesses; they are in custody on remand awaiting trial; they are detained as illegal immigrants; they are incarcerated for breaches of administrative regulations such as pass-laws, curfews; they are imprisoned for 'crimes' of homelessness, wandering, vagrancy; they are detained, interned or imprisoned under security regulations as 'dangerous to the State' or as hostages; they are imprisoned for breaches of regulations on compulsory education.

International minimum standards concerning deprivation of liberty are intended to lay down principles which have to be observed for the deprivation of liberty on any grounds, thus ultimately enabling detainees to have their case heard by a judicial authority, giving them the possibility to challenge the grounds for detention, *i.e.* its lawfulness.

The essential principles relating to deprivation of liberty can be summarized as follows: (1) both the grounds and the procedure for deprivation of liberty have to be provided for by law; furthermore, arbitrary deprivation of liberty is prohibited even if based on national law; and (2) every person deprived of liberty is entitled to judicial appeal proceedings to challenge the lawfulness of his/her detention. The underlying reasoning is to enable courts to determine the grounds, the procedure, and the conditions of detention, in other words, to guarantee judicial supervision over all forms of deprivation of liberty.

Obviously, one has to make a distinction here between detention leading to criminal proceedings, which include a decision on the lawfulness and necessity of detention at least in principle, and detention on other grounds, where judicial proceedings may be restricted, if not non-existent.

If deprivation of liberty can be ordered at the mere discretion of an authority, if such an authority does not have to give any information on persons detained, if detained persons have no recourse to any outside authority to lodge a complaint and nobody else can do it on their behalf, and if the authority ordering deprivation of liberty does not have to justify its acts to anybody, there is no possibility of protecting detainees; widespread occurrences of detention under such conditions are a recurrent topic on the agendas of international bodies concerned with the protection of human rights. Frequently such detentions are 'justified' as 'emergency detention', 'executive detention', 'security detention', 'preventive detention'.

A particularly difficult situation is that experienced by large numbers of detainees — including children — held in conditions of states of emergency. The declaration of emergency enables states to derogate a large part of their obligations to observe human rights, and the international minimum standards are reduced to a few basic rights, such as the right to life, prohibition of torture, prohibition of retroactive penal laws.

The issue of the rights of detainees is often postponed till the end of the emergency period or the release of detainees, then responsibilities of officials for torture or responsibilities of the government for mass detention without legal grounds emerge as issues of law. Efforts to intervene on behalf of the detainees frequently fail. However, there are possibilities of invoking violations of fundamental human rights nationally and internationally because international law provides not only grounds to bring complaints for the treatment of individuals, but also grounds to challenge the national laws justifying violations of human rights. Apart from the use of legal procedures, non-governmental organizations with increasing frequency resort to 'mobilization of shame' campaigns, by breaking the rule of silence about the fate of victims and exposing violations committed.

An issue of particular relevance for children is facilitating intervention on their behalf by their immediate family, relatives, lawyers or welfare officials. The lack of information on and from persons detained under states of emergency places an obstacle upon the initiation of any proceedings on their behalf. Protection of children is dependent upon their legal guardians acting on their behalf. Consequently, the immediate notification of the family when taking a child into custody and details of its whereabouts should become an obligation for the agency which took the child into custody. That is an essential pre-requisite for according any protection to the children detained.

The interpretation of the UN Standard Minimum Rules in the Secretary-General's outline of United Nations' minimum standards on the treatment of detainees is particularly relevant for children:

> The Standard Minimum Rules recommend that an untried prisoner shall be allowed immediately to inform his family of his detention and shall be given all reasonable facilities for communication with his family and friends and for receiving visits from them, subject only to such restrictions and supervision as are necessary in the interest of the administration of justice and of the security and good order of the institution. This right of the detained person is to be regarded as an effective indirect means of

preventing torture and ill-treatment, since the family and friends of the detainee, after communicating with him, may lodge appeals against the order of detention on his behalf, retain a counsel for him or take other effective action to terminate the illegal detention or ill-treatment.[2]

According to Part E of the UN Standard Minimum Rules, added in 1977, the protection as envisaged for persons detained in connection with criminal proceedings extends to persons detained without a criminal charge, thus including persons detained under emergency or security regulations.

On a number of occasions the Inter-American Commission on Human Rights dealt with cases where information was non-existent or scarce, thus 'missing' persons and 'missing' information formed the substance of the case. Cases involving children included the following two:

Case 7822 (Guatemala)
Iride del Carmen Marasso Beltrán de Burgos, aged 30, a citizen of both Chile and Italy, married to a citizen of El Salvador, was arrested by security forces along with her son, Ramiro Ignacio Burgos Marasso, aged one and a half, on April 25, in her home. The security forces took them to the investigations section of the Guatemalan National Police and no charges have been brought against them. At the time of her arrest, Mrs. Marasso Beltrán de Burgos was 8 months pregnant. There are eye-witnesses to the events. No more has been heard of them, and there is fear for their lives.

Case 2553 (Argentina)
It is public knowledge that on November 24, 1976, at approximately 1.30 p.m., an armed confrontation took place between the joint forces and the occupants of a farm located on Calle 30, between 55 and 56, in La Plata. This house was the residence of Daniel E. Mariani, his wife Diana E. Teruggi, and their three-month old daughter, Clara Anahi.

According to a newspaper report and reports from neighbors, the house — where the child was — was completely surrounded by the joint forces before the confrontation which lasted for several hours.

On the day following the event, an oral report was made to the 5th Police Precinct that the child's name did not appear in the summary proceedings along with the names of those who had died and who had been identified by the police.

On March 3, 1977, a written reply was received to one of the notes presented to the Chief of Infantry Regiment No. 7, Colonel Conde, reporting that the child's whereabouts were unknown, but that Police Headquarters of Operations Area 113 was continuing the investigation.

Dr. Sambucetti initiated proceedings No. 36.792 in Juvenile Court No. 2. Reports were obtained from the Children's Hospital, the Fire Departments, the Regional and Police Units. All replies were negative, and the police were informed that no minor had been at the place where the incident occurred.

After a year of continuous and anguished searching, the child's whereabouts are still unknown. She has not been found alive or dead, and there is no explanation for her disappearance.

The Commission is in possession of a newspaper account of the events in reference during which Clara Anahi Mariani disappeared, and has also received a number of negative replies from the Argentinian authorities as to the child's whereabouts.

Abuelas de Plaza de Mayo became a symbol of persistence in pursuing the cases of the 'missing children in Argentina'. Information became available to a larger extent only after the emergency powers had been ended in December 1983. Tracing the missing children years after they 'disappeared' is by all criteria a difficult task. Amnesty International reports, *inter alia*, on the case of Paula Eva Logares:

> She was kidnapped with her parents, Monica Grinspon de Logares and Claudio Ernesto Logares, in Montevideo, Uruguay on 18 May 1978 when she was just 23 months old. They were all returned illegally to Argentina where the parents were seen by a number of former prisoners in a secret detention centre in the province of Buenos Aires. Both remain 'disappeared'.
>
> In 1980 Paula's grandmother, Elsa Pavón de Aguilar, received information indicating the little girl was alive, living with a former policeman, Ruben Luís Lavallen, and his common-law wife, Raquel Leiro, who claimed her as their natural daughter.
>
> On 13 December 1983 a legal action was initiated by the grandmother in a juvenile court in order to regain custody of the child. The court issued an order preventing the Lavallen couple from leaving the country but then the judge declared himself incompetent to act on the case. The case then went to a Federal Court which began a criminal investigation of the case. During the course of these investigations it was shown that the Lavallens had forged the child's birth certificate and that their account of the birth was somewhat suspicious: Raquel Leiro had given birth unexpectedly at a friend's house and a police doctor, who worked with

Lavallen at the Brigada de San Justo, used as a secret detention centre, attended her. The couple refused to undergo paternity tests. Genetic tests carried out in June 1984 on the orders of the judge at the Immunology Unit of the Durand Hospital on the grandmother and the child revealed a 99.5% certainty that the two were related biologically.[3]

Protection of rights of detainees and prisoners

The general principle concerning the rights of detainees and prisoners asserts that they retain their human rights. Deprivation of liberty curtails their freedom, and the exercise of their rights is regulated by strict prison rules. Yet, the international and national legal sources affirm their rights and lay down procedures for ensuring their observance.

The United Kingdom, for example, reserved the right not to recognize the full extent of the rights of 'persons lawfully detained in penal establishments', children and adults alike. The survey of England and Wales carried out within the framework of the DCI Exploratory Study includes the following quotation from the British regulations: *'Prisoners in British prisons have no rights, only privileges. Exercise, human companionship, minimum standards of accommodation, sanitation, light and ventilation are deemed to be privileges to be granted or taken away.'*

The practice of the Supreme Court of India represents the opposite approach to the rights of prisoners. The Supreme Court spelled out its attitude towards the rights of prisoners and the protection thereof on two occasions: *'. . . a prisoner retains all the rights enjoyed by a free citizen excepting only those necessarily lost as an incident of imprisonment'*, and *'judicial supervision protects the prisoner's diminished fundamental rights if they are flouted, frowned upon, or frozen by the prison authority'.*

The general approach of protective legislation is to provide safeguards for specific rights of prisoners, taking the internationally adopted minimum standards as guidelines. Those provisions are supplemented by additional obligations and duties of the authorities, followed by the establishment of prisoners' complaint procedures, procedures for the supervision of prison conditions by independent agencies, and penal sanctions against officials for the abuse of power.

An important distinction regarding the rights of detainees and prisoners is 'positive discrimination' or 'reverse discrimination' in favour of children. The general principle of human rights' law prohibits discrimination on any grounds. Applied to rights of prisoners, this means the exercise of rights without distinction on any grounds. However, the protection of children as a specially vulnerable group requires that special measures be undertaken for their benefit. A recently elaborated Draft Body of Principles for the Protection of All Persons under Any Form of Detention and Imprisonment reaffirms that protection should be applied to all detainees and prisoners without any distinction, and then adds:

> Special measures solely designed to protect the rights and dignity of children, young persons, pregnant women, nursing mothers and sick and handicapped persons shall not be deemed to be discriminatory, provided that the need for, and the application of, such measures be always subject to review by the judicial authorities.[4]

The nature and scope of ill-treatment of detainees and prisoners is evidenced by the large proportion.of complaints from prisoners to all the existing international organs empowered to receive individual complaints for violations of human rights. Furthermore, the number of international efforts to outlaw the worst types of ill-treatment testifies to the need of intervention in the treatment of detained and imprisoned persons. Most of them focus on torture, inhuman and degrading treatment or punishment.

Torture is defined as

> ... any act by which severe pain or suffering, whether physical or mental, is intentionally inflicted on a person for such purposes as obtaining from him or a third person information or a confession, punishing him for an act he or a third person has committed or is suspected of having committed, or intimidating or coercing him or a third person, for any reason based on discrimination of any kind, when such pain or suffering is inflicted by or at the instigation of or with the consent or acquiescence of a public official or other person acting in an official capacity.[5]

Such a lengthy description of the nature and scope of torture is, unfortunately, desperately needed to provide grounds for the establishment of accountability and punishment of public officials who resort to torture.

Closely related acts frequently inflicted upon persons detained or imprisoned are inhuman treatment (deliberate causing of intense suffering), degrading treatment (gross humiliation of the victim before others or forcing the victim to act against his/her will), and — especially relevant to children and also prohibited — corporal punishment. Corporal punishment has been expressly prohibited by the UN Standard Minimum Rules and also by the Protocols to the Geneva Conventions, which extend the prohibition to conditions of armed conflict.

Corporal punishment of imprisoned children is frequently reported in DCI national surveys, but it is seldom recognized legally. One of the exceptions is Hong Kong, where corporal punishment of children exists in three forms provided by the law:

> Any use of force against a person, save in exceptional circumstances or as specifically sanctioned by the law, is . . . a criminal offence. The exceptional circumstances include cases where the use of force occurs: . . . in the course of the lawful correction of the child by its parent or of a pupil by its teacher, provided that the correction is reasonable and moderate considering the age, health and sex of the child.
>
> For a limited number of offences a court may order a male offender to be punished by caning . . . Such punishment is limited in the case of an offender:
> (a) under the age of 14, to 6 strokes;
> (b) between 14 and 17, to 12 strokes; and
> (c) above 17, to 18 strokes.
>
> Rules or Regulations made under the Prison Ordinance, the Detention Centres' Ordinance, and the Training Centres' Ordinance also contain powers to punish male inmates for disciplinary offences by caning. In no case are more than 18 strokes permitted, and caning is carried out under supervision with medical advice.
>
> [Report of the United Kingdom on the implementation of the ICCPR, CCPR/C/1/Add.37, pp. 82–3.]

According to the Criminal Procedure Act of 1977, 'juvenile whipping' is accepted as a penal sanction in South Africa. In Nigeria, rules on prison discipline include flogging as a disciplinary measure; the juveniles are not excluded. Flogging in Pakistan has already been mentioned. Those are exceptions. Most national laws follow the requirements of international minimum standards for the treatment of detainees and prisoners and prohibit corporal punishment.

The European jurisprudence on human rights determined that the penalty of corporal punishment constitutes degrading treatment of children and juveniles and therefore violates the existing international minimum standards. The well-known decision in the Tyrer Case included the following assessment:

Judicial birching humiliates and disgraces the offender and can therefore be said to be degrading treatment or punishment. This is particularly evident in the procedure used for birching in the present case, including the fact that persons between 14 and 21 years have to strip off their trousers when being birched. In continuation, the Commission concluded that birching as a punishment is an assault on human dignity which humiliates and disgraces the offender without any redeeming social value.[6]

It is important to note that the European Commission, in its extensive jurisprudence concerning ill-treatment of detainees and/or prisoners, included the age as a factor to be taken into account in determining whether a particular act of the officials violates the international minimum standards prohibiting inhuman, cruel and degrading treatment. A specific assessment has to take into account 'all the circumstances of the case, such as the duration of the treatment, its physical or mental effects and . . . the sex, age and state of health of the victim.[7]

The national survey of Nigeria reveals that the maintenance of prison discipline and punishment of offenders is largely dependent upon decisions of the Superintendent of the prison. He decides whether a prisoner will be punished and in what way. There does not seem to be any possibility of lodging a complaint against his decision. In an interview a boy said: *'Yes, I have been punished once. I was given six strokes of the cane. I was involved in a fight over food.'*

In India a large number of children in prison suffer from beatings by the prison staff: *'twenty per cent of the boys have expressed strong dislike of beating practised by the prison staff responsible for exacting work from them and for the maintenance of the general discipline and also against the use of abusive language'.*

The surveys did not include descriptions of the existence and effectiveness of complaints procedures. However, occasional references to the defencelessness and helplessness of children in prison have been made throughout the empirical surveys.

It would be difficult to envisage an effective procedure whereby the imprisoned children themselves initiated complaints. Most of them have no access to legal assistance, insufficient knowledge of laws and regulations and fear revenge by prison guards. It seems better to attempt to develop *complaints procedures on behalf of* children, enabling families as well as defense counsels, social workers, child welfare organizations, especially those bodies having first-hand knowledge of prison conditions and treatment of children and a mandate for the protection of children. It would also seem essential to make it a public duty to the reporting of gross violations of the rights of children deprived of liberty. The lack of knowledge about children in prison has been repeatedly cited as a major obstacle throughout the national surveys; public awareness of children in prison as a social and political problem is far from widespread. This is reflected in the relatively small number of complaints relating to the treatment of children in prison, but in the appalling pictures of prison conditions emanating from such cases.

Safeguards against ill-treatment of prisoners, suggested from the jurisprudence of international bodies dealing with individual complaints, would include keeping records on taking into custody, interrogations, treatment and any other acts relevant to the prisoners, and obligatory *medical examinations*, which allow the possibility of the prisoner requesting an examination by a medical officer outside the prison system. Evidence on the state of health of prisoners was deemed by the Human Rights Committee as indispensable in proceedings concerning allegations of torture. Obviously, it raised the issue of the burden of proof and access to the evidence needed. The Committee asserted that parties to such proceedings — the victim and the State — are not in an equal position as to access to evidence, and added: 'frequently the state alone has access to relevant information'. The rule of the burden of proof in such conditions attributes responsibility to the state, unless it provides evidence to which the victim does not have access. Such a rule also suggests the obligation of the state to investigate all cases of alleged ill-treatment of prisoners. The Committee stated that the ICCPR implied that 'the state party has the duty to investigate in good faith all allegations of violations of the Covenant made against it and its authorities'.[8]

The principle of separation of children in custody from adults

The international human rights law embodies the principle of segregation of children deprived of liberty from adults in two explicit provisions:

> Accused juvenile persons shall be separated from adults and brought as speedily as possible for adjudication. [International Covenant on Civil

and Political Rights. article 10. paragraph 2(b).]
Juvenile offenders shall be segregated from adults and be accorded treatment appropriate to their age and legal status. [International Covenant on Civil and Political Rights, article 10, paragraph 3.]

Those provisions are unconditional requirements relating to treatment of children, which means that states are not allowed to deviate from them for whatever reasons (such as insufficient capacity of specialized facilities, difficulties in transportation to specialized facilities, 'exceptional' or 'very brief' imprisonment or detention with adults). The International Covenant on Civil and Political Rights (the ICCPR) has been ratified by seventy-seven states and it represents a part of the universally applicable human rights law. Furthermore, the reporting and supervision procedure for the implementation of the ICCPR makes possible an assessment as to what extent its provisions — specifically, the rule of separation from adults of children deprived of liberty — have been implemented in practice.

States party to the ICCPR are obliged to report on the implementation of the obligations embodied in the ICCPR, and their reports are scrutinized by the Human Rights Committee. Besides discussing and commenting upon individual reports, the Committee periodically issues General Comments on topics and problems of relevance to the ICCPR as a whole. It is worth while to quote the specific references the Committee made to the rule of separation in Article 10:

> Subparagraph 2(b) of the article calls, *inter alia*, for accused juvenile persons to be separated from adults. The information in reports shows that a number of states are not taking sufficient account of the fact that this is an unconditional requirement of the Covenant. It is the Committee's opinion that, as is clear from the text of the Covenant, deviation from States' obligations under subparagraph 2(b) cannot be justified by any consideration whatsoever . . . There are also similar lacunae in the reports of certain states with respect to information concerning juvenile offenders, who must be segregated from adults and given treatment appropriate to their age and legal status . . . Thus, for example, the segregation and treatment of juvenile offenders should be provided for in such a way that it promotes their reformation and social rehabilitation.[9]

Thus, both the text of the ICCPR and its authoritative interpretation by the Committee oblige states to separate children deprived of liberty from adults.

The international legal provision on the separation of children in custody from adults is valid even in wartime conditions. Protocol I to the Geneva Conventions of 1949 specifies that children have to be detained separately from adults. The only exception allowed is accommodation of family units. Article 77, paragraph 4 reads as follows: 'If arrested, detained or interned for reasons related to the armed conflict, children shall be held in quarters separate from the quarters of adults, except where families are accommodated as family units'.[10]

The international minimum standards set by the ICCPR and additionally by the United Nations Standard Minimum Rules for the Treatment of Prisoners are interpreted as the minimum acceptable to the international community.[11] This means that states departing from rules embodied in those standards commit human rights' violations.

States are entitled to depart from the internationally accepted minimum standards by submitting reservations to the relevant provisions. The number of such reservations relating to the principle of separation of children in custody from adults is relatively high, showing that states are aware of the obligatory nature of that principle, but that a large number are not able, or willing, to implement that principle in their laws and practices.

It is important to note that some countries lodged reservations not because of a lack or insufficiency of specialized facilities, but as a matter of policy.[12] The Netherlands can be singled out for its resolute attitude expressed in the Report on the implementation of the ICCPR:

> Since the drafting of the Covenant, opinions on the treatment of prisoners have changed significantly, and the principle of segregating adults from juveniles as set out in this article is no longer so widely recognized. International forums are increasingly coming to the conclusion that there is a need for selection to be based on personality criteria rather than on age. [CCPR/C/10/Add.3, p. 17]

While the Netherlands could be quoted as an example of straightforward rejection of the principle which seems to be rooted in the international law on the rights of the child, its attitude is widely shared among West European countries and embodied in the wording and practice of the European Convention on Human Rights and the European Standard Minimum Rules for the Treatment of Prisoners. The European Standard Minimum Rules have been accepted as the yardstick to be followed by the member states of the Council of Europe for the treatment of imprisoned persons, and they do *not* require the separation of children in custody from adults. The Rules demand that young prisoners are detained 'under conditions which protect them from harmful influences and which take account of the needs peculiar to their age', and include age as *one* of the factors to be taken into account when allocating prisoners to different institutions.

Reports of governments on the implementation of the ICCPR offer a basic source of information on the manner in which governments interpret their obligations as to the treatment of imprisoned children, especially of the obligation to separate children from adults. A large number of reservations to that provision testifies to the inability or unwillingness of some 20 per cent of the governments which ratified the ICCPR to implement that rule. States' Reports include an account of the treatment of imprisoned children, even those of states which reserved the right not to apply the principle of separation.

Such information is valuable and readily available. However, it is often incomplete and therefore does not provide sufficient data enabling an observer to judge what is the practice in the respective countries. Practically every country included the principle of separation of children in custody from adults, with large variations in defining minimum age, age limits for children placed into specialized institutions and exceptions to the principle of separation.

It is worth mentioning that sometimes States' Reports present the information on the treatment of children within the adult penal system in a manner raising doubt as to whether they reflect the actual practice. Two examples may be cited:

— The government of India describes criminal proceedings against minors in the following way: '. . . they are tried by the special courts in a different atmosphere assisted by honorary social workers without any kind of fear that they are undergoing a trial. Their proceedings are conducted in a friendly manner without any kind of hostile atmosphere' (CCPR/C/10/Add.8, p. 18).
— The government of Chile excludes the possibility of imprisonment being harmful to the dignity of prisoners in the following terms: 'It is hard to imagine how loss of dignity could occur when the basic principle of the Chilean criminal order is to rehabilitate the convicted person and to equip him to play a dignified role in society' (CCPR/C/Add.25, p. 32).

It is difficult to verify the actual rules which guide the treatment of children within the penal system at a particular time and place, not only because departures from legal rules cannot be ascertained in practice, but because legal rules themselves are sometimes contradictory. The legislation in Morocco, for example, as described by the government itself in its Report to the United Nations on the implementation of the ICCPR, contains a contradiction with respect to the very possibility of the imprisonment of minors. The Report first states that 'minors (persons under the age of sixteen years) are liable only to one or more of the following preventive or re-educational measures', and then lists placement in charge of parents or guardians, probation, placement in educational or vocational training institutions or into the care of public welfare service, or finally into an establishment for juvenile delinquents of school age. Thus, persons under sixteen years of age should not be imprisoned at all. However, the description of prison regulations includes the following rule: 'Every prisoner under 16 years of age shall be completely separated by day and night from all adult prisoners' (CCPR/C/10/Add.2, pp. 15 and 18).

Notes

1   *Study of the Right of Everyone to be Free from Arbitrary Arrest, Detention and Exile*, UN Publication Sales No. 65.XIV.2, New York, 1964.
2   *Human rights in the administration of justice*, Note by the Secretary-General, UN Doc. E/AC.57/24, 22 April 1976.
3   *The Missing Children of Argentina: A Report of Current Investigations*, Amnesty International, Doc. AMR 13/02/85, July 1985, p. 4.
4   *Draft body of principles for the protection of all persons under any form of detention or imprisonment*, UN Doc. E/CN.4/Sub.2/395, 28 June 1977.
5   Cf. Convention against torture and other cruel, inhuman, or degrading treatment or punishment, UN Doc. E/CN.4/1984/72; Declaration on the Protection of All Persons from being Subjected to Torture and Other Cruel, Inhuman, or Degrading Treatment of Punishment, General Assembly Resolution 3452 (XXX), 9 December 1975; Torture and other cruel, inhuman, or degrading treatment or punishment in relation to detention and imprisonment, General Assembly Resolution 3453 (XXX), 9 December 1975.
6   ECHR, Tyrer Case, Opinion of 14 December 1976, pp. 14–15.
7   ECHR, App. No. 8586/79 of 10 October 1980; and App. No. 8324/78 of 12 December 1980.
8   Views of the Human Rights Committee under Article 5(4) of the Optional Protocol to the International Covenant on Civil and Political Rights concerning Communication No. R.7/30, 15th session, 29 March 1982, para. 13.3.
9   General Comment 9 (16) of the Human Rights Committee, UN Doc. CCPR/C/21/Add.1, 26 August 1982, pp. 5–6, emphasis added.
10   Protocol Additional to the Geneva Conventions of 12 August 1949, and relating

to the protection of victims of international armed conflicts (Protocol I), adopted on 8 June 1977, entered into force on 7 December 1978.

11 The *Standard Minimum Rules for the Treatment of Prisoners* represent, as a whole 'the minimum conditions which are accepted as suitable by the United Nations'. They define the category of young prisoners to include 'at least all young persons who come within the jurisdiction of juvenile courts'; in addition the Rules specify: 'As a rule, such *young persons should not be sentenced to imprisonment*' (emphasis added). The rules also include an explicit provision on separation: 'Young prisoners shall be kept separate from adults.'

Standard Minimum Rules for the Treatment of Prisoners, adopted by the First United Nations Congress on the Prevention of Crime and the Treatment of Offenders, and approved by the ECOSOC resolution 663 C (XXIV), 31 July 1957 and 2076 (LVII), 13 May 1977.

12 Other reservations are:

Austria: 'Article 10, paragraph 3, of the Covenant will be applied provided that legal regulations allowing for juvenile prisoners to be detained together with adults under twenty-five years of age who give no reason for concern as to their possible detrimental influence on the juvenile prisoner remain permissible.'

Denmark: 'In Danish practice, considerable efforts are made to ensure appropriate age distribution of convicts serving sentences of imprisonment, but it is considered valuable to maintain possibilities of flexible arrangements'.

Finland: 'Finland declares that although juvenile offenders are, as a rule, segregated from adults, it does not seem appropriate to adopt an absolute prohibition not allowing for more flexible arrangements . . .'.

Netherlands: 'The Kingdom of the Netherlands subscribes to the principle set out in paragraph 1 of this article, but it takes the view that ideas about the treatment of prisoners are so liable to change that it does not wish to be bound by the obligations set out in paragraph 2 and paragraph 3 (second sentence of this article)'.

United Kingdom: 'Where at any time there is a lack of suitable prison facilities or where the mixing of adults and juveniles is deemed to be mutually beneficial, the Government of the United Kingdom reserves the right not to apply article 10(2)(b) and 10(3), so far as those provisions require juveniles who are detained to be accommodated separately from adults, and not to apply article 10(2)(a) in Gibraltar, Montserrat and the Turks and Caicos Islands in so far as it requires segregation of accused and convicted persons'.

The following States' Reports have been used as a source of information for this study: *Austria*, CCPR/C/6/Add.7 of 27 April 1981; *Bulgaria*, CCPR/C/1/Add.30 of 12 July 1978; *Canada*, CCPR/C/1/Add.43 (vols.I and II) of 10 May 1979, and CCPR/C/1/Add.62 of 15 September 1983; *Chile*, CCPR/C/1/Add.25 of 27 April 1978, and CCPR/C/32/Add.1 of 7 May 1984; *Colombia*, CCPR/C/1/Add.50 of 28 November 1979; *Costa Rica*, CCPR/C/1/Add.46 of 24 August 1979; *Denmark*, CCPR/C/1/Add.4 of 29 March 1977, and CCPR/C/1/Add.19 of 3 January 1978, and CCPR/C/1/Add.51 of 29 November 1979; *Finland*, CCPR/C/1/Add.10 of 15 April 1977, and CCPR/C/1/Add.32 of 23 August 1978; *France*, CCPR/C/22/Add.2 of 10 May 1982, and CCPR/C/22/Add.4 of 30 January 1984; *Germany, F.R.*, CCPR/C/1/Add.8 of 30 November 1977; *India*, CCPR/C/10/Add.8 of 13 July 1983; *Italy*, CCPR/C/6/Add.4 of 21 May 1980; *Jamaica*, CCPR/C/1/Add.53 of 3 October 1980; *Japan*, CCPR/C/10/Add.1 of 14 November 1980; *Morocco*, CCPR/C/10/Add.2 of 19 February 1981; *Netherlands*, CCPR/C/10/Add.3 of 16 March 1981; *Romania*, CCPR/C/1/Add.33 of 31 August 1978; *Spain*, CCPR/C/4/Add.5 of 6 June 1979, and CCPR/C/32/Add.3 of 15 August 1984; *United Kingdom*, CCPR/C/1/Add.35 of 15 September 1978, and CCPR/C/1/Add.37 of 15 November 1978, and CCPR/C/1/Add.39 of 28 February 1979, and CCPR/C/1/Add.17 of 21 September 1977; *Yugoslavia*, CCPR/C/1/Add.23 of 14 March 1978, and CCPR/C/28/Add.1 of 6 June 1983.

6 Deviations in national laws from the principle of separation of children in custody from adults

The principle of separation, in spite of being laid down in the relevant international legal instruments, has not been adopted by a number of countries as the operational rule for the treatment of children in custody. Though most countries declare their adherence to the principle, objections to its unlimited application and limitations to its implementation in practice make deviations from the principle of separation almost more widespread than the implementation of the principle itself.

On the level of international law, as has already been shown, there are numerous reservations to the principle of separation. What follows is a comparative analysis of deviations from that principle in national laws. It begins with a survey of basic legislative acts which set forth the principle and — more often than not — allow departures from it. These 'escape clauses' allow law enforcement agencies to place children in custody together with adults if there are insufficient separate facilities, temporarily etc. A lack of provision for supervision of that part of the legislation amounts to condoning violations of the principle of separation by the law itself.

The second part of the analysis of the operation of the principle of separation in national laws discusses the main grounds for justifications of deviations from the principle of separation as established in the empirical part of the research. In addition, a separate chapter is devoted to the subject of children placed in adult prisons together with a parent, usually the mother.

Such an analysis demonstrates the necessity to take a second look at the principle of separation of children in custody from adults. Our research shows that *exceptions come close to overruling the principle itself*. However, we have to repeat here that analyses of the separation of children in prison from adults have never been carried out before on a comparative basis, which was one of the motives for undertaking the exploratory study. Consequently, while results show that the principle has not been implemented fully and thus requires more stringent rules for its observance, the conclusion of the study is different: we interpret the non-implementation of the principle of separation as another argument in favour of alternatives to imprisonment for children.

Table 9 analyses the general rule on separation as provided by most of the laws and adds the exceptions provided by the law itself. Even a cursory look at the table demonstrates the extent to which the law enforcement agencies actually enjoy leeway in deciding upon the placement of children in their custody.

If the rights and interests of children are taken as the basic factor for decision-making, the rule would be the opposite to the one identified by cross-national research: instead of placement with adults if separation is not possible, the rule would be that *law enforcement agencies should not take children into custody unless they can implement the rule of separation*. It could be safely assumed that such a rule would eliminate a significant proportion of the imprisonment of children.

An example of the actual interpretation and application of the rule of separation is given below by means of quotations from the information on Jamaica. First, the governmental report on the implementation of the rule of separation in the law is cited, followed by that part of the DCI survey dealing with the actual operation of the same rule:

> Arrangements shall be made by the Commissioner of the Police for preventing a juvenile while detained in a police station, or while being conveyed to or from any criminal court, or while waiting before or after attendance in any criminal court, from associating with any adult . . . [CCPR/C/1/Add.53, p. 13].
>
> *The legislation of Jamaica requires 'separate provision' for the incarceration of children. Prison officials, empowered to enforce the legislation, do not stress the 'separate provision', but the additional term 'as far as possible'. Due to 'the physical structure of the prisons and the chronic overcrowding' the implementation of the 'separate provision' is virtually impossible.*

Moreover, it is not only the principle of separation of children from adults in prison that has been restricted by the vaguely worded 'escape clauses', specific exceptions have been written into national laws. The major types of limitations of the principle of separation identified in the countries surveyed can be classified as follows:

(1) non-separation from adults can be beneficial, or at least not harmful for children, and specific cases have to be dealt with on their own merits; thus the principle of separation is rejected in

Table 9   National legislation on the imprisonment of children: the rule of separation from adults and exceptions to it

Country	Legal rule on the imprison- ment of children	Legal rule on the separation of children from adults in penal institutions	Exceptions provided by the law itself
Austria	in specialized institutions	inmates up to 25 separated from adults	'if possible'
Bulgaria	separation from adults	classification of inmates by other criteria except age	'degree of danger to society'
Canada	in specialized institutions	not uniform: federal state generally up to the age of 21	'as far as practicable'
Chile	in specialized institutions	offenders under 20 to be separated	security regulations
Colombia	complete separation from adults	juveniles never to be held in 'common prisons'	detention of juveniles at 'secure places' including prisons and police cells
Costa Rica	complete separation from adults	inmates under 17 to be kept apart at all times	no exception in law
Denmark	separation not mandatory	separation in general; flexibility kept	pre-trial detention in local prisons
Finland	separation not mandatory	separation as far as possible and con- sidered necessary	the same rule applies to all types of dep- rivation of liberty
France	separation in principle	children under 16 to be separated	exceptions for pre- trial detention
Germany, F.R.	in specialized institutions	inmates under 24 to be separated	'if possible'
India	in specialized institutions	children to be kept separately at reformatories	exceptions: under- trials, short-term sen- tences, etc.
Italy	semi-liberty in principle	juveniles under 25 to be separated	transitional period: the new system being implemented
Jamaica	complete separation	young prisoners to be detained separately	'as far as possible'; pre-trial detention: 'safe places'
Japan	in specialized institutions	inmates up to the age of 26 to be separated	imprisonment: 'as far as possible'; pre-trial detention: except in 'unavoidable cirumstances'

Table 9 (*continued*)

Morocco	complete separation	prisoners under 16 to be separated from adults	'wherever the existing arrangements permit'
Netherlands	separation not mandatory	separation not mandatory	the same rule applies to all types of deprivation of liberty
Nigeria	separation	children under 16 to be separated from adults	'as far as practicable'
Pakistan	rule unclear	reformatory or prison at discretion of the court	separation not mandatory
Romania	in specialized institutions	persons under 18 to be separated	corrective labour in collectives; pre-trial detention
South Africa	rules vague	unconvicted persons under 18 and convicted under 21 to be separated from others	'as far as possible'; pre-trial detention: 'places of safety'
Spain	complete separation	separation of children and adults compulsory	no exception provided in law
Switzerland	in specialized institutions	separation of children from adults in detention required	transitional period: legislation to be implemented by federal constituents
Thailand	separation in principle	separation by type of offence and age; age limit 16	pre-trial detention
United Kingdom: Scotland	in specialized institutions	persons under 21 to be separated from adults	no exceptions provided in law
United Kingdom: England & Wales	in specialized institutions	separation rules for numerous age groups	except for 'any temporary purpose'; pre-trial detention: discretion of local authorities
Yugoslavia	in specialized institutions	separation rule applicable to inmates under 27	'if possible'
Zaïre	in specialized institutions	separation of children under 16	placement at the disposal of the Executive Council

favour of keeping *the option of 'flexible arrangements'*, which does allow for individualization of treatment, but also for large margins of discretion for the authority empowered to make the decision;

(2) *the lack or inadequacy of existing facilities* is invoked as an obstacle to the implementation of the principle of separation, with the justification that — if separated from adults — children would be incarcerated in conditions of virtual solitary confinement;

(3) categorization by age shows variations in the definition of children, juveniles, young offenders, adolescents, etc.; in some countries, the minimum age for the penalty of imprisonment (deprivation of liberty in a penal facility) has been raised to fifteen, sixteen or even eighteen, and the policy pursued is *controlled mixing within the category of youngest inmates* (aged sixteen to eighteen, or eighteen to twenty-one); moreover, there are examples of policies and practices rejecting the separation of prisoners exclusively, or predominantly by age;

(4) rejection of the criterion of age is perhaps most visible in the treatment of *'unruly children'*, a widespread exception to the right of children to special procedures and specialized treatment; 'unruly' children are those who are deemed to require adult-type treatment because of the nature of the offence committed, their general behaviour and life-style, or by their disruptions of the institutionalized treatment if confined with their own age-group;

(5) the most widespread rejection of the principle of separation by age applies to the *treatment of female inmates*. Not only the practices of most of the countries surveyed, but also expert opinions and experiences of the researchers indicate the need to treat women as a category merely to be set apart, without any additional separation within the group. It includes not only keeping girls and adult women together, but also mothers and their children, in female departments of prisons.

The option of 'flexible arrangements'

Deciding on the treatment of each child on the basis of his/her needs and life prospects would, at first sight, seem ideal. Yet, such individualization of treatment requires a qualified staff, varied facilities and continuous supervision over the impact of the treatment upon the child. The experiences within the DCI Exploratory Study show the general lack of staff, insufficient and overcrowded facilities and absence of supervision of the treatment of children in penal institutions. Discretion in deciding upon the fate of a child has not therefore been supplemented by the necessary personnel and infrastructure. Moreover, large margins of discretion make outside supervision practically impossible because of the lack of uniform standards which could be applied as criteria for evaluation.

Lack or inadequacy of existing facilities

The development of international standards encounters the obstacle of non-existence of infrastructure needed for their implementation. Some states did reserve the right not to apply the rule of separation because of insufficient facilities, but a larger number agreed to apply the rule of separation in their laws, though they do not apply it in practice stating that it is for the benefit of the children. Declarations of intent, and legislation based on them, have no impact on the children who get imprisoned. Most of them are not aware of the fact that they are entitled to separation from adults. The gap between law and practice largely remains unchallenged.

The mere implementation of the rule of separation of children from adults in penal institutions does not ensure better conditions for the imprisoned children. A testimony to that effect comes from the report on conditions in Nigeria:

> *The Borstal alternative as a means of punishment is regarded by the inmates and society as penal servitude no less disgraceful than being in an adult prison. Indeed, the Borstal officials themselves regard the inmates as 'young prisoners' and they are so treated. A boy aged thirteen summarized his experiences in one sentence: 'This is not home, is it?'*

The underlying idea of the DCI Exploratory Study has been that children should not be imprisoned at all; although reality warns us that such a principle might be impossible to implement, the basic principle of non-imprisonment of children is supplemented by an additional one: children should not be imprisoned unless the State can ensure specialized facilities and appropriate treatment.

Such an approach sheds doubt on the acceptability of the implementation of the rule of separation in prisons if that is the only measure taken. More often than not, separation of children within adult penal facilities places them in conditions dangerously resembling solitary confinement. The dilemma has been explicitly noted in the Report of the United Kingdom (Gilbert Islands) on the ICCPR: 'The alternative (segregation of juveniles from adults) would be cellular confinement, which might well amount to solitary confinement' (CCPR/C/1/Add.37, p. 75). The dilemma is frequently resolved at the expense of detained or imprisoned children: to keep them separated from adults, the authorities keep them completely isolated.

More evidence on virtual solitary confinement of incarcerated children comes from the survey of the United States: *'While most States require that youths held in jails be separated from 'sight and sound' of adult offenders, this criterion is often loosely constructed and poorly enforced. Frequently, it results in children being isolated in conditions far worse than those of adult prisoners.'*

Different age classifications

National regulations on age classification for the purposes of the system of criminal justice are varied to the extent of non-comparability:

In Nigeria children are persons up to four years of age, pesons aged fourteen to seventeen are young persons; for the purposes of penal treatment, persons under sixteen are juveniles and the rule of non-imprisonment in adult facilities applies to them. Legally, persons aged sixteen to twenty-one are to be kept in borstal institutions. In practice, borstals are used for persons under sixteen and up to the age of twenty-three.

In Za2ïre children are persons under sixteen and they are entitled to treatment as children, which includes non-imprisonment in adult penal facilities. However, regulations for the maintenance of discipline in adult institutions refer to children under fourteen when specifying types of punishment. Before 1978, the cut-off point between children and adults was eighteen, and all persons under eighteen were to be treated as children.

In Pakistan the national laws distinguish the following categories: youthful offenders are persons under fifteen, juveniles are those up to eighteen, and adolescents persons above eighteen and under twenty-one. The penal laws refer only to the males; there are no provisions for girls and women. It is not possible to determine the impact of legislation on the penal treatment of children, because the legislation on borstal institutions and prisons has not been changed since the 1890s, thus juvenile wards house inmates in the aged ten to twenty-one.

In Scotland children are outside the adult penal system up to the age of sixteen and can be dealt with only by social welfare legislation. The exception is the treatment of children on the basis of 'an unruly certificate', on which children aged fourteen to sixteen can be subjected to adult-type penal treatment, which includes imprisonment. The new legislation of 1980 prohibits imprisonment of persons under twenty-one, but it has not been possible to determine whether 'unruly children' will remain an exception.

In the Netherlands, the age range of imprisoned youth is sixteen to eighteen, exceptionally up to twenty-one. The national survey finds such a solution acceptable: 'There is no reason to think that this form of incarceration is harmful either to the children or to the adults because of a minimal difference in age. Most of the adults in these facilities are eighteen years old . . . I have talked to boys detained in such facilities and to the staff of one of these institutions. Neither of them judges this situation unfavourably.

There is also an account on the non-desirability of the separation of prisoners solely by the criterion of age in the report on children in prisons in West Germany: '*A separation of the younger prisoners from the older ones ('baby group') was not considered useful. The physical age alone was not considered to be an adequate criterion for the group set-up; all experiments in this respect have failed.*' However, two interviews conducted with children in adult prisons within the same survey and by the same team of researchers in West Germany refute the thesis on non-desirability of separation of children from adult inmates by bringing out one of the worst aspects of keeping children in adult prisons: a prison is a criminal education centre. The early social experience of children has been emphasized by all psychologists as a determinant of the formation of their attitudes and life-styles. The exposure to adults convicted of crime in conditions of isolation from any other influences does result in children adopting and frequently absorbing what they learn. Two examples from the same report on West Germany: '*a sixteen-year-old boy: 'I have learned a lot of criminality here which one cannot learn outside'; a fourteen-year-old boy has learned 'how to perform proper break-ins'.*'

'Unruly' children

Grounds for classifying a child as 'unruly', criteria for such classification, margins of discretion and possibilities for protecting the rights of such a child are extremely varied.

In Switzerland, the Society for Juvenile Penal Law demanded that the option of transferring 'extremely difficult' or 'dangerous' children to adult facilities be retained in the new draft of the Penal Code: '*The experience shows, alas!, that in certain cases all the educational and therapeutic measures fail and the release (of such a child) cannot be envisaged for reasons of public security. Their placement in an adult penitentiary should remain* ultima ratio *in the instruments of juvenile penal law.*'

In Canada:

> *During the years 1981–82 at least 134 children under the age of majority in their province (under sixteen, seventeen or eighteen years of age) were admitted to provincial prisons for adult offenders. . . . the legislation in every province specifies conditions under which a child can be placed in an adult institution. They can be placed in adult prisons when they are considered too dangerous to be accommodated with other children, when they have been convicted of a serious crime or when trial has been held in an adult court.*

The certificate of unruliness in some countries enables law enforcement authorities to deal with a child as if he/she were an adult. Moreover, such certificates can be issued by the police. An example of such a practice comes from Scotland:

> *The majority of children who find themselves in adult penal settings reach there on grounds of 'a certificate of unruliness' and are either on remand awaiting trial or already tried and awaiting sentence . . . An individual sheriff must be satisfied that the child (aged fourteen–sixteen) is of a character so unruly or depraved that he or she cannot be committed safely to the care of the local authority. There has so far been no official guidance as to the precise interpretation of these terms. This makes grounds for appeal hard to establish and creates difficulties for contesting a court decision. Senior police officers also have power to issue a certificate of unruliness . . .*

In Nigeria, a child can be imprisoned if the family or a social worker deems the child to be 'unruly': '. . . *at least five of the children interviewed (fifty children aged twelve to eighteen were interviewed) claimed that they were taken before magistrates by relatives who found them to be beyond control. Sometimes social welfare officers are the prosecuting agencies, but then they only act on information or complaints from families and relatives.*'

In England and Wales the practice of imprisonment of children based on 'certificates of unruliness' met with severe criticism even among the authorities. The Employment and Social Services Sub-

Committee reviewed the practice and found out that 40 per cent of the children imprisoned on remand, when brought before a judge, receive non-custodial sentences. The Sub-Committee concluded: *'We condemn in the strongest possible terms the use of certificates of unruliness as a means of achieving secure accommodation. We recommend that the practice of remanding young persons to adult prisons should cease forthwith.'*

The response of the government of New Zealand to the DCI request for information on penal custody of children in adult facilities includes a description of court practice and raises the question of the value of the introduction of certificates of unruliness:

> In New Zealand a court may remand a young person to penal custody if the court is of the opinion that no other course of action is desirable, considering all the circumstances. However, the court generally does not record the reason(s) for its decision, and there is therefore little information available as to what circumstances characteristically lead the court to form such an opinion. For these reasons, it is not clear whether the introduction in New Zealand of some form of certificate of unruliness provision would reduce the number of young persons remanded in penal custody.

To deem a child to be 'unruly' means in practice to deprive him/her of the right to be treated as a child. The offence committed or child's behaviour are sufficient to place the child among adults. One of the worst aspects of the use of 'unruliness' is the general lack of information on the grounds and criteria applied in the specific case. That means that no appeal against such a decision is possible (even if allowed, it cannot have any impact if the decision is within the discretion of the organ which made it and no reasons are stated for it); moreover, the rights and interests of such a child cannot be protected. Frequently children are punished because of the failure of the family to bring him/her up properly, or because of the failure of the penitentiary system either to rehabilitate or to deter such a child.

However, the use of 'unruliness' raises the question of principle: if such children are deemed to be 'difficult', is their placement in an adult facility an appropriate treatment? Such children obviously need special treatment, and incarceration with adults can generally do little more than victimize them as the most vulnerable inmates, or criminalize them by teaching them how to perform crimes.

It seems necessary to keep the option of separating children who disrupt order and discipline in children's or juvenile facilities in order to protect other children, but not to leave the 'separated' children without any protection. The dilemma has been expressed in the national survey of Costa Rica:

> *The purpose of removing from the population of an institution dedicated to rehabilitation those who are not only unrehabilitable, but who interfere in the rehabilitation of others may, in the author's opinion, constitute a valid reason for departing from the principle of separation of adults and minors, assuming that the individual evaluation is correct and such cases are so infrequent as not to permit the existence of a distinct juvenile unit for this category of inmates. It is undoubtedly a dangerous principle, since it could easily lead to abuse of transfers as a form of punishment or in order to ease the operation of the juvenile centre by eliminating 'problem' inmates.*

7 Punishment for sins of their parents: babies in prison

Children who are kept in prison with their mothers, fathers or both parents are perhaps the most widely known instances of children in adult prisons. They also form one of the most controversial groups. Different principles for the treatment of children contradict each other: the principle of separating children in custody from adults is opposed to the principle of non-separation of families in custody; the principle that children should never be imprisoned, that there is always a better alternative, may contradict the principle that the treatment of the child has to be decided upon by the criterion of his/ her best interest, which may be custody with the parent(s), provided that prison conditions are satisfactory.

Moreover, the issue is regularly confined to the problem of mothers with their babies, and thus falls within the framework of the treatment of female inmates, where the rule of separation by age has not been as firmly upheld by specialists and legislators as the one for male inmates.

> *The reasoning behind the non-separation of female inmates by age in Scotland, in spite of the fact that Scotland is a rare exception in having a specialized female institution for juvenile offenders, runs as follows: 'They [the young and old female inmates] share the same living accommodation and are treated in the same way. The staff believe this is helpful because older women have a calming influence on the youngsters and as a result trouble rarely arises in the remand unit.'*

The only country for which the DCI obtained information on babies imprisoned with their fathers was Thailand. Pierre Toutain, a French journalist published an account of 'the prison of children' (so named because of the large number of children therein) in Bangkok. He wrote: 'The children are subject to the sexual caprice of other prisoners and are even forced into prostitution by prison warders.' The imprisonment of children with their fathers stems from the principle of the father having the responsibility for the children who have to follow him wherever he goes.

Non-separation of girls from older women has been advocated as beneficial by numerous sources used in the DCI Exploratory Study. The United Kingdom (England and Wales) report to the United Nations on the ICCPR includes an authoritative statement on its desirability:

> Moreover, in certain cases complete segregation is not considered necessarily desirable. Older women, who are less likely to be committed to a criminal way of life than adult males, can have a stabilizing influence on girls if they are allowed to associate at certain times, e.g. at work in the case of girls over school-leaving age. The Advisory Council on the Penal System in its report on Young Adult Offenders, published in 1974, took the view that young women need not be separated from older women (Recommendation 25). [CCPR/C/1/Add.17, p. 13.]

Such assertions have to be discussed with extreme caution. One has to take account of the fact that female inmates represent a minority of the prison population; girls are brought into the penal system much less frequently than boys. Therefore, incidents of abuse are statistically less visible. It does not mean that they do not exist.

Valuable evidence comes from interviews with girls imprisoned with adult women:

> *Colombia: 'The ICBF (Instituto Colombiano di Bienestar Familiar) officer informed me that they [girls] are not segregated from adult inmates. These are usually lesbians and the young girls are generally raped on arrival, he reports. In a matter of three days, the girls will learn the vocabulary used by the adult inmates.'*
> *Austria: a girl aged seventeen, answering the question on what was the most difficult thing about living in prison, said: 'The fact that we have to be together with adults; this leads to constant trouble.' Another girl of the same age answered: 'Trying to get on with the other prisoners.' Their answers to the question on sexual activities in the prison were evasive: 'I'm not answering this question,' and 'I would rather not talk about it.'*

The issue of mothers in prison with their children shows the limitations upon attempts to ascertain the dimensions of the problem by quoting prison statistics. With respect to mothers with children, the existing data more often show the capacity of the existing mother-and-child prison departments. An illustration is given in the survey of Germany, F.R.:

> *In fact, around June 1983, forty-one mothers and fifty-two children in the Federal Republic lived together in confinement. This figure, however, would only be significant if it were known what proportion those women represent out*

of the total number of women actually eligible for this kind of accommodation. Unfortunately, no data exist as to how many of all imprisoned women in the Federal Republic (approximately 1,400 in June 1983) have one or more children under school age.

The national survey of Nigeria brings the problem of children in prison with their mothers from the level of quantification of the problem to the level of addressing the issue as a matter of principle: *'official records have revealed that there are 240 such children [in prison with their mothers] in female annexes of all the prisons in Nigeria. This figure may seem insignificant, but one cannot lose sight of the fact that these children have committed no crime, but are being indirectly punished because society has not yet devised a solution.'*

The problem of mothers with small children has usually been reduced to the controversy between those asserting that separation of the child from his/her mother is worse than living in prison, and those claiming that the life in prison can never be anything but detrimental to the child. Simplified to two opposing views, that controversy has not been resolved. The interviews with mothers incarcerated with their children, with prison staff and the research carried out show both positive and negative aspects of keeping children in prison with their mothers, without a clear-cut consensus on the principle. However, they do reveal a whole set of conditions which have to be met if the stay of the child in prison is not to be an obstacle to its development.

An extensive study into the problem of mothers imprisoned with their children has been carried out in the DCI survey of Germany, F.R. Some excerpts are given below:

The possibility of keeping children with their mothers in prison ... is restricted by a series of conditions. First of all, the child should be under school age, which means that it must be younger than six; secondly, the prison conditions should be adapted to the well-being of the child; and thirdly, the child's well-being should be guaranteed by the youth welfare office.

The requirement of the well-being of the child in particular has led continuously to quarrels between supporters and critics of the modern mother-and-child prison establishments. According to an inquiry made in 1983, in which the staff of mother-and-child prison establishments were asked to state reasons in favour and against keeping children in prison with their mothers, the following points were emphasized:

(1) in favour — a sudden separation of mother and child can be avoided, so that no estrangement takes place; placement of the child in a children's institution can be avoided; a positive mother–child relationship can be

developed or maintained; the mother learns or continues to care for, bring up, and feel responsible for the child, regular care of the child is ensured; and during imprisonment the framework for the future support can be provided.

(2)   *against — the environment of a prison is usually not made clear to the child; the closed establishment hinders the freedom of movement and spontaneity of the child; considerable retardation in the development of the child may occur; the child shares the dependence and powerlessness of the mother, exemplified by her lack of access to the keys; living together with a large number of mothers and children in a closed establishment means a heavy stress for all concerned; the male element is missing, resulting in a purely female upbringing; the relationship with the outside world, including other family members, is made more difficult or may be completely severed.*

While the negative aspects of imprisonment of children with their mothers involve a variety of factors, the positive ones are confined solely to the mother–child relationship. Therefore, the option suggested by the International Seminar on Children in Adult Prisons, non-imprisonment of pregnant women and mothers with small children, seems an ideal solution.

Nevertheless, improvements to existing conditions have to be advocated as immediately applicable ameliorative measures, while keeping the option of introducing a prohibition of the deprivation of liberty of mothers with small children. Existing institutions are so varied that no universal formula could be suggested — in some, even the basic necessities of life are lacking, in others material conditions are satisfactory and more contact of children with the outside world would be the improvement needed.

The diversity of the existing conditions experienced by children in prison with their mothers is shown below by a selection of findings in the DCI national surveys. First, different national policies with respect to allowing mothers to keep the children with them in prison are outlined; secondly, the diversity of prison conditions in the countries surveyed is shown by a selection of observations and interviews from the DCI surveys; and thirdly, the process of deciding upon the imprisonment of pregnant women or mothers with dependent children is briefly tackled, and finally the recommendations of the International Seminar on Children in Adult Prisons are mentioned.

National policies on babies in prison with their mothers

In the United Kingdom, the policy of allowing mothers to have babies with them in prison is not uniform; two extremes can be identified: in Scotland, the policy seems to be to encourage mothers to have their children with them in prison, in England to separate mothers from their babies as soon as possible.

The observation data on Corton Vale in Scotland include the following description —

> *Pregnant women have full ante-natal care in the institution and are transferred to the local maternity hospital at the time of birth. Babies are accommodated with their mothers, and indeed this is encouraged if children are very young. Every effort is made to ensure that mother and child relate normally. The staff welcome having babies in the institution; they believe it to be important for the child's development to remain close to the mother and consider it helpful to the mother to have support and guidance at that time. It is also believed that the presence of a baby has a stabilizing influence on other inmates.*

The national survey of England includes the relevant policy documents and regulations concerning mothers and babies in prison. Two excerpts:

> *The Prison Rules state that: 'The Secretary of State may, subject to any conditions he thinks fit, permit a woman prisoner to have her baby with her in prison, and everything necessary for the baby's maintenance and care may be provided there.'*
>
> *The Standing Order 13 of 1983 (as amended) states — inter alia — the following: 'All pregnant women and mother with young babies should be made aware that their babies may be considered for admission to a mother-and-baby unit in a prison. A baby should normally be admitted only temporarily to a unit: (a) in a closed prison if he would attain the age of nine months before the mother's earliest date of release or by the date of her likely transfer to open conditions, or (b) to a unit in an open prison if he would attain the age of eighteen months before her earliest date of release. If a baby in prison is not eligible to stay with his mother, separation should take place within the first four weeks if the baby is not being breast-fed, or at the end of the first four weeks if he is being breast-fed . . .'*

The DCI survey of England emphasizes negative aspects of such a policy:

There are only three mother-and-baby units, and priority is given to women who give birth during their sentence, although the governor of the prison has the power to remove any baby at any time. After pregnancy subtle pressure is used, encouraging abortion, discouraging keeping the baby in prison. The policy for long-term prisoners seems to be to remove the child as soon as possible after birth. . . . The fear of losing the right to keep one's baby is a constant sanction for good behaviour.

Children cannot stay in prison with their mothers in Jamaica. '*Children are not incarcerated with their mothers. If, consequent to their mother's imprisonment, they are found in need of care and protection by a Juvenile Court, they will be placed in foster care or a children's home.*' In Denmark: '*Mothers can bring their babies into the prison and keep them until they are twelve months old. . . . Only very few mothers choose this option, and none of the prisons — open or closed — have special facilities for mothers with babies.*'

In the Netherlands the mother decides whether her child will stay with her in prison, or with friends or relatives if there are any. Apparently, the mother has a say in the treatment of the child within the prison — in the use of the prison medical facility or an outside hospital, in the planning of the child's meals. The sole mother interviewed by the national researchers made three complaints: '*she [the baby] should have more contact with her father; she should have more fresh air [only one hour per day in the prison] and she should have more toys [now she has only the toys which her mother knitted]*'.

In Thailand:

Children are not allowed to stay with their mothers in prison. Only new-born babies can stay with their mothers in prison; those over three years of age will be sent to stay with relatives or to the Department of Social Welfare until their mothers are released. . . .

According to the report by the Correction Department, there were 124 children [kept in jail because a parent is an inmate]. They were in various jails for women throughout the country and the majority of them were at the Bangkok detention centre for female inmates. Most of the children are babies. Some were born in prison. These children are not supposed to stay with their mothers once they reach the age of three. However, according to the Nation Review *survey (29 May 1984) some children born to inmates have stayed with their mothers in jail until they were six years old. They must stay in the cells together with their mothers.*

According to the Nation *survey, life in Thai jails and prison conditions generally have gone from bad to worse because of acute financial constraints. Sleeping quarters at most detention centres are old and below the standard required by the United Nations. Prisoners are packed in jails at 20 per cent above their capacity. Because of financial constraints it is impossible to allot special places for the mothers and their babies. To support these children, the prison has relied on its own funds and outside donations. Thus the facilities for children are inadequate.*

The information on children in prison with their mothers in Pakistan is contradictory, even about the basic legal postulates. According to the Prisoners Aid Society, mothers are entitled to keep their children with them until the child is three years of age. Information was nevertheless provided about a girl who —due to administrative negligence — spent eleven years in prison with her mother. A survey of the mother-and-child problem in the Pakistani *Herald* of June 1984 states that boys can remain in prison with their mothers up to the age of ten, while girls can stay in prison indefinitely. That survey mentions a case of a girl of fifteen who spent twelve years of her life in prison with her mother. Prison conditions are appalling. Women giving birth in prison have no access to an obstetrician. They have to rely on assistance of another inmate, and infant deaths have frequently been reported.

In Nigeria mothers are allowed to keep their children with them in prison until the children reach eighteen months. Inmates on remand awaiting trial are excepted; older children can therefore be found in prison with their mothers. An excerpt from the observation of Enogu prison, Women's Wing, housing eighty-six women: *'The babies appeared to be well fed. They shared their mother's bed in the cell, which housed a minimum of sixteen inmates. . . . The cells are badly ventilated. . . . The children are given baby food and the resident doctor pays regular visits.'* Interviews with mothers imprisoned with their children reveal anxiety concerning possible stigmatization of their children by the stay in prison. One mother stated: *'You carry your child everywhere. There is nowhere for her to go. There are no toys or books. . . . Maybe people will abuse her because she lived in prison and call her a prisoner when she is older.'* Another mother shares those worries: *'I want him [her nineteen-month-old son] to be taken out of prison. I do not want people to call him a prisoner.'* A third mother objects to the prison conditions: *'We can only wash at week-ends. I used to wash his clothes every day at home. . . . No, there is no hot water. . . . There is nobody here to leave him with. Everything here is different from outside. . . . No toys. No contact with other children.'*

Prison conditions for mothers with children

In Costa Rica, a women's prison includes a special unit called a 'cradle house' (*Casa Cuna*) for children whose mothers are imprisoned there. The conditions are apparently good: *'The staff knew of no reported cases of adverse consequences for the child of residence in the institution. Indeed, it was said that, given the socio-economic background of most of the children admitted, it is possible that the situation of many of them actually deteriorates upon their return into the community.'*

Prison conditions in Austria are apparently good, judging by the criteria of material conditions only (food, sanitation, space, etc.), but interviews with mothers staying in prison with their children reveal the impact of imprisonment on the children. A mother of a ten-month-old baby states: *'The child is normally developed and interested in everything. But it does not laugh much and often seems dejected. That would certainly be different outside the prison.'* A mother of an eighteen-month-old baby says about its reactions: *'It shows a strong urge to go out. It is quite happy if a woman prison officer takes it with her. I think it would go even with strangers, if only it could go out. It is quite mad about keys and always wants to open the door.'*

There is a description of the Female Penitentiary Complex of Madrid in the observation data included in the national report on Spain. The prison itself was built in 1934 as an asylum for the poor, later converted into a prison hospital and ultimately into a prison for women. Women can have their children in prison, according to the legislation, until the children reach the age of six (compulsory school age). The researchers concluded that: *'the mothers' department, in its material and architectural aspects, is not an adequate place — it has not been meant for that — for the life of children under six years of age.'* Though living conditions were largely determined by the inadequacy of the building itself, a programme of outside pre-school education for children was introduced in 1983 and shows good results: *'The fact that some of the children went to school outside has been a positive experience. A favourable evolution in their psychological development has been observed owing to the contact with children of their age in another environment.'*

A description of prison conditions from the survey of Chile:

In Tres Alamos there were no special provisions or programmes for inmates, nor were there any recreational or educational activities. Medical attention was provided only for pregnant women and then only during the final months of pregnancy. At the time of giving birth they would be put in the medical ward and stayed there for one week, permanently guarded by two armed men. The children born in prison did not get special food. Milk, vitamins, and other essential foodstuffs had to be provided by the Red Cross or by relatives of prisoners. . . . In addition [to seventeen minors aged between fourteen and eighteen] there were five children of both sexes only some months old. These children were born in prison, their mothers having been detained in the women's section of Tres Alamos. Conditions in Tres Alamos were very bad. In the women's section 120 prisoners lived in a wooden block with facilities for fifty persons. Normally, ten or eleven prisoners slept in one room, six of them in berths and others on the floor. There were no doors, so that if it rained water flooded in. There was no space for eating, prisoners had to eat in the open air. There were four toilets, three of which functioned, no warm water; nor were there any special provisions for children and babies.

The national survey of Zaïre includes a description of mothers imprisoned with their children in the central prison at Kisangani.

Among the women we found two mothers whose children were with them. One of them had two children with her, aged five and three. In addition, she had six other children. The children who were in prison with her were not very well because they were not used to it. She could have removed them from prison, but there was nobody to look after them because she was a widow. She had been arrested because of a problem concerning a plot of land —stellionat She thought that if she did not leave prison soon, the education of her children would suffer. She had no special regime because she had children.

Excerpts from the national survey of India:

The children of women on remand always remain with them, even when the mother is engaged in some assigned work (under the rules, those on remand are not supposed to be put to work), but the children of convicted women also remain with them in all prisons except one which is a model women's prison.

In one prison, the children were seen eagerly playing with used match sticks, empty match boxes or other tit-bits they could find in their mother's cells. At another, the children who managed to get a ruler or a pen from the room where their mothers were being interviewed were unwilling to give up their possessions, which they took as their only playthings. Officially, the absence of any toys for children was explained as a security measure. But obviously toys can be procured which need not be used as injurious instruments for a child or its mother.

Interviews with mothers incarcerated with their children in South

Africa show appalling conditions of detention. The women interviewed were all imprisoned for violations of 'pass laws' and/or influx
control regulations. One of them said the following:

> *When the police arrested me, I was given no choice as to what to do with my*
> *children. I was never taken to the Aid Centre or given any advice by anyone.*
> *Both children were ill when I went to prison. They were vomiting and had*
> *diarrhoea. I was allowed to take them to the prison hospital where I saw a nurse*
> *who gave me some medicine. It was not the right medicine for their problems. I*
> *saw no doctor. There were many of us in a cell — about thirty to forty. There*
> *were no benches in the cell and we were each given a mat and two blankets for*
> *sleeping. We slept on the mat on the cold cement as there were no beds. . . . The*
> *children stayed with us all the time. When I was busy cleaning floors and walls, I*
> *would tie the baby on my back and the older one would just stand next to me. . . .*
> *We received far too little food and I needed special baby food, like lactogen or*
> *nestum, for the baby. If we asked for more food, it was refused.*

Deciding upon imprisonment of women with small children

Differences between national policies on the imprisonment of
pregnant women and mothers with dependent children and diverse
prison conditions in the countries surveyed would at first sight
prevent any universally applicable solution to the problem. Yet, there
is one: non-imprisonment.

Arguments against the separation of a small child from its mother,
or against the keeping of a small child with its mother in prison, have
been and will remain a topic of study and controversy. The
International Seminar on Children in Adult Prisons analysed the
issue and a possible contribution of the DCI Exploratory Study in
terms of a policy proposal. An agreement was reached in the
following suggestion:

> *There was discussion about the advantages or otherwise of keeping children in*
> *prison with their mother (or father). It was generally accepted that mothers with*
> *young children, or who were pregnant, should not be put in prison. If they were*
> *to be sent to prison, then the system should be adapted to make it possible for the*
> *child to be with the parent with a minimal risk. There are comparatively few*
> *women in prison, even fewer mothers, and therefore special facilities should be*
> *provided in the relatively rare event of imprisonment of the mother being*
> *inevitable. The alternative to imprisonment should always be considered first.*
> *Imprisonment of mothers with or without children should be a last resort and*
> *should be carried out in special conditions.*

There are indications of such a policy already being followed by national courts, though only in just a few countries. Generally, the fate of the child of a mother facing or experiencing imprisonment has not received sufficient attention from legislators, judges or law enforcement agencies.

The procedure of deciding upon a custodial sentence for a pregnant woman or a mother with a small child should take more account of the fate of the child. According to the information collected by the DCI Exploratory Study, awareness that the child is being indirectly punished is generally lacking. An exception is found in the court practice and current legislative proposals in Austria.

> *The decision whether mothers may be permitted to have their small children with them rests with the prison management, subject to the approval of the Federal Ministry of Justice. Children born in prison are usually left with their mothers. But in any case the consent of the child-welfare authorities must be given. A mother can appeal to the Ministry of Justice against the decision of the prison management whether or not to let her child stay with her. Contrary to the precise stipulation of the law [a child may stay in prison until a year old, unless it jeopardizes the health of the child] at the present time a small child is left with its mother until the age of three. After that it is sent to relatives, or if necessary to a home. . . .*
>
> *Furthermore, the question of the child's board-and-lodging is taken into account by the competent penal court when considering whether to reduce the sentence by converting custodial sentence into a conditional one.*

Another exception is Costa Rica: *'the existence of dependent children is a factor which the judge in charge of the mother's case takes into consideration in deciding whether imprisonment, whether before trial or upon sentencing, is necessary'.*

The practice of the United States is interesting because of its substantially different attitude on decision-making with respect to imprisonment of mothers with dependent children. The existence of small children does not seem to be a mitigating factor in a decision on imprisonment. However, it may be a factor in defining abandonment of the child by its parent. The Supreme Court of Utah decided, for example, that a mother who committed a criminal offence and is subsequently imprisoned has voluntarily relinquished her parental rights: while committing the crime she must have been aware of the possibility of imprisonment and thus of being forced to abandon her child. A similar attitude has been adopted by the Appellate Court of New York which held that a mother's inability to continue regular contacts with her child, resulting from her own transgressions, can be determined as abandonment. Moreover, a similar attitude has been accepted for a father: the Texas Court of Appeals held that a man who committed a crime knowing of his wife's pregnancy and his own possible imprisonment for the crime had shown such indifference to his parental responsibilities that the state could have presumed a voluntary abandonment of his child.[1]

Note

1   Gomien, D., 'Prisoner Mothers, Babies and the State', unpublished seminar paper, Cornell Law School, Spring 1984.

8 Protection of children within the system of criminal justice

The problems encountered by children who are brought into the adult system of criminal justice are enormous and diverse. The varying laws, practices and experiences of the countries surveyed do not diminish the validity of the universal finding of the researchers — though different, the problems of children are beyond their ability to assert and protect their rights and interests. Therefore, special protection and assistance is indispensable.

A common feature revealed in all the national surveys is the lack of protection of children in the pre-trial stage of criminal proceedings. Extensive powers of the police, vague provisions for the protection of rights of arrested or detained persons and practically non-existent accountability of officials directly or indirectly responsible for ill-treatment of children caused the taking of children into custody and their pre-trial detention to be emphasized as a primary area of concern for the protection of children.

When the child is brought before the judge, its chances of having a fair trial are legally guaranteed. Practically, most children have no assistance, and their right to defence is seriously jeopardized. Considering the frequent non-existence of legal representation of children and the obstacles to their securing effective defence on their own, the DCI exploratory study revealed an emerging consensus on the necessity of having *juvenile judges* act *in loco parentis*. It has been realized that unless there is an agency specifically appointed to act for the benefit of children in the system of criminal justice, most proposals intended for the benefit of children will have no effect.

A child in prison — the main focus of the study — is a responsibility of the state concerned. According to the initial assumptions of the project, the exercise of the state's responsibility should be evaluated by the criteria used to determine whether parents are fit to care for their children. The following summary of results of national surveys brings up a few possible criteria for such an evaluation: those which states themselves profess as objectives of the incarceration of children.

Children in custody

Police custody and pre-trial detention has been singled out by most researchers participating in the DCI Exploratory Study as the problem urgently needing attention and legal regulation. Usually, police custody is deemed to be so exceptional and brief that it is left out of legal guarantees for the rights of children.

Accounts of unacceptable treatment of children before they have been brought before a judge are found in most of the national surveys. Three are quoted below:

> *Jamaica: 'The young person comes into contact with and under the influence not only of hardened adult criminals but also hardened young prisoners, convicted or on remand and recidivists. And this before his case has been heard, much less decided.'*

> *Thailand: 'Every child accused of committing an offence, either petty or capital, must be confined during the investigation process in the police station. There we have found that children are put in the same cell as adults, though it is forbidden by law.... Because of restricted premises and a limited budget it is very difficult for police officers to follow the letter of the law.'*

> *Colombia: 'Children under twelve may not be imprisoned. If they are detained by the police, they are placed under the supervision of minors' defenders* (defensores de menores). *A police station for minors operates in Bogotá. It is called the Comisaria de Menores.... On occasion, children under twelve may be held overnight at an ordinary police station. Abuses are reportedly common when children stay overnight at a police station. It is said that children have to surrender whatever money they have in their pockets before being released.'*

For all the countries covered by the exploratory study it has been found that the police may and do take children into custody. It was not possible to ascertain the frequency of such instances, the duration of the custody, the safeguards against abuse of children. Nevertheless, it was possible to infer from the information available that too little is known about it, which implies that police treatment of children, including custody, falls outside any supervision or complaint proceedings. The information obtained is unfavourable: most national surveys claim that children are not separated from adults during police custody, and quite a few mention the beating of children as a common method of interrogation.

In principle, police custody is legally confined to twenty-four or forty-eight hours in most countries (police decision), while the extension of custody has to be decided upon by a public prosecutor or a court of law. It is generally justified (in law, again) by the need for police investigation. Pre-trial detention may actually mean the prolongation of police custody or removal to a prison or a youth custodial institution, but this has — in most countries — to be decided upon by the court. The duration of pre-trial detention has not been quantified in the report because of the lack of data: in many countries inconsistencies have been reported between the legally permissible and the actual duration of police custody. However, data on the latter are not available. The situation is further complicated by the differing legal institutions: the term 'preventive detention', for example, stands for totally different types of incarceration in different countries.

An exception to the lack of information on the use of custody of children is Denmark.

> *According to the data for the period January–September 1981, 199 persons aged fifteen to seventeen were remanded in custody, out of a total of 3,039 persons. The average length of time they spent in local prisons [or in youth institutions] was sixty-four days . . . 46 per cent of the persons aged fifteen to seventeen who were charged for a criminal offence in that nine-month period were detained during police investigations . . . 42 per cent of the detained persons aged fifteen to seventeen were arrested for a maximum period of 24 hours (police decision), 0.3% were in custody for additional periods of three times 24 hours (court decision), and 3.6% were remanded in custody (pre-trial detention, court decision). The total number of detained persons aged fifteen to seventeen was 2,574.*

Children in police custody and pre-trial detention are subject to interrogation, the meaning and implications of which they often do not understand. An important safeguard has to be the protection of children against self-incrimination. The general principle of the protection of detainees asserts the right of the suspect or the accused not to testify against himself. Children require additional protection: ideally, the principle should be that children should not be interrogated unless the defence counsel is present to assist the child. However, most children do not have defence counsels; the absolute minimum should therefore be not to interrogate children unless a judicial official, preferably a juvenile judge is present. The implementation of such a rule is fairly simple: national laws embodying such a principle declare any evidence gathered in violation of such a rule inadmissible.

An example of the necessity to protect children from self-incrimination is given in the DCI survey of *South Africa*:

> *The Appellate Division case of S. v Mpongoshe illustrates the inability of two fifteen-year-old youths to comprehend the consequences of a plea of guilty to a serious charge and the lack of protection afforded ... Fortunately these children were legally represented and their legal adviser explained to the court that despite their inclination to plead guilty, he was certain that they did not comprehend the meaning of sabotage in terms of the relevant legislation. In the meantime, the court had already questioned the accused (as it may do), elicited damaging admissions, and sentenced them to five years' imprisonment.*

Two practically universal features of pre-trial detention of children are evident from the national surveys: (1) pre-trial detention exposes children to the worst violations of their rights, at the same time that those children are to be presumed innocent because they are awaiting trial; and (2) legally, pre-trial detention of children is exceptional, and most states do not enact detailed regulations for the treatment of children; in practice it is widespread and prolonged. Frequently, national researchers reported that *the majority of children in prison were awaiting trial.* The duration of pre-trial detention uncovered was up to two or even three years.

The conditions of such detention are evaluated as unacceptable in most of the DCI surveys. With respect to the principal focus of the study — separation or non-separation of children from adults — it has been emphasized that if separation has been implemented, which is an exception, it virtually puts children in conditions of solitary confinement:

> *Germany, F.R.: 'isolation (often twenty-three hours a day in a solitary cell, interrupted by a one-hour walk)', of two to three months' duration;*

> *Netherlands: 'The whole day is spent in the cell, except when the police want to interrogate the boy. If possible, the latter can spend half an hour a day in the open air'.*

> *France, pre-trial detention: '... the minors are kept twelve to twenty-four out of twenty-four hours in cells. In fact, the "walk" and othe "activities" are not obligatory'.*

> *Denmark: 'Persons in pre-trial detention are sometimes held twenty-three hours a day in the cell, except for short visits to the toilet. The twenty-fourth hour consists of two half-hour walks in the open air in narrow cage-like walled yards with wire netting on top. There are examples of fifteen to seventeen-year-olds*

being detained before trial under such circumstances.'

Costa Rica: 'The most disturbing aspect of their detention was the complete lack of physical exercise and virtual twenty-four-hours-a-day confinement to their cell. The first minor reported that, in twenty-four days of detention, he had been out of his cell only twice a day for one hour each time.'

United Kingdom (England and Wales): 'In some prisons, and in police cells, prisoners may be locked up for twenty-three hours a day.'

The legislation of Germany, F.R. requires youths (children aged fourteen to eighteen) to be separated from adults in pre-trial detention, and the detention itself has to be executed so as to provide the children with educational opportunities. The national survey of Germany identifies the gap between legal provisions and actual practice:

Apart from a few exceptions, however, the arrangement of the remand sentence hardly fulfils the legal requirements. It is mainly guided by the object of securing the procedure, by the risk of the escape of the detainee, by the gravity of the charge and the danger of repetition, and it is brought into line with the remand sentences for adults with the corresponding isolation (often twenty-three hours a day in a solitary cell, interrupted by one hour's walk). . . . Only in a few cases is the period of remand for juveniles executed in juvenile prisons, where the relevant educational facilities exist. The number of youths on remand is much higher than the number of youths actually convicted and sent to juvenile prisons. . . . On a selected day, 31 January 1983, there were 852 prisoners aged from ten to eighteen held on remand.

The rule of separation of children from adults in police custody is often not implemented because of lack of will and material conditions. However, an example of a solution designed to observe the rule of separation despite inadequate conditions come from Costa Rica:

When a juvenile is taken into custody during the night or weekend and detained in a police station, the usual practice outside San José is not to detain them in cells, but in the station's administrative area. In Puntarenas, they are kept in an enclosed inner courtyard of the Guardia Civil headquarters, and on occasion are put in an unoccupied office or store room at night. In other offices of the Guardia Civil they are kept in the troop's recreation room. In the Cartago headquarters of the Guardia Civil they are kept in a chapel, and in the San Carlos office of the judicial police they are kept in the detectives' desk area.

Table 10   Applicability of the rule of separation of children from adults to police custody and administrative or security detention

Country	Applicability of the rule of separation to police custody of children	Imprisonment of children on grounds other than suspicion of or charged with a criminal offence
Austria	no	Administrative offences; aliens
Bulgaria	no	Security and administrative offences
Canada	no	Administrative offences; aliens
Chile	no	Military and security orders; internment of anti-social persons
Colombia	no	Procedure for the expulsion of aliens
Costa Rica	yes	no
Denmark	no	Administrative offences; aliens
Finland	yes	no
France	no	Administrative offences; aliens
Germany, F.R.	no	Detention of children in need of education
India	no	Detention of children in need of care
Italy	no	Measures of detentive security
Jamaica	no	Preventive detention; detention of vagrants; detention for the purpose of education and welfare
Japan	no	Detention of aliens
Morocco	no	Detention by virtue of parental punishment
Netherlands	no	Administrative offences; aliens
Nigeria	no	Detention of beggars, vagrants
Pakistan	no	no
Romania	no	Security and administrative offences
South Africa	no	Security regulations; administrative offences; restrictions of freedom of movement and residence
Spain	no	no
Switzerland	no	Administrative offences; aliens
Thailand	no	no
United Kingdom: Scotland	yes	no
United Kingdom: England & Wales	no	Administrative offences; aliens
Yugoslavia	no	Administrative offences; infractions
Zaire	no	Detention of vagrants and beggars
West Bank	no	Military and security orders

Table 10 shows the information available on the existence of the rule of separation in detention which is not 'imprisonment' in the narrow meaning of the word. The information in the table is not complete. However, we have listed what is available in an attempt to analyse the operation of this rule.

The first column in the table shows whether the general principle of separation is applied to police custody. On numerous occasions researchers remarked on the existence of a rule which is not observed in practice. Still, we were interested in determining whether any rule exists at all. It is obvious that separation of children from adults in police custody 'as a rule' exists only in a small number of countries. Again, we have not treated the rule as existing if it allows for exceptions (e.g. 'if possible', 'unless circumstances require otherwise'), but only if the rule specifies the conduct which police officials have to adopt in dealing with children.

The second column is a sketchy picture of how children are treated in administrative and security detention. Not all the national surveys included the information needed. For countries marked with 'no' either the assertion was that there is no such detention or we could not ascertain whether detention other than in connection with criminal offences exists. However, where we could uncover such detention, it usually did not provide for any protective measures in favour of children. The information available has been presented here to alert the reader to a practice of detention of children which is not widely known, and which, according to the information available, is in violation of the essential international standards for the protection of children in custody.

Children in court

The Children in Adult Prisons Study referred to criminal proceedings only from the viewpoint of deciding upon or control over the imprisonment of children. However, sufficient information has been gathered on legal proceedings to allow for the following conclusion: one of the major deficiencies of the criminal justice system is the almost complete lack of institutionalized representation and protection of the rights of the child.

The empirical material gathered within the study reveals that the right to counsel does not exist as an enforceable right for children suspected of or charged with criminal offences. While most countries have provisions on the right to a counsel, the realization of that right is in practice confined to private engagement of legal counsel by the child's family. Free legal aid exists in an increasing number of countries, but its scope does not cover all the cases of children in conflict with the law.

The same conclusion has been reached within the UNITAR study previously mentioned, which consisted of sixty reports on the status of children under national law. The conclusion with respect to legal representation of children in proceedings against them deserves to be quoted:

> The right to counsel is becoming more important because of the informality of juvenile court proceedings (in most states it seems proceedings against juveniles are held in special courts or separate courtrooms) and the concomitant lack of adherence to standard procedural safeguards generally applicable to adults. Although the motivation behind the relaxation of formal rules in juvenile courts has been the search for flexible and individualized or non-punitive treatment of children, the system actually (because of heavy case loads, unsuitable and inadequate staff and resources) works to their detriment: children end up with less, not greater protection than adults.

It goes on to emphasize that 'procedural safeguards have been given up for benefits which, by and large, have not materialized', and adds with respect to punitive treatment of children that various measures are 'all based on a promise of rehabilitation within the system which it is not sufficiently equipped to fulfil.'[1]

It is not possible to compare the implementation of the right to defence of the accused, including children, because most of the data available relate to the legal formulation of the right. The proportion of the accused which avail themselves of that right is not known for the majority of the countries surveyed. However, it is worth emphasizing that the lack of defence for children within the adult penal system is evident in a sufficient number of instances to indicate that more often than not children have no legal assistance during the proceedings against them.

> *The report from Spain includes interviews conducted with thirty-three juvenile inmates. Of these, only four had some help from a lawyer during the proceedings.*
>
> *The report from South Africa explains the lack of legal assistance in the following terms: 'Most juveniles accused would fulfil the requirements for free*

legal aid, yet most of them have never heard of free legal aid. Many accused juveniles are not even aware of their right to a lawyer. Even if they are, they do not contemplate engaging an attorney because of the expense. One can only speculate about the chances of a fair trial for a young child alone in court conducting his/her own defence within the complex technical principles of the criminal procedure.'

The interviews conducted with young inmates in India (age range eleven to eighteen) confirm that legal assistance to children is provided by the families. Out of 234 children interviewed, 39 per cent stated that legal aid was arranged for them by their families; the other children had none.

Two major conclusions may be drawn from the empirical material collected:

(1) most of the countries surveyed have separate juvenile courts to deal with young offenders;
(2) most of the countries also have additional provisions concerning legal assistance or special juvenile counsels, social workers or welfare officials.

Also, in most of the countries children in practice do *not* get assistance during the criminal proceedings. It may be generally asserted that assistance to the child depends on the involvement of its family. Children without support and assistance from parents and relatives do not get much assistance if they have to rely upon legislative provisions on the possibility of assistance. Many have been imprisoned without even knowing what assistance they might or should have had.

Differences in legal systems prevent summarized comparisons between legal aid to and representation of minors, but in spite of variations in penal proceedings against children, the common feature of practically all systems is an emphasis on the role of the juvenile court and/or juvenile judge.

Its role is twofold: the traditional task of protecting the interests of the state/society is coupled with the requirement to take account of and protect the rights and interests of the child.

A good example of provisions on the special role of the juvenile court is the legislation of Jamaica:

Where a juvenile is brought before a juvenile court, it shall be the duty of such a court to explain to him in as simple language as possible the reason for his being before the court.

Where a juvenile is charged before a juvenile court with any offence, it shall be the duty of the court to ascertain the defence, if any, of the juvenile so as to put, or assist the juvenile and his parents or guardian in putting such questions to any witnesses as appear to be necessary.

Where a juvenile is charged with any offence, and admits the offence so that the court is satisfied that the offence has been proved, the court shall record a finding to that effect and, before sentencing the juvenile, shall obtain such information as to his general conduct, home surroundings, school record, and medical history as may enable it to deal with the case in the best interest of the juvenile.' [CCPR/C/Add. 53, p. 19]

Children in prison

Throughout the report indications of detrimental effects of prison upon children have been given, as well as descriptions of the inability of children to assert and protect their rights within the system of (adult) criminal justice.

The present section will not repeat the topics already dealt with, but will focus on particular two problems of children in adult prisons: labour and education. Analyses of the implementation of the general purpose of imprisonment — to (re)educate inmates and prepare them for self-supporting and law-abiding lives — made within the empirical section of the exploratory study confirm that imprisonment is not a good alternative from the viewpoint of rights and interests of children.

While observations and empirical surveys speak about the over-all lack of education of imprisoned children, quite a number of them identified conditions of forced labour. These require an analysis of imprisonment as a negation of its own purpose: instead of schooling, prisons 'offer' manual labour. Forced labour of imprisoned children has to be denounced as a violation of a whole range of their rights. The issue has been raised by the national survey of Pakistan:

It may be mentioned here that under the Factories Act no person under the age of seventeen can be made to work more than seven hours a day, and not more than three and a half hours at a stretch without at least one hour's break in between. The maximum working time per week for such children is forty-two hours. Since these rules were made keeping in view the physical limitations of a child of that age, it would be more humane to apply those rules to child prisoners as well.

Child prisoners in Pakistan work ten hours per day. The report of Great Britain for Hong Kong shows that prisoners — children not excluded — also have to work ten hours a day: 'Imprisonment with hard labour may not be imposed as a punishment for a crime. A convicted prisoner may, unless excused by the medical officer, be required to do useful work for not more than ten hours a day and may be paid for his work at approved rates' (CCPR/C/1/Add.37, Report by Hong Kong, pp. 83–4).

The exploitation of child labour has been prohibited by the ICCPR and the ICESCR, i.e. by general international law and by a number of ILO conventions. Yet, information about the exploitation of child labour in prison is not sufficiently known. Children are victimized by being treated as if they were adults. An example of such inconsistency in the law itself comes from Pakistan:

> *Women and juvenile prisoners are required to perform one-third of the tasks fixed for hard and medium labour for adult male convicted persons. The actual tasks might be lighter, but they entail nine hours' steady work for even the juvenile prisoners . . . under the Factories Act no person under the age of seventeen can be made to work for more than seven hours a day.'*

Accounts of the neglect of the education of child prisoners as a result of their work come from India and Yugoslavia:

> *There is no schooling for juvenile remand prisoners at any place; as such, no time is fixed for it. At some prisons . . . trained teachers competent to impart elementary literacy are employed, but they are mostly found helping the administration . . . [child prisoners] work, not towards their own rehabilitation, but to help the management make ends meet. The grant per child per month is in the ranges of Rs. 75–100 ($US 9–12). Obviously, the children earn nothing . . . How can the State itself ignore their rights to education and stoop to the shameful exploitation of child labour?*
>
> *[In Yugoslavia,] penal institutions have to rely on prisoners' labour for income needed to maintain the institution. The system of funding for the penal institutions envisages the income to be generated by inmates' work . . . The work of inmates has to generate sufficient income, because a substantial part of the salaries of the prison staff depends directly on the economic effect of prisoners' labour. The legislation states that every prisoner capable of working is obliged to work, and no specific provision is added with respect to minors. The prison authorities have discretion regarding the relief of those minors who are attending school of their obligation to work.*

While most national laws set a minimum age for imprisonment

and a higher minimum age for imprisonment including hard labour, it is interesting to note a determination of an upper age-limit for prison labour without a corresponding lower age-limit in the legislation of Romania: 'After the age of sixty in the case of men and fifty-five in the case of women, convicted persons are not required to work while serving their sentence'. The minimum age for imprisonment is fourteen but the general obligation to work is set at sixteen. The law stipulated the general obligation of all convicted persons to work (the minimum age for imprisonment is fourteen) and educational training and remuneration as a reward for good behaviour: 'the convicted person is required to perform useful work for which he is suited. Convicted persons also receive educational training, incentives and remuneration where they prove to be hard-working, disciplined and of good behaviour' (CCPR/C/1/Add.33 at p. 11).

Education of imprisoned children may be a good indication of the realization of the *purpose of imprisonment* in practice. If the essential aim is to enable children to lead a normal life after release, the period of imprisonment should be used to enable them to do so.

The UN Standard Minimum Rules for the Treatment of Prisoners spell out the purpose of imprisonment in rule 58: 'The purpose and justification of a sentence of imprisonment or a similar measure deprivative of liberty is ultimately to protect society against crime. This end can only be achieved if the period of imprisonment is used to ensure, so far as possible, that upon his return to society the offender is not only willing, but able to lead a law-abiding and self-supporting life.'

An additional rule makes education of young prisoners compulsory: 'The education of illiterates and young prisoners shall be compulsory and special attention shall be paid to it by the administration (rule 77, para 1).

An obvious consequence of those rules, which 'represent, as a whole, the minimum conditions which are accepted as suitable by the United Nations' (rule 2), is the possibility of testing the implementation of the purpose of the imprisonment of children by analysing whether, or to what extent, prison treatment enables children to lead a self-supporting life after release. The principal foci of attention should therefore be education and vocational training.

Table 11 shows the existence and extent of compulsory education of imprisoned children. Only provisions relevant to the education of children in adult facilities are included, thus leaving aside the regimes of specialized institutions for the custody of children, which were beyond the terms of reference of this project.

Notes

1 Mamalakis Pappas, A., *Law and the Status of the Child*, pp. LII–LIII.

Table 11 Labour, education and vocational training of children in adult prisons

Country	Compulsory education	Compulsory labour	Education during imprisonment	Labour during imprisonment	Vocational training
Austria	Up to the age of 15	6 hours per day with adults	Instruction twice a week	Manual labour	Courses twice a month
Chile	No	No			
Colombia	No obligation of the State to provide facilities	No	Choice between education and work together with adults depending on facilities		
Costa Rica	No	No		Inmate has to agree to work	
Denmark	Yes, in State prisons; no. in local prisons	40 hours a week: choice between education, work and vocational training			
Finland	No	No		Inmates entitled to do work of their choice and keep the income	
France	No	No	Adult-type courses a few times a week	Manual labour	
Germany, F.R.	Yes	No	General education and training courses	Work directed towards vocational training	
India	No	Yes	Conditions varied	Manual labour Hard labour	No
Italy	No	Yes	Prison-schools: separate institutions	Work is a part of the re-educational treatment	
Jamaica	Compulsory literacy courses				
Japan	Up to the age of 18	Imprisonment with forced labour a penalty			

Table 11 (*continued*)

					Work directed towards vocational training
Netherlands	1½ hours per day compulsory	Yes	6 hours per day voluntary		
Nigeria	Up to the age of 16	No	4 hours instruction per day	Not applicable	Children above 16 taught trades and skills
Pakistan	No	9 hours per day	No formal education	Manual labour Hard labour	No
South Africa	No	Yes	Literacy courses conditions varied	Manual labour	Conditions varied
Spain	Yes	No		Work is a right of inmates	
Thailand	No		Adult education programme		Training workshops
United Kingdom: Scotland	Up to the age of 16	Yes	Remedial classes; daily & evening classes	5 hours a day: inmates allocated to work/ training workshops	
United Kingdom: England & Wales	No	No	Conditions varied	Prison regulations require 10 hours of work a day	
Yugoslavia	Yes	Yes	Conditions varied	Manual labour	Conditions varied
Zaire	No	Yes	Civic and revolutionary education	Manual labour Forced labour	No

9 Responsibility for the victimization of children in adult prisons

The purpose of bringing up the issue of responsibility for the treatment of children in the system of criminal justice, particularly in prisons, can best be explained by posing a simple question: to whom can one complain concerning the treatment of children — within the prison system, locally, nationally, internationally? In other words, are there bodies whose terms of reference include the protection of the rights and interests of children within the system of criminal justice which could supervise the implementation of the existing principles and norms designed to protect the rights of children, initiate specific actions to assist children in having their rights observed or act on behalf of children, and — ultimately — suggest changes necessary to prevent criminalization and victimization of children?

One has to bear in mind that those most in need of protection are frequently kept ignorant of their rights, and are unable to do anything to protect themselves. DCI national surveys reveal practices of incarceration of children as young as five or ten:

> *In South Africa a child as young as seven could be arrested, detained, tried, convicted, and sentenced... in Pakistan any child above ten can be ordered to be kept in prison... in Colombia children under twelve can be held overnight at an ordinary police station ... in Canada a respondent to the DCI questionnaire reported that five boys, ages five to sixteen, were detained an average of forty days in an adult penal facility in Newfoundland ...*

Those are some of the instances reported; one cannot help wondering how many more woud be identified if the information on children in adult prisons were collected systematically.

Conclusions of the International Seminar on Children in Adult Prisons held in Florence included an assertion that legislation on the protection of children from and within the criminal justice system is indispensable, but insufficient: *'monitoring and supervision are crucial problems of protection of rights of imprisoned children. No laws, however well drafted, can have beneficial effects for children unless their application is supervised.'*

The necessary components for establishing violations of rights of children and punishing those responsible would be: (1) identification of persons responsible for securing compliance with the laws and regulations asserting the rights of children deprived of liberty; (2) establishment of a procedure for the enforcement of those standards, including penalties for non-compliance; (3) keeping registers containing all relevant information about children who are incarcerated; (4) establishment of inspection and/or supervisory services. Most countries have legislation determining penalties for law enforcement officials who infringe the rules for the treatment of inmates. Some examples follow:

> *In Costa Rica the Penal Code makes an offence the concealment of detainees by authorities, and it also imposes penalties on any public official who abuses his office by committing an arbitrary act prejudicial to somebody's rights; in Japan the Penal Code defines a special type of crime as the abuse of authority by public officials, and it lays down special criminal procedures and penalties for public officials who resort to coercion, physical violence and maltreatment (two to ten years of imprisonment); in India the issue of cruelty to prisoners is dealt with by the Prisons Act which stipulates that in case any excesses are committed against a prisoner, the prison administration is held responsible. . . .*

In Colombia there is a specific assertion of responsibility for non-compliance with rules concerning children:

> It shall be prohibited to hold a juvenile under sixteen years of age in places other than [a secure place separate from a common prison] or special establishments for juveniles. Any infringement of this prohibition shall render the official issuing the order for remand in custody and the warden or head of the establishment concerned liable to dismissal and to disqualification from public office and the exercise of public rights for a period of one year; such penalty shall be imposed summarily by the appropriate superior official, simply on presentation of proof that the breach has been committed. [CCPR/C/Add. 50, p. 19.]

The last quotation invokes the initial assumption of this chapter: the process of identifying the responsible person is dependent upon an agency empowered to start proceedings, and the existence of proof of violation of the rights of a child. It therefore seems more important to focus on monitoring and supervision than to cite legislation which might, or might not, be implemented in practice.

Supervision of the prison system

DCI surveys generally conclude that there is a lack of any supervision of prison conditions and treatment in the respective countries, not even by the prison authorities, let alone by independent outside bodies. The problem of supervision of prisons in general goes far beyond the issue of imprisoned children, and has itself been a subject of considerable concern.

The most difficult aspect is, again, what happens in police stations or lock-ups before a child is brought before the judge. The scope of the problem is outlined in the national survey of Pakistan:

> *Use of force by the police is a common feature. It may be mentioned that a majority of child delinquents belong to the class of 'street children' and, as such, lack the support of any guardian or relative. Consequently, any injustice to them goes undetected and unpunished. The duty of regular inspection of police stations is badly neglected by superior officers. Although recommendations and suggestions for improvement of conditions for confinement are being made by individuals and social agencies, the matter of incarceration in police stations particularly in reference to children is being badly neglected.*

Accountability of the police brings up a range of problems far beyond the treatment of children. As far as children are concerned, a specific arrangement has to be added to any general regulations of the police work — the time children can be kept incarcerated should be reduced to an absolute minimum, and children should be brought before a judge as soon as possible, preferably within twenty-four hours.

The relevance of bringing the child before the court is connected with the already mentioned proposal on the protection of children in the criminal justice system, *viz.* that juvenile judges should act *in loco parentis.* A role for judges in the supervision of prison treatment and conditions of imprisonment of children has already been envisaged in a number of countries at least in principle.

The most common form consists in empowering the juvenile judge to exercise supervision over the execution of the penalty. In France 'the judge who passed the sentence is responsible for keeping the convicted person's progress under review and ensuring the individual application of judicial sentences by deciding on the main aspects of treatment in prison' (CCPR/C/Add.2, p. 20). Similar provisions exist in numerous other national legal systems. All the same, the results of the research collected in the DCI project demonstrate that the law is often not observed in practice:

> *In Costa Rica, the legislative provision is similar: 'every juvenile court [has the duty] to visit the establishments for the confinement of minors in his jurisdiction at least once a week'. However, the practice is different: this provision is virtually a dead letter as far as provincial juvenile judges are concerned . . . While the judges do not make regular visits to minors detained . . . the social workers attached to their courts do. Moreover, the juvenile courts' social workers have a centralized administration, with a national director and supervisor, who regularly visits the provincial courts and detention centres. This system has undoubtedly aided in preventing or detecting and rectifying problems.*

> *In Jamaica, supervision of prison conditions is entrusted to the Board of Visitors; while that body has the duty 'to see that the welfare of prisoners is taken care of', the practice is different: 'This body hardly ever meets.'*

> *In Yugoslavia, legislative provisions entrust supervision of the execution of juvenile imprisonment to juvenile courts: 'judicial control of the execution of sentences is explicitly provided by the legislation concerning minors, but in practice juvenile courts have no role at all in the supervision of the execution of the imprisonment of minors . . . visits of judges to prisons are organized and conducted routinely once a year'.*

The UN Standard Minimum Rules require regular inspection of penal institutions. The European Standard Minimum Rules went a step further and laid down the necessity of control of prison conditions and treatment by judicial or other duly constituted bodies, outside the prison administration, by visits of such bodies to prisons and authorizing their access to prisoners. Modalities of supervision of prisons in the countries surveyed are extremely varied. The DCI surveys identified five major types:

(1) *supervision by ombudsman-type bodies* (Denmark, Finland);
(2) *executive supervision* (by the Ministry of Justice in Japan, by the Ministry of Internal Affairs in Yugoslavia);
(3) *boards of visitors* (England, Jamaica, Morocco);
(4) *judicial supervision* (United States);
(5) *supervision by public prosecutors* (Bulgaria, Romania).

No suggestions as to the type of supervision best suited for the protection of children can be made because most national surveys assert that the system of supervision employed does not function effectively.

Monitoring of prison conditions and treatment

Access to information on children in adult prisons has been singled out throughout the DCI Exploratory Study as the key to the protection of the rights of imprisoned children. This book shows to what extent information is scarce, incomplete, confidential or inaccurate. However, a promising sign has been the willingness in a significant number of countries approached to grant access to prisons to national researchers conducting DCI surveys.

Protection of the rights of imprisoned children demands that monitoring of their treatment and conditions be made not only a legitimate field of activity within assistance to children, but a public duty. Unless there is information on the (ill) treatment of children in prison, it is impossible to implement a scheme securing the rights of those children. As has already been stated, the problem is the protection of children, persons whom the law recognizes as a group entitled to special protection because they are not able to assert and enforce their rights — in prison least of all.

The Florence seminar concluded that *'monitoring at local, national and international levels has to be recognized formally as an integral and indispensable part of protection of the rights of children'*. Moreover, monitoring of the effectiveness of the prison system is a pre-requisite for upholding or changing it, if it does not achieve its objectives. Most proposals of alternatives to imprisonment are based on the established inability of the prison system either to rehabilitate or to deter offenders. Particularly with respect to children, specialists generally agree that imprisonment is a totally unacceptable solution.

Irrespective of arguing the case against imprisonment of children as a matter of principle, it is still necessary to devise methods to secure monitoring of prison conditions affecting children because there are only a few tendencies towards the replacement of imprisonment by alternatives which exclude the deprivation of liberty.

The necessity for monitoring the conditions and treatment of persons deprived of liberty has repeatedly been asserted as an essential condition for their protection. A recent compilation of non-governmental information submitted to the United Nations on violations of the rights of detainees and prisoners ends with the following conclusion of the UN Secretariat: 'Despite the intensity and frequency of violations of the human rights of detainees, it is difficult to quantify violations and establish patterns . . . mainly because of the atmosphere of secrecy that generally surrounds them'.[1] The DCI surveys show that a number of countries do not allow access to prisons, and publication of information about prison conditions is an indictable offence.

No public duty to monitor prison conditions and treatment is by international treaties, but the United Nations has asserted it in quasi-legal instruments. The Code of Conduct for Law Enforcement Officials states, *inter alia*, that the work of law enforcement officials should be subject to public scrutiny. Moreover, it imposes the duty to report violations of minimum human rights standards 'within the chain of command or outside it, if no other remedies are available or effective'. Additionally, it asserts that the mass media may perform monitoring functions by bringing the violations of the rights of detainees and prisoners to the attention of the public.[2]

Possibility of complaints by or on behalf of children

The right to submit complaints against violations of rights has been firmly established in international human rights law. Generally, the ICCPR asserts the right to an effective remedy against acts violating human rights, including those committed by persons acting in an official capacity. Specifically, the UN Standard Minimum Rules lay down the right of detainees and prisoners to submit requests and complaints to the director of the institution, the inspector of prisons, the central prison administration, a judicial authority or to another competent authority.

The right is not exercised by most detained or imprisoned children. Some of the reasons are indicated in DCI surveys of Yugoslavia and Chile. In Yugoslavia:

> *Possibilities for minors to institute proceedings for the protection of their rights during imprisonment are lacking. The existing regulations allow a wide margin of discretion to prison authorities in deciding upon all issues of the conditions of imprisonment . . . The low educational level of the imprisoned minors includes their lack of knowledge about their rights and the possibilities for their protection. The traditional authority of the prison personnel and the frequent use of corporal punishment make it even more difficult.*

The national survey of Chile explains the lack of complaints by detainees by the pattern of political repression:

The sectors of society which are most victimized by political detention of minors are poor sections, poblaciones *and students.*

The repression is today extended to the very poor sectors of society, to people who are unfamiliar with their legal rights and who are so used to arbitrariness that they do not make complaints, or who lack means to inform solidarity organizations.

The UN Committee on Crime Prevention and Control repeatedly emphasizes the exercise of the right of prisoners to submit complaints as a key recommendation for the systems of criminal justice. A recent set of recommendations includes '. . . the strengthening of inmate grievance procedures by ensuring to prisoners the right of recourse to an independent authority at both the national and international levels.' In addition, the Committee singled out detention in police custody and in prison custody before trial as areas where detainees are least protected.

Children need the option to have complaints submitted on their behalf by the family, a defence lawyer or a social welfare body to make up for their legal and actual inability to protect their rights. A number of countries have established special bodies with the mandate to protect the rights of children within the system of criminal justice (for example, Defensor de Menores). Others make the protection of children within criminal justice a task of juvenile courts. However, there is a need to recognize the right to initiate proceedings and invoke remedies on behalf of children deprived of liberty for individuals or organizations acting for the benefit of children. The standing to initiate such proceedings is limited to the victim or his or her family. Such a method leaves children who have no family to act for their benefit without anybody to assist them.

Notes

1 *The administration of justice and human rights of detainees.* Question of human rights of persons subjected to any form of detention and imprisonment. Synopsis of material received from non-governmental organizations in consultative status with the Economic and Social Council, prepared by the Secretariat. U.N. Doc. E/CN.4/Sub.2/1984/13. 5 June 1984, para 60.
2 *Code of Conduct for Law Enforcement Officials.* Annex to the General Assembly Resolution 34/169. 17 December 1979.

10 Alternatives to imprisonment existing in the countries surveyed

Children in adult prisons need protection from abuse by prison guards and adult inmates. Separation from adults ameliorates their circumstances, but children are still exposed to the hardship of prison life. Finally, it has frequently been established that prisons neither rehabilitate nor deter — another incentive to consider imprisonment from the viewpoint of its possible replacement by alternatives not involving deprivation of liberty.

Movements for alternatives to imprisonment exist in countries which differ by any criteria one might use. Research on Africa shows, for example, that imprisonment had been 'imported' together with colonialism. Research on Great Britain shows a variety of small-scale projects attempting to deal with juvenile delinquents by counselling or community work, instead of the official policy of 'short, sharp shock' of imprisonment, which has frequently been determined as being too shocking. In the United States formal judicial procedure has been replaced by 'teenager courts' in some small-scale experimental projects attempting to enable juveniles to contribute to the reduction of delinquency without involving adults.

The DCI surveys often departed from a mere analysis of prison conditions and asserted the need to replace imprisonment as a method for dealing with children and juveniles. Three examples below show a high degree of similarity in the identification of reasons for the substitution of imprisonment:

> *The survey of prison conditions for children in Pakistan includes the following conclusion by the researcher: 'Theories regarding criminal justice have differed on many points, but there has been unanimity on the need for independent institutions where efforts can be concentrated on the welfare of the juvenile. That some societies still tolerate the existence of juvenile wards in prisons and jails only points to the fact that children have become victims of their neglect.'*

> *The survey of the Federal Republic of Germany correlates the negative effectiveness of juvenile imprisonment and the trend to build additional prison*

facilities which assure the use of imprisonment in the future: 'The worst preventive effects are produced by imprisonment for no fixed duration and juvenile punishment. This knowledge has, however, not yet led to any obvious consequence in the jurisdiction by avoiding the sentencing as juvenile punishment or by reducing it. What is more, the tendency in the whole Federal Republic (in the individual federal states) is towards creating new space for confinement by building new prisons. Instead of the money flowing into the extension of ambulant help, it flows into the ten times more expensive stationary section. There, 'the medicine which has proved to be ineffective is applied over and over again in ever greater doses as a compulsory therapy.'

In the United States, the Juvenile Justice and Delinquency Prevention Act of 1974 was enacted 'in response to the documented failure of the juvenile justice system' based on repression/imprisonment while neglecting prevention of delinquency. The implementation measures for the new law include incentives for the federal states to develop delinquency prevention programmes, 'particularly community-based programmes and services which would reduce the use of costly and unnecessary incarceration of youth.'

Evidence of the utilization of outdated prisons and prison regulations has been found throughout the project: in India some of the prison buildings are older than 250 years; in Denmark nineteenth-century prisons are still used today; in Pakistan laws on reformatory schools and borstals originate from 1897 and 1926 respectively; in Japan the Prison Law of 1908 is still in use. Even a cursory look at recently adopted national and international legislation shows that conceptions on the treatment of offenders have changed radically, especially with respect to the treatment of young offenders. By the utilization of prisons we are — to borrow the words of Marshall McLuhan — trying to do today's job with yesterday's tools.

The existence of alternatives to imprisonment in a growing number of states is an encouraging sign of the changes on the level of governmental policy for dealing with delinquent children. The examples of the alternatives to imprisonment have been described both in the national surveys and in the states' reports on the implementation of the ICCPR. The following extracts may be quoted as illustrative of the current changes in policies, laws, and practices:

United Kingdom (England and Wales): the reasoning behind the legislative changes introducing alternatives to imprisonment by the replacement of the deprivation of liberty with community service was described by the then Minister of State at the Home Office, Leon Brittan, in 1979 in the following terms: 'it is obvious, from common sense, from experience, and from research, that teaching anyone to come to terms with the community in which he lives must for the most part be better done in that community'. The Powers of the Criminal Courts Act 1973 empowers the court which has convicted a person of an offence punishable with imprisonment to make a community service order requiring him to perform unpaid work for not less that forty or more than 240 hours. The court has to explain to the offender the purpose and the effect of the community service order and the offender has to give his consent. The actual work is carried out under the instructions of the probation officer.

United Kingdom (Scotland): according to the Community Service by Offenders (Scotland) Act of 1978, courts in Scotland have the power to make community service orders for offenders over the age of sixteen and also to make unpaid work a provision of the probation order. The work consists of forty to 240 hours of unpaid work for the benefit of the community over the period of up to one year, but [unlike the system applied in England and Wales] the supervision is not carried out by probation officers, but by the social work department of the local community where the offender resides.

Jamaica: by the Criminal Justice (Reform) Act of 1978, community service orders have been introduced as substitutes for the penalties of deprivation of liberty, thus giving the court an additional option for non-custodial sentencing besides probation, probation with compulsory attendance of a training centre and suspended sentences with or without supervision. The community service orders resemble the scheme devised in the United Kingdom, with the addition of the requirement that community service should not interfere with school attendance of the offender. However, the national survey stresses the hesitant utilization of alternatives to imprisonment by juvenile courts because of the insufficiently developed infrastructure for the implementation of such measures. An opinion of a Justice of the Appeal is cited to that effect: 'There is little hope of convincing judges that deterrence as a central principle of sentencing policy should be rejected in favour of reform when the machinery for effective reform is non-existent.'

Italy: alternatives to custodial sentencing of minors have been developed by the application of semi-liberty regimes and the release of young inmates on trust to the social services. The semi-liberty regime consists of allowing an inmate to spend a part of the day outside the prison establishment, participating in educational or work activities. Release on trust to the social services may be granted to juvenile inmates (and adults) for the period equal to the rest of the custodial sentence based on 'verified behavioural characteristics', and it includes the participation of the former inmate in a community programme of education, work and social integration.

France: a legislative decree of 26 January 1983 was devised to 'mitigate the rigours of prison life' and combat the over-population of prisons. It advocates greater use of alternatives to imprisonment and introduces a new sentencing option — community service. The previously existing alternatives included various forms of semi-liberty and probation, with the addition of 'providing the person with such welfare and educational assistance as he may require'. The social and educational assistance has been introduced to eliminate the discrepancy between the need for assistance of the juveniles in danger, and repression against juveniles in breach of the law. The national survey includes the following conclusion on the insufficiency of the traditional societal response to juvenile delinquency: 'The response is inadequate frequently enough; because the first phase of the intervention consists of superficial measures, while the subsequent repressive phase is ineffective.'

Denmark: a description of a successful case of replacing imprisonment by a non-custodial sentence best explains the necessity of its introduction. A director of a prison describes the fate of a former inmate, a boy aged sixteen, who was serving his sentence in that adult prison. 'It soon became necessary to consider placement outside the prison, because his need for attracting attention from other inmates, whose average age is twenty-seven, resulted in his bad behaviour. Among his fellow inmates he chose negative models for his own conduct in many situations. He wanted to show that he himself was 'able to', but in reality he was not a tough guy. On the contrary, he was a dependent, uncertain, and — in private — rather reasonable young person. With excellent support — even financial — from the local social welfare authorities a family care arrangement was established, and a relevant job was found. During four months the child — for he was and is nothing but a child — has lived under this alternative to imprisonment, and things have gone very well.'

11 Sources of information on children in adult prisons used in this book

It has not been the purpose of the DCI exploratory study on Children in Adult Prisons to establish that children are sent to prison and find themselves placed together with adults. The point is that, although such occurrences are known, they have never been consistently analysed and thereafter challenged from the viewpoint of the rights and interests of the child.

The results of the study have confirmed the initial assumption: every country explored revealed the imprisonment of children together with adults in some form. Moreover, empirical research showed to what extent children in prison have been neglected as a social, political and human rights problem.

The study shows the scope of the existing information on the nature and extent of the problem: we have found that lack of information may be as indicative as abundance. The logic has been well described by the researcher on Canada: *'It was assumed that if this practice [the imprisonment of children with adults] occurs with any great frequency, it is likely that responsible officials will deny the practice (since all the countries have legislation prohibiting it), but that volunteer (i.e. non-governmental) organizations will be aware of it.'*

Sources of information have therefore been (1) national surveys carried out in the selected countries by independent researchers, (2) information supplied by governments to the United Nations on the implementation of essential state obligations relating to the rights of the child, (3) governmental responses to the request for information by the DCI and (4) information collected by non-governmental organizations, primarily Amnesty International. Table 12 shows which of the first three sources of information has been used for each country covered by the exploratory study. Information from non-governmental organizations has been gathered for all of them.

The selection of the countries for in-depth investigation has been a combination of choice and necessity: it was regarded as indispensable to include countries from different parts of the world and in different stages of development, while it was necessary to narrow the selection to those countries where researchers willing and able to carry out the national survey could be found.

Table 12   Sources of information on children in adult prisons used
in this book

Country	National survey DCI Project	State's report on the ICCPR	State's report on the ICESCR	Information supplied by the government
Austria	yes	yes	yes	no
Bangladesh	yes	no	no	no
Bulgaria	yes	yes	yes	no
Canada	yes	yes	yes	yes
Chile	yes	yes	yes	no
Colombia	yes	yes	no	no
Costa Rica	yes	yes	no	yes
Denmark	yes	yes	yes	yes
Finland	yes	yes	no	no
France	yes	yes	no	yes
Germany. F.R.	yes	yes	yes	yes
India	yes	yes	yes	no
Italy	no	yes	yes	yes
Jamaica	yes	yes	no	no
Japan	yes	yes	no	no
Morocco	yes	yes	no	no
Netherlands	yes	yes	yes	yes
Nigeria	yes	no	no	no
Pakistan	yes	no	no	no
Romania	yes	yes	no	no
South Africa	yes	no	no	yes
Spain	yes	yes	yes	no
Switzerland	yes	no	no	no
Thailand	yes	no	no	no
United Kingdom	yes	yes	yes	yes
United States	yes	no	no	no
Yugoslavia	yes	yes	yes	no
Zaïre	yes	no	no	no
West Bank (Occupied Territories)	yes	not applicable		no

Differences among the national surveys carried out according to
the uniform research plan are immense: as a rule, not all the
information envisaged by the research outline could be obtained, but
the quality and quantity of information ultimately collected also
varies. The diversity of information on some topics and on some
countries obviated any cross-national comparison. The final analysis
has therefore been confined to those topics and countries where the

existing information permitted it. This has been the first attempt to collect data on the nature and scope of the imprisonment of children with adults world-wide, and the study marks only the end of the first phase of the project. Thus it was deemed important to raise the relevant issues, even if the data gathered could not substantiate any meaningful conclusions.

Wherever possible, the information collected was checked against other sources. Table 12 shows for which countries this has not been possible, since only one source of information was available. Usually, the information from the national surveys has been compared with governmental reports to the United Nations. Discrepancies between the two have been noted in the report. However, the national surveys have primarily focused on describing the practice of incarceration of children with adults, while governmental reports on the implementation of international human rights instruments generally describe the existing legislation. We hope that our combination of information on the legislation and the practice will be an incentive to devote more attention to the actual application of the law and its impact on children.

The exploratory study has a double objective: to shed some light on the nature and the dimensions of the problem of imprisoned children. The first part of the objective has been somewhat easier to realize because the nature of the problem could be illustrated by fragmentary data and qualitative analysis. However, with respect to the dimensions of the problem little could be done at this stage. The reason is illustrated by data on the existence or the lack of basic statistics on children in adult prisons given in Table 13. Statistics on children in adult prisons are virtually non-existent. This again shows the overall lack of attention to the problem of delinquent children; while it is known that they may be kept in adult facilities, contrary to both international and national regulations, little is known even as to the mere numbers of such children. The fragmentary information collected within the DCI Study shows that numbers extend to thousands in many countries. Still, those are approximations.

An important explanation for such a lack of statistical information is the *law* itself: in most countries imprisonment of children in adult facilities is contrary to the law. That is why the collection of statistics has not been envisaged. At best, one can get an assessment that 'imprisonment of children in adult facilities does occur exceptionally'. Checking whether exceptions have replaced the rule is sometimes virtually impossible.

Table 13   Available information on the existence of statistics on imprisoned children

Country	Statistics on child juvenile delinquency	Statistics on imprisoned children obtained in the DCI exploratory study	Statistics on children in adult penal facilities			
			police custody	pre-trial detention	prison sentences	detention on other grounds
Austria	yes	Province of Vienna only	no	yes	yes	no
Canada	yes	yes: not uniform	yes	yes	yes	yes
Chile	yes	yes	yes	yes	yes	security/political
Colombia			no information			
Costa Rica	yes	Province of San José only	yes	yes	yes	not applicable
Denmark	yes	yes	yes	yes	yes	yes
Finland			no information			
France	yes	yes	yes	yes	yes	no information
Germany. F.R.	yes	yes	yes	yes	yes	no information
India		Estimate of total number	no	no	yes	no information
Italy			no information			
Jamaica			no information			
Japan	yes	Total number			no information	
Morocco	yes	Estimate of total number			no information	
Netherlands	yes	yes	yes	yes	yes	yes
Nigeria	yes	Total number of convictions	no	no	yes	no information
Pakistan			no information			
Romania			no information			

Sources of information 133

						security: confidential
South Africa	fragmentary	yes; exception; security	no	yes	yes	
Spain			no	yes	yes	no information
Switzerland		yes; not uniform	no	yes	yes	no information
Thailand	yes	Total number of convictions			no information	
UK: Scotland		yes	no	yes	yes	no information
UK: England & Wales	yes	yes	yes	yes	yes	yes
USA	yes	Not uniform; fragmentary	no	incomplete	yes	no information
Yugoslavia	yes	Not uniform; incomplete	no	yes	yes	fragmentary
Zaïre	partial	incomplete	no	partial	yes	no information
West Bank		Data confidential			not applicable	

Table 14   Access to prisons granted or denied within the DCI project and comparison of legally determined minimum age for imprisonment and the actual lowest age of children found in prison

Country	Access to prison for DCI national surveys	Legal minimum age for imprisonment	Estimated minimum age of children with adults (excluding children in prison with mothers)
Austria	access granted	14	14
Canada	no information	14/16	not known; under 16
Chile	access denied	16	not applicable for security detention
Colombia	access granted	16	no information
Costa Rica	access granted	16	12
Denmark	no information	15	15
Finland	no information	15	no information
France	access granted	13	presumably under 10
Germany, F.R.	access granted	14	14
India	access granted	16	11
Italy	no information	14	no information
Jamaica	access granted	14	no information
Morocco	access denied	16	9
Netherlands	access granted	16/17	16; exception: aliens
Nigeria	access granted	12	12
Pakistan	access granted	15/10	10
Romania	no information	14	no information
South Africa	access granted	7/10	7
Spain	access granted	16	16
Switzerland	no information	15	no information
Thailand	access denied	16	7
UK: Scotland	access granted	14/16	14
UK: England	access granted	14/16	14
Yugoslavia	access denied	16	no information
Zaire	access granted	16	no information
West Bank	access denied	not applicable	12

An encouraging result of the national surveys is the fact that states which deny access to prisons and prisoners to bona fide researchers have become an exception. The majority of countries approached with the request for access to prisons where children are kept granted it. Not surprisingly, there are exceptions.

The relevance of access to prisons can be seen from a comparison between the minimum legally determined age for the imprisonment of children and the actual ages of children found in adult prisons.

Perhaps such information will be as interesting for the states concerned as it was for the researchers conducting fieldwork. That information is also summarized in Table 14.

The issue of access to prison is generally not regulated by law: thus granting or denying access is subject to discretion of a particular law enforcement official. According to the information collected within the DCI Exploratory Study the only country which has regulations on the access to prison and inmates by researchers and by the media is Denmark.[1]

Notes

1   *Circular on Public Access to Penal Institutions and Local Prisons under the Prison and Probation Administration*. Department of Prison and Probation of the Ministry of Justice , 13 September 1978. The Circular forms a part of the Danish Rules of Custodial Treatment which were supplied in English translation by the Danish government to the DCI.

12 Alternatives to imprisonment of children

Daniel O'Donnell

The research carried out on behalf of Defence for Children in twenty-seven countries failed to identify even one which has succeeded in completely eliminating the detention of minors with adults. Yet this important finding should not obscure the progress which has been made in some areas. The report on Canada indicates that one province, Quebec, has nearly eliminated the detention of minors in provincial prisons for adults. Only nine persons under the age of eighteen were admitted during the period 1981–82. The report on the United States indicates that, although the problem is very grave in many states, successful deinstitutionalization campaigns in two states, Maryland and Pennsylvania, have led to the complete elimination of detention of minors in adult facilities. In Lyons, France, a delinquency prevention programme and related reforms reduced the number of minors detained during adjudication by 50 per cent.

In Argentina the transfer of juvenile detention centres from military to civilian control following the return to constitutional government in 1984 led to an ambitious programme of deinstitution-alization of minors, particularly those in pre-trial detention. In Costa Rica research carried out on behalf of DCI in 1983 indicated that the detention of minors with adults had been successfully eliminated from most parts of the prison system, but persisted in four regional detention centres. It was estimated that seventy to one hundred minors were detained in these centres per year. However, upon receipt and study of the DCI report, the government took a series of steps designed to reduce the problem even further, including reduced use of pre-trial detention, temporary confinement of juvenile offenders in homes for needy children, allocation of additional resources for the transfer of juvenile prisoners and strict regulations concerning the maximum duration and conditions of confinement of minors temporarily admitted to 'multi-use' facilities.

The elimination of the detention of minors with adults is possible, as the preceding examples suggest, but is a complex process. Reform efforts which fail to take this into account, however well-intentioned, run the risk of unforeseen set-backs. The Danish report provides but one example of this risk: the present problem of minors detained in adult facilities was attributed by the DCI researcher to the premature closure of juvenile facilities resulting from a reaction against the use of indeterminate sentences and a campaign in favour of deinstitutionalization.

Comprehensive efforts to eliminate the detention of minors with adults should include four basic components: *political commitment, legal norms, planning* and *supervision*.

The importance of a high-level political commitment to the elimination of the detention of minors is reflected in a passage from the report on Morocco:

> *Various off-the-record conversations have led us to believe that the conditions of detention, sanitation and overcrowding of delinquents in the minors' quarters are so deplorable that an investigation would require long preparations by the administration before the facilities could be 'visitable' . . . This proves, on one hand, that the administrators are very aware of the intolerable conditions of detention, whose consequences are not limited to minors, and yet that none of them individually is able to budge the weight of the administrative machine in order to bring about the least improvement of a situation recognized as truly alarming.*

The elimination of the detention of minors with adults invariably requires the co-operation of diverse agencies and branches of the government, including one or more of police agencies, prosecutors, child welfare agencies, prison authorities, public defenders and the juvenile courts. The difficulties which arise in seeking effective co-operation among them are one reason why a firm, high-level policy commitment is indispensable to successful reform in this area. In addition, in federated countries the very different situations reported in various states or provinces illustrates another reason why a firm, high-level decision is necessary. Finally, the need in some cases to devote substantial resources to improving the infrastructure necessary to guarantee effective protection of this right is another reason why a firm commitment on the ministerial level at least is required for effective action.

The historical survey of the treatment afforded minors in detention included in the report on France provides numerous examples of the critical role which the press and public opinion can play in creating the necessary commitment to effective substantial changes in official policy.

The second component is normative action, that is, the adoption of laws and administrative rules and regulations designed to protect minors from detention with adults. There can be no doubt that the lack of a clearly defined legal duty concerning the separate detention of minors and adults contribute to poor practices, the abuse of discretion and a lack of appreciation of the importance of the principle of the detention of minors in separate facilities. On the other hand, many DCI investigators agreed that the real problem was not with the legislation in force but rather with the fact that it is so widely ignored.

Indeed, the experience in some cases suggests that the adoption of absolute norms can be counter-productive: if compliance is impossible the norm becomes inoperative and in time is forgotten. As already mentioned, in Costa Rica the law provides that all orders of juvenile court judges must be obeyed 'immediately'. Hence prison authorities were obliged to transfer minors to juvenile centres immediately upon receiving a transfer order. Since this was materially impossible because of the lack of petrol for official vehicles to undertake long voyages every time a transfer was ordered (in many areas the entire monthly quota would be required for a single transfer), correctional authorities were left with no other guideline than the vague and subjective notion that transfers should be effected as soon as possible. While some managed to reduce delays to a minimum, in other institutions delays of weeks or months were common. Paradoxically, the administrative regulation adopted in 1984 after receipt of the DCI report, which allows detention in 'multi-use' facilities for up to sixty-four hours will probably be more effective in reducing the detention of minors in such centres than the still existing but unenforceable norm concerning transfers. The same principle, it is suggested, may be applicable to the broader problem of prohibiting the detention of minors with adults: laws which are too far removed from reality lose force, and may even create, in reality, a situation of normlessness. At the same time a minimum of absolute norms must be upheld — the weakness of relative or qualified norms, especially those incorporating vague concepts like 'possibility' or 'necessity' is also notorious.

Ideally the approach should be to improve the physical and administrative infrastructures to maximize the real possibilities of complying with the internationally recognized principle of separate detention of all minors, then adopt enforceable norms, administrative as well as legislative, which oblige the responsible authorities to make the most of the possibilities offered by the system. Precisely what such norms should be is perhaps not a question to be answered in the abstract. Should circumstances dictate that the general prohibition be expressed in qualified terms, however, it is worth recalling that the qualifications may include procedural as well as substantive elements such as a requirement that all cases of minors detained in adult facilities (without direct contact) be reported to or approved by a high-ranking authority.

It should also be borne in mind that the normative component of a comprehensive reform plan is not limited to the basic principle of prohibiting the detention of minors with adults, but extends to a vast number of related questions such as decriminialization, police powers to detain for questioning, the issuance of identity documents, juvenile court procedure and others. Only two specific recommendations will be made here: first, that police should have no power to detain minors for questioning without first bringing the minor before a juvenile court, and second, that the law should expressly recognize that custodial sentences are a last resort, to be imposed only when no non-custodial sentence would be appropriate for the individual in question.

The third component of a successful reform effort is the incorporation of human rights criteria into planning in the administration of justice and the correctional system. The need for this would seem self-evident: the separation of adults and minors in detention depends not only on the law in force but also on the efficiency of the juvenile courts in avoiding delays in adjudications, the capacity and location of juvenile institutions, the availability of transportation, the efficiency of social workers in identifying alternatives to detention. All of these depend in turn on the allocation of human and material resources in the planning of criminal and juvenile justice systems.

Yet planners often have only the vaguest idea of the needs and rights of the juvenile prisoners, even though the realization of these rights and fulfilment of these needs should be among their main preoccupations. This ignorance is one of the explanations for the substandard conditions prevailing in many penal institutions, including overcrowding, dark and humid cells, poor sanitation, violence among inmates, the lack of physical exercise, inadequate diet and a host of other evils. It is the reason why administrators are so often frustrated by external factors in their efforts to improve respect for the rights of prisoners. What are so often perceived as financial obstacles to respect for the rights of prisoners are often, upon closer examination, the consequences of planning errors or deficiencies. Even delays in adjudication and under-employment of alternatives to detention can often be explained, at least in part, by poor planning in the distribution of judicial resources.

Planners very often lack even adequate data concerning indices of delinquency, the characteristics of juvenile offenders and similar factors necessary to make reliable predictions about the need for judicial or correctional resources, or to design preventive, decriminalization, diversion or alternative sentencing programmes. It is necessary, therefore, to give priority to the incorporation of children's rights criteria into the relevant planning processes and to make concerted efforts to begin compiling and publishing comprehensive statistical information concerning juvenile delinquency and related matters.

The last element of a comprehensive plan for the prevention of the detention of minors with adults is supervision or follow-up. Widespread non-compliance with the law was reported to be a major cause of the detention of minors in many countries. Once legislation is reviewed to ensure that it is in conformity with the needs and possibilities of the society, it is necessary to create an efficient mechanism for ensuring compliance with the relevant laws and regulations. Although an inquiry into the reasons therefore would take us far afield, it is obvious that the 'normal' mechanisms for ensuring respect for the law are too often inadequate, and that special mechanisms for protecting the rights of juvenile prisoners are required. Such mechanisms should not only be charged with supervising compliance with the law *per se*, but more generally with overseeing the welfare of juvenile prisoners. They should, for example, detect unanticipated problems in the operational aspects of the system in force, or the need to adopt it to qualitative or quantitative changes in juvenile delinquency.

There is probably no limit to the types of mechanisms which could fulfil this function. The requirement that juvenile court judges regularly visit juveniles in detention is a useful mechanism for detecting violations of the rights of juvenile prisoners. The creation of children's ombudsmen, like the one functioning in Norway, is another. In Costa Rica, the human rights procurator, a kind of ombudsman functioning within the framework of the Ministry of Justice, has succeeded in causing some improvements in the conditions of the detention of minors. The rights of children in

detention would seem to be a natural area of concern for governmental human rights commissions, where they exist. The mandate of
official child welfare agencies could also easily incorporate the
protection of the rights of children deprived of their liberty. Finally,
as investigators in more than one country suggested, non-governmental
human rights organizations could clearly play a crucial role in
investigating the conditions in which children are detained, where
the government gives them the freedom of action necessary to make a
positive contribution in this regard.

Alternative to pre-trial detention of children in adult facilities

A difference between pre-trial detention and imprisonment with
adults is that pre-trial detention with adults is largely attributed to the
lack of capacity or inadequate distribution of juvenile centres, while
a variety of more specific causes come into play in deciding upon and
enforcing imprisonment. This difference is of considerable importance to the search for alternatives to the detention of minors with
adults.

In those countries where there is a serious gap between the overall
capacity of juvenile institutions and the demonstrated 'need' or
where the geographical distribution of juvenile centres is patently
inadequate, it may be impossible to envisage solving the problem
without a commitment to the construction of new facilities or the
adaptation of existing buildings to this use. In developing countries
where inadequate facilities constitute an insurmountable obstacle to
effective protection of the rights of juvenile prisoners and the
national economy does not permit financing necessary improvement,
the international community has an obligation to provide the
assistance required to bring these nations to the threshold where they
are able to shoulder these responsibilities.

However, the possibilities of finding alternatives which do not
require the construction of new facilities are often underestimated.

The first type of action to be considered is delinquency prevention.
Prevention is obviously the ideal alternative, as it not only spares
juveniles the ordeal of detention of any kind, but also protects the
rights of their potential victims and the moral interests of potential
delinquents. The encouraging results of small-scale delinquency
prevention programmes identified by the DCI researchers show a

decrease — sometimes by 50 per cent — of the 'need' for detention of minors. While those programmes are as a rule limited in scope and experimental, the practical benefit they have demonstrated is obvious.

The second type of action to be considered is the *diversion* of certain forms of conduct from the juvenile justice system to social service programmes. Poverty is the cause of a great deal of juvenile delinquency throughout the world. Juveniles are arrested, adjudicated and incarcerated in vast numbers for vagrancy, begging, prostitution, exercising 'street work' illegally, use of public transport without payment, and of course theft. Yet how can society presume to 'rehabilitate' those whose 'crimes' are an intimate part of their daily struggle for survival? These are clearly social problems best addressed through programmes designed to aid needy children rather than the juvenile justice system. In the words of the Florence Declaration, prisons are being employed to do the work of child welfare institutions; social assistance is being replaced by repression.

Obviously, not all who commit thefts are motivated by compelling necessity and it would be utopian to suggest that property offences, which account for well over 50 per cent of all juvenile delinquency, be eliminated from the jurisdiction of the juvenile courts. What is suggested is that the need for rehabilitation as opposed to the need for assistance in meeting one's basic material needs should be employed as the criterion to distinguish between those minors who shall continue to be handled through the juvenile justice system — and institutionalized only if the judge deems this necessary to accomplish rehabilitation — and those who should be diverted to appropriate welfare programmes. In considering the possibilities for reducing the 'demand' for juvenile detention facilities the optimal separation of functions between the juvenile justice and welfare systems should be a critical consideration. If necessary, steps should be taken to give welfare agencies the resources necessary to assume the full responsibility for all cases not appropriate for treatment in the juvenile justice system.

In some cases, decriminalization without diversion to other social programmes may be indicated. In South Africa, 40 per cent of the entire prison population is imprisoned under the notorious 'pass law' regulations, which apply only to the non-white population. This is an exceptional example of a case where repeal of unjust legislation would have a profound impact on the 'need' for detention facilities, but less dramatic possibilities for decriminalization undoubtedly exist in other countries. Many countries have already eliminated the so-called 'status offences' (conduct which can lead to the institutionalization of minors, but which is not criminal for adults) such as truancy or being beyond parental control. Those which have not should give careful consideration to this possibility, especially if overcrowding of juvenile facilities is resulting in the detention of juveniles in adult facilities.

Pre-trial detention is only justified in order to ensure the individual's presence at adjudication, to prevent tampering with the evidence, or, exceptionally, to protect society from an extremely vulnerable individual or to guarantee the safety of a minor living in an especially dangerous environment. Two lines of action are suggested by this statement of principle.

The main justifications for pre-trial detention, applicable to adults as well as minors, take on a special significance when minors are concerned. Minors are not, as a rule, fully autonomous members of society but rather are under parental care and authority. Thus the determination whether pre-trial detention is necessary implicitly — and in many countries explicitly — depends on an evaluation of the home environment.

In Costa Rica, authorities in the province where there was the highest incidence of pre-adjudication detention with adults attributed the high incidence of detention to the situation of semi-abandon in which many of the juvenile offenders live (single-parent families with parental alcoholism, drug use, prostitution, etc.). In some cases it was even difficult to locate a member of the immediate or extended family willing to accept responsibility for the minor. This suggests that increased use of social workers to identify and, in appropriate cases, reinforce familial resources as an alternative to detention could make a useful contribution to reducing the demand for detention facilities.

Secondly, it is necessary to review compliance with those principles concerning appropriate use of pre-trial detention, that is, to review the functioning of juvenile courts. Indeed, continuous or periodic review of the functioning of juvenile courts should also encompass two other factors directly linked to the detention of minors with adults: the duration of juvenile proceedings, particularly relevant if the child is being detained, and the use made of various types of sentences by the courts. Review of the functioning of juvenile courts is particularly needed for three reasons. First, juvenile justice tends to be one of the most neglected areas in the judicial system;

secondly, because of the unusual degree of discretion vested in juvenile courts; and, thirdly, because of the low visibility of juvenile justice.

It would be inappropriate here to suggest any particular model for reviewing the operation of juvenile courts, yet it is appropriate to suggest that the review have two dimensions. The first would be the creation of some body — an administrative entity within the judicial branch, a legislative committee or an office within the executive branch — directly responsible for overseeing the operation of juvenile courts. By detecting and drawing attention to deficiencies and irregularities in their performance it would help promote uniformity and efficiency, supplementing the system of appeals to higher courts, which tends to be particularly ineffective where juvenile courts are concerned. In addition, statistics concerning the detention of minors, juvenile delinquency and the operation of juvenile courts should be compiled and made available to the public, allowing independent analysis by concerned academics, organizations and individuals. Juvenile justice reform is greatly handicapped by the lack of reliable and comprehensive data at present, both nationally and internationally.

The combined effect of these methods, delinquency prevention, diversion or decriminalization, increased use of judicial social workers to facilitate pre-adjudication release in parental custody and increased scrutiny over the operation of juvenile courts, may make an appreciable contribution to reduction of pre-trial detention of minors and their detention with adults in particular. Still, it is possible that the pressure to detain minors with adults will not be completely relieved, especially when the phenomenon is linked to the distribution of juvenile detention facilities rather than their capacity *per se*. The question of to what extent, and in what circumstances detention in a juvenile sector of a 'multi-use' detention facility is acceptable then arises. It will be recalled that both the Standard Minimum Rules for the Treatment of Prisoners and the Draft Standard Minimum Rules for the Administration of Juvenile Justice require that minors be detained either in separate institutions or in 'separate parts' of an adult institution.

Here the empirical studies conducted for the DCI perform a valuable service in demonstrating how extremely difficult it is to eliminate multiple risks inherent in the detention of minors in essentially adult facilities. Absolute separation from adults is almost impossible to maintain in practice; reception areas, cafeterias, indoor or outdoor recreation areas and work or educational programmes offer some of the most common opportunities for direct contact. Even if separation is maintained, the interests of the minors are often sacrificed to those of the majority in countless ways, including diet, exercise, recreation and educational programmes. Furthermore, the area dedicated to minors is often too small to permit adequate classification and segregation of minors according to age, reasons for detention, potential danger for other minors, etc.

Thus while it is probably unrealistic to propose an absolute ban on the detention of minors in such centres, it is imperative to recognize that it should not be a regular practice but a last resort, to be employed only when all other avenues have been explored, and to control their use when it cannot be avoided.

The ways in which the recourse to such centres may be avoided are as varied as the circumstances which cause it. In the first instance, it would seem appropriate to classify juveniles for whom pre-trial detention is considered necessary according to dangerousness. For those less prone to violence, temporary residence in homes for non-delinquent needy children would be definitely preferable to detention in a penal institution.

Given the risks involved in the detention of minors in 'multi-use' centres, it would seem appropriate to do so only when dangerous minors are concerned. Foremost among the regulations needed where the detention of minors in 'multi-use' facilities is indispensable is a clear limit to the duration of such detention. Experience shows that flexible limits such as 'as soon as possible' offer little or no protection against prolonged detention in dangerous circumstances. Regulations should also emphasize that compliance with minimum guarantees such as daily exercise cannot be suspended because of the need to separate minors from adult prison population, and should guarantee that separation from adults does not in practice result in solitary confinement. Finally, given the exceptional nature of this measure, it would be appropriate to require special authorization to resort to it or perhaps regular visits by a juvenile judge or child welfare agency to assure adequate protection of the rights of minors confined in such institutions.

Alternatives to the imprisonment of children with adults

When imprisonment with adults affects specific sub-categories of minors and reflects deliberate policies, these must be carefully reviewed to determine the extent to which they are consistent with the best interests of the child. It should be stressed that policies which in theory may be justified in terms of the interests of the child are not necessarily motivated by or compatible with the interest of the child in practice.

For example it has been suggested that a flexible age limit may be justified, not strictly speaking because it is in the 'best interest' of the child, but because it may be a more reliable and humane way of determining which individuals within a certain border-age merit treatment as adults and which should still be considered minors. Opinions will differ because the risk of abuse of discretion cannot be eliminated from such discretionary norms although it can be reduced by the introduction of procedural safeguards and definition of the parameters within which such discretion may operate. However, assuming *ad arguendum* that a flexible age limit is recognized as legitimate for this purpose, it is imperative to ensure that it is not used for other purposes. The common practice of automatically reclassifying as adults minors charged with certain offences in order to impose the heavier punishments reserved for adults is clearly an unacceptable use of the flexible age limit.

A three-fold classification of prisoners into juveniles, young offenders and adults rather than the traditional separation into minors and adults is preferred in many modern penal systems. Nevertheless, in at least one country, the Federal Republic of Germany, where 'intermediary' institutions may house individuals as young as fifteen and as old as twenty-five, abuse of younger inmates was considered a serious problem by the DCI researcher. Although it would seem imprudent to condemn the use of 'intermediary' institutions categorically, as an exception to the rule prohibiting the detention of minors with adults it should be allowed only to the extent conditions can be created to guarantee that such detention will be without prejudice to the interests of the minors concerned.

In many countries the housing of infants with their mothers in prison is allowed only under strictly controlled conditions. On one hand, infants are admitted to the prison only when it is the sole alternative to separating the child from its natural family; on the other, every effort is made to provide the admitted children with special diets, regular medical care, pleasant surroundings and frequent contact with the 'outside world'. In other countries, however,

DCI researchers found that mothers and children detained together received no special treatment and indeed were confined in conditions which were deplorable even for adults. Such a situation obviously can never be considered in the 'best interests' of the child.

Examples could be multiplied. The conclusion, which bears repeating, is that all practices purportedly justified as being in the interest of the minors detained with adults should be carefully scrutinized to determine whether they are fully consistent with the rights of the child in practice as well as in theory.

When detention of minors with adults after adjudication results from the limited capacity of juvenile institutions, two types of actions should be considered. Diversion and decriminalization, described above, will obviously have a beneficial effect on overcrowding. The second approach is greater reliance on non-custodial sentences.

Although it is the link between non-custodial sentences, overcrowding and the imprisonment of minors with adults which retains our attention here, as a general principle non-custodial sentences should always be substituted for custodial sentences whenever possible, even when there is no risk of detention with adults.

The types of non-custodial sentences available are well-known. Community service is an important alternative, as it involves none of the dangers which even detention in a juvenile facility may pose to many juvenile offenders, including not only exploitation or victimization but also 'education in crime'. Where institutionalization is not deemed necessary, community service constitutes one way of avoiding the inequity of fines. Since many juveniles turn to crime because of acute poverty, especially in developing countries, and since non-payment of fines usually results in imprisonment, the use of fines as 'alternatives' to custodial sentences may in reality contribute to the detention of large numbers of minors for whom imprisonment serves no legitimate purpose. The DCI researcher in Colombia reported that many minors were imprisoned in Bogota for inability to pay amounts as small as two or three United States' dollars. In Scotland 1,680 persons under the age nineteen were jailed for failure to pay fines in 1982, half of all those in this age group remitted to penal institutions. The periods of detention for non-payment of fines ranged from a week to three months or more, the average being three weeks.

Successful community service programmes have the additional advantage of aiding in the rehabilitation of certain offenders by reinforcing a positive self-image and aiding in reconciliation with the community. They also have the advantage, particularly relevant in developing countries, of not requiring large investments of public funds and even — although this should not become a dominant consideration lest community service programmes be distorted into a pretext for exploiting youth labour — of allowing young offenders to make a modest but constructive contribution to the development of the society.

'Mediation, arbitration and the encouragement of the peaceful settlement of disputes' between the minor and the injured party is another valuable alternative to custodial sentences. In Costa Rica this has become an increasingly important alternative, even though not formally recognized by the code of juvenile justice; 'abstention' is the method of reconciliation or peaceful settlement of disputes effected through the intervention of the juvenile judge, with the assistance of judicial social workers.

The researcher on Zaïre also reported that certain types of cases involving minors are left to the tribal authorities to be resolved by traditional dispute-settlement methods. This alternative, which in the case of Zaïre is not a true alternative sentence but a form of diversion or deference to a traditional legal system, eliminates the risk of incarceration since the use of prisons is alien to such traditional systems. In addition, where still viable, traditional dispute-settlement mechanisms are generally recognized as being more effective than modern penal systems in reintegrating the offender into society, providing some form of compensation for the injured party and in general restoring harmonious social relations. Like community service then, arbitration or mediation can be an attractive alternative to fines, when the court determines that a period of rehabilitation in a total institution is not required. Another advantage which these two have in common, in contrast to the more traditional probation, is their relative low cost.

Probation is a well known alternative sentence which permits the offender to remain at liberty on condition that he or she report regularly to a social worker. A series of other conditions may also be imposed, including school attendance.

The idea of conditional liberty, which may be withdrawn if the conditions are not respected, tends to predominate in probation programmes for adults. When juveniles are concerned it is more appropriate to emphasize the supportive aspect of probation, the giving of assistance, counselling and moral support necessary to help the individual avoid recidivism. It is particularly indicated where the minor's personality and behaviour traits do not indicate a need for institutionalization, but where the supervision and support normally provided by the family is deficient, or where the family actually constitutes a cause of the juvenile's behaviour problems.

Warnings or admonitions have also been endorsed as a valuable alternative to custodial sentences, albeit with the condition that the warning is given by a judge or magistrate rather than by the police. This reflects concern about the situation reported in England, where the police 'caution' juveniles arrested for minor offences rather than refer them to juvenile court and the 'caution' enters the juvenile's police record as a conviction. Considering the far-reaching consequences of criminal records, convictions without fair adjudication of all the circumstances of the case by a competent authority is a high price to pay for the immediate benefit of avoiding the risk of incarceration. This is especially so since institutionalization is not a penalty to be imposed, withheld or bargained away at the discretion of authorities but rather an instrument of rehabilitation to be resorted to only when needed. Moreover, the warning is likely to have a more lasting and constructive effect when administered by a judge, the representative of justice, rather than the police.

Confinement in private homes for children is another alternative which merits brief mention, although it is not strictly speaking a non-custodial alternative. Since such homes are invariably intended for juveniles only, the alternative, while custodial, eliminates all risk of contact with adult prisoners for the minors directly concerned. At the same time it reduces overcrowding in official juvenile centres, thus indirectly reducing the risk of 'overspill' of juveniles into adult facilities within the state correctional system.

Reliance on private institutions may be particularly useful where the centralization of state juvenile facilities causes local or regional problems in the accommodation of juvenile offenders. Private juvenile homes may not only eliminate the risk of detention with adults, but also offer conditions of detention far superior to those prevailing in official institutions. They may also diminish the risk of stigmatization of the minor, since many private homes are intended principally for needy children rather than juvenile offenders.

13 Summaries of DCI country surveys

Randy Goodman

In order to give the reader some indication of the breadth of material brought to light by the researchers in the country reports, the Advisory Panel for the study on Children in Adult Prisons decided to prepare abstracts of them. It was not intended that these be point-by-point summaries of the reports, but rather that they give an overview of the situation, allowing the reader to determine which of the country reports he or she would like to study more closely. The abstracts were prepared with the assistance of Kathleen Rimar and Willie J. Wheaton of the Human Rights Clinic at the Faculty of Law and Jurisprudence of the State University of New York at Buffalo.

The task of preparing the abstracts was made somewhat difficult by the differences in style, structure, presentation and content of the various reports. As a result, they are not uniform from these standpoints. Some of the country studies gave detailed descriptions of the juvenile justice system as well as the prison system, whereas others tended to concentrate on prison statistics and the researcher's observations. The focus of the research differed from country to country: some researchers chose to examine the situation of minors of certain ages more closely, believing mixing of children with adults was more likely to occur in these age groups; other researchers chose to examine the possibility of mixing all relevant age groups. Not all researchers used eighteen as the age of majority; where the national age of majority was lower, some researchers applied that age.

The availability of details on institutions, including the conditions within institutions, varied from report to report. In addition, there were great divergences in the information given as to the way in which children came to be incarcerated; some researchers took into account those children placed in institutions for 'status' offences or as a result of neglect proceedings when compiling statistics and examining facilities available to children, while others either did not explicitly state that they had done so or actually did not do so. Many of the researchers conducted interviews with children in prison, but the summaries of these have not been included in the abstracts. Information about mothers with children was on the whole not consistent.

No short summary could adequately reflect the flavour of a report. Many of the researchers gave some information about the economic, social and cultural conditions in their countries. These factors are quite important for an understanding of prison conditions, the effect of incarceration and even the effect of mixing children with adults, as well as in understanding government programmes for reform. However, because of space limitations, these could not be discussed in the abstracts. Another issue stressed by some researchers but not included in the abstracts is government efforts at reform. Some researchers were quite positive about efforts being made, while others were critical of government policy in this field.

Despite these shortcomings, the Advisory Panel believes the abstracts will be useful to the reader, and at a minimum, will alert him or her to the content of the country studied. It is hoped that those with an interest in a particular country will contact the DCI Secretariat and request the full country study.

Austria

Scope of the report

Children who commit criminal offences in Austria are placed in two distinct categories. Children under the age of fourteen are referred to as '*Unmuendige*' (minors). Minors are considered too young to be criminally liable, and are consequently never punished. Children between the ages of fourteen and eighteen are referred to as '*Jugendliche*' (juveniles). Punishable offences committed by juveniles are usually subject to the same disciplinary measures as those applied to adults. An exception relates to life imprisonment, to which only adults may be sentenced.

Mixing of adults and minors in penal facilities

As a general rule there are no juvenile prisoners housed with adult prisoners. The female prison at Schwarzau in Steinfeld is a special case. Since it is rare for juvenile females to be convicted of criminal offences, there is no special prison for juvenile females. There is only the one female prison in Austria, Schwarzau, which was visited by the researcher in 1983; only six of the 133 prisoners were juveniles. The prison authorities affirmed that this ratio of juveniles to adults is typical in Schwarzau.

In principle, all juvenile males convicted of a crime are sent to the one prison facility in the country for juveniles. This prison is located in Gerasdorf, and all juveniles sentenced to imprisonment for six months or more are sent there. Although theoretically there is no mixing of juveniles and adults in Austrian prisons, prisoners aged eighteen to twenty-four may make special application to be sent to Gerasdorf, which is known for its special educational programme and instruction. Consequently, frequent requests are made by young adults to be sent to Gerasdorf; available information indicates, however, that only in exceptional cases are eighteen to twenty-four year olds actually assigned to this juvenile facility.

There are a few isolated cases (no exact figures known) where juveniles are incarcerated in a prison or jail with an adult. These exceptional occasions have occurred while the juveniles were awaiting trial, or when the sentence was less than six months.

Mothers with children in prison

For an adult or juvenile woman to give birth while in prison is a rare occurrence in Austria. However, the female prison at Schwarzau does have a mother–child department in which some mothers live with their small children. During this researcher's visit in 1983, there were four mothers living in this department with four children. The ages of these children ranged from five months to two years. The authorities stated that young children have rarely been at the institution in recent years because social workers usually attempt to place them with families.

In the mother–child department, the women are housed in three prison rooms, each with a maximum capacity of accommodation for two adults and two children.

Mixing of ages in the female prison

At the Schwarzau prison, the juveniles have contact with the adult women during working hours, because they all participate in the ordinary work done at the prison. There is often contact during the exercise period. There are no other possibilities for contact, as the juvenile girls sleep in separate rooms from the adult women. There have been no reports of assaults, threats, sexual attacks or homicide in prison. Incidents of assault or prison violence are rare in Austria. Only a few incidents of assault have been reported at the juvenile prison at Gerasdorf, where a small number of adults aged eighteen to twenty-four are also imprisoned.

Bulgaria
Scope of the report

There are two sections in this report. The first is a summary of national legislation pertaining to juvenile delinquency. The second provides a description of the organizations which have been established to implement punitive or educational measures.

The Penal Code in Bulgaria differentiates between those under fourteen years of age (minors) and those between the ages of fourteen and eighteen (youth). Minors are not considered responsible for their offences, and are consequently only subject to educational measures. Delinquent behaviour committed by those between fourteen and eighteen years of age can be punished, if it is deemed that such youths were capable of recognizing the nature and importance of their acts and could have controlled them.

Penal procedures call for the accused to have the assistance of a lawyer. The cases of minors and youth are held in closed session, and participation of the parents is obligatory.

Various punitive and educational measures have been imposed on juvenile delinquents. The Penal Code holds that if an infraction of the law does not constitute a public danger, then educational measures are to be applied. Since most infractions committed by minors fall into this category, penal sanctions for minors are rare.

Punishment for convicted youths is aimed at re-educating them and preparing them for productive work in society. Such punishment can consist of disciplinary actions, deprivation of freedom or prohibition to work in certain professions.

Juvenile delinquency and institutions for minors and youth

Acts of juvenile delinquency in Bulgaria mainly involve offences against the person and stealing (particularly of motor vehicles). Between 75–80 per cent of juvenile offences involve the theft of goods, such as alcohol and cigarettes. Some 10–15 per cent of the young people who are found guilty of delinquent acts come from homes where the parents are either divorced or have serious problems. Thus, a considerable proportion of juvenile delinquency is attributed to problems relating to the socialization process in the family. Another recognized cause of illegal behaviour among young people is alcoholism.

The government, with the assistance of social organizations, has established several types of organizations equipped to deal with various aspects of juvenile delinquency. 'Commissions' exist to control anti-social behaviour by persons eighteen years of age or younger. These are state organizations represented by all departments and committees dealing with children's issues. They are directed by the Central Commission within the Procurate General Department, under the Attorney-General. Their principal functions are to ensure the welfare of children and to implement educational measures. The Commissions are also empowered to take action against parents who are shown to have neglected their children. Pedagogical Departments are State Departments which are supervised by persons possessing a higher education degree in pedagogy. These departments cannot impose coercive sanctions, but are designed to effect educational measures for minors and youth. Temporary Detention Houses are social assistance institutions attached to the People's Departmental Councils. In most cases, minors and youth are confined to these establishments for fifteen days only. Finally, there are two reformatories — one for boys, which can accommodate 200 children; the other for girls, is equipped for twenty persons. These institutions provide general school education curricula, as well as technical and professional training facilities.

Canada

Scope of the report

Canada is a federation of ten provinces and two territories. There are widespread differences between these regions in the implementation of the Juvenile Delinquency Act (JDA, 1909, revised in 1926). This Act remains the principal federal legislation governing juvenile behaviour. In Canada, the age of majority varies significantly: in six provinces and both territories, a minor becomes an adult on the sixteenth birthday. In two provinces, seventeen-year-olds are considered as adults, while in two other provinces the age of majority is reached at eighteen.

Children in prison with adults

Table 15 indicates the age of majority for each province and territory and the number of offenders among the adult and juvenile population.

Table 15 Number of admissions to provincial institutions for adults in Canada, by province and age at admission, 1981–2

Province	Age at admission (years)			Total	Total
	<16	16	17	<18 yrs.	all ages
Newfoundland (17)*	11	22	138	171	1,978
Prince Edward Island (16)	n.a.	n.a.	n.a.	88	878
Nova Scotia (16)	n.a.	n.a.	n.a.	540	4,327
New Brunswick (16)	3	228	314	545	4,078
Quebec (18)				9	21,620
Ontario (16)	17	3,276	3,518	6,811	24,562
Manitoba (18)	n.a.	n.a.	n.a.	58	5,669
Saskatchewan (16)	1	188	388	577	5,923
Alberta (16)	11	537	989	1,537	15,253
British Columbia (17)	n.a.	n.a.	n.a.	244	8,401
Yukon Territory (16)	0	9	33	42	453
Northwest Territories (16)	2	24	70	96	766

* Age of majority with respect to the criminal justice system in that province given in parentheses.

Each province has laws forbidding the placement of children in adult institutions. However, children are placed in adult prisons by court order, as the legislation in every province also specifies conditions under which minors can be placed in adult institutions. This practice is permitted when minors are considered too dangerous to be housed with other children, when they have been convicted of a serious crime, or when their trial has been held in an adult court. There is also evidence that some minors are detained briefly — no more than four days on the average — in local lock-ups and jails, where they may come in contact with adult prisoners. This happens mostly in the remote areas of the North, where the lock-ups are the only facilities available for holding minors awaiting transportation to a juvenile facility, which is often several hundred miles away.

This report did not examine living conditions or the specific situations of minors in the various provincial prisons. The research indicated that no serious problems exist in these institutions, even in the cases where minors and adults are incarcerated together.

Chile

Scope of the report

The report includes a comprehensive assessment of the situation in Chile, with regard to juvenile delinquency, the detention and punishment of minors. The investigation focuses on minors who are detained for either political reasons or criminal offences, over the years 1973–84. The analysis comprises a legal, socio-economic, political and human rights perspective. Special attention is devoted to the conditions in secret detention centres and documented cases of detained and/or tortured minors. Cases of mothers imprisoned with their babies or young children are also examined. Finally, interviews with two minors detained in the Puento Alto prison shed light on conditions there. Additional information pertaining to this prison is provided by former detainees and social workers.

The report points out the difficulty in obtaining precise and accurate statistics on detained and tortured minors, although their number is known to have increased during the past five years. The sources for data and other facts include publications of human rights' organizations, various journals and testimonies of prisoners and former prisoners.

The Vicaria de la Solidaridad is the only organization to have begun the process of data collection on imprisoned minors as a distinct category. Although other organizations exist which work with and for minors, they do so by approaching the minors as indirect victims, e.g. as children of prisoners, children of 'disappeared' persons, etc. They do not, therefore, deal specifically with child-prisoners.

Minors in detention centres

Since September 1973, two types of detention centres have existed in Chile — public and secret. Both types are found throughout the country. Beginning in 1973, a large number of prisons, police stations and public buildings served as public detention centres. Minors were detained with adults, and political prisoners were not segregated from convicted criminals. All prisoners were subject to the same internal discipline. During the 1974–76 period, several camps were established in various parts of the country where political prisoners of juvenile age were detained.

Most minors were released at the end of 1976, on the occasion of a general amnesty. Some had been detained for up to three years without trial. The number of minors detained for political reasons declined in 1977–8. However, since 1979 there has been a significant increase in the detention of minors on political grounds.

Allegations concerning the torture of minors are widespread. Such torture has reportedly been inflicted in secret detention centres, police stations, military barracks and even in cars which are specifically equipped with sophisticated torture instruments.

New secret torture centres were established between 1980 and 1984, although minors have been kept in these centres for shorter periods than was previously the case. The government, responding to pressure from human rights organizations, confirmed the existence of eleven of these torture centres. Subsequently, they were sanctioned by legislation enacted in May 1984 (known as the 'anti-terrorist law').

Chilean law defines a 'minor' as any person under twenty-one years of age. However, criminal responsibility begins at the age of eighteen, and in certain cases at sixteen. Minors under sixteen cannot be held criminally responsible.

According to Article 29 of Law 16.618 (1967), minors who are convicted of a crime can be: (a) placed in the charge of their parents or guardians; (b) placed in restricted liberty; (c) placed in an educational institution; or (d) placed in the charge of someone who has offered to assume responsibility for his/her education.

Specific findings

In 1979, there were seventy-seven reported cases of detained minors. The twenty-two girls and fifty-five boys varied in age from nine months to eighteen years. The following year there were eighty-one such cases (thirty girls and fifty-one boys), ranging in age from forty days to eighteen years. In 1981, ninety-nine cases were reported (twenty-seven girls and seventy-two boys), ranging between eight months and eighteen years of age. The number of cases rose to 115 in 1982 (thirty-seven girls and seventy-eight boys), aged from three to eighteen years. In the majority of these cases no criminal charges were filed, and those arrested were released shortly thereafter, without having been tortured (see Table 16 for the data between May 1983 and September 1984).

The report examines conditions in the Puento Alto Detention Centre, where some 150 children were detained in 1983. The centre is

Table 16 The most recent data on detained and tortured children
given in the report on Chile, 1983–4

| | May–December 1983 | | January–September 1984 | |
	Detained	Tortured	Detained	Tortured
Girls	45	15	61	22
Boys	292	103	265	191
Total number known	337	118	326	213

operated by the police, and beatings and other forms of physical
aggression are common. Homosexual relations between guards and
detained minors are a regular occurrence, and newly-arrived minors
are often raped by those already in detention. Food is lacking in both
quality and quantity. Hygienic conditions are poor — there are
frequent outbreaks of scabies, as well as plagues of rats and
cockroaches. There is no electric lighting in the rooms, and no
medical or dental care is provided. Although there is a school, no
regular instruction is available; the only course taught is at the level
of first-year secondary school. In July 1983, only twenty-six of the 500
institutions providing rehabilitation programmes to minors were
operated directly by the state. Thus, the 474 institutions operated by
private agencies were caring for 98.4% (46,900) of the minors in need
of such assistance.

Colombia

Scope of the report

This report deals with children held in penal facilities where adults
are also incarcerated and where at least visual and auditory
communication between minors and adults is possible. Information
is based on an examination of the relevant legislation in Colombia,
as well as conditions in three different prisons. Until recently, all
persons under the age of eighteen were considered as minors under
the law. The age of penal responsibility was lowered to sixteen
because of the increase in serious crime by juveniles. Children under
the age of sixteen are now considered to be minors according to
Colombian penal law. Minors, though criminally responsible, may
not be incarcerated with adults. Juveniles over the age of sixteen are
criminally responsible. They are treated as adults under the

Colombian Penal Code, even though the age of majority is still eighteen years.

There are some rare cases where children as young as twelve years of age are incarcerated, although usually they are only held overnight at an ordinary police station. However, in such cases where young minors are kept overnight at a police station, abuses are common. These minors are often required to surrender whatever money they have to adult prisoners or to corrupt jailers. It must be emphasized, however, that it is not customary for twelve to sixteen-year-old minors to be housed in jails or prisons with adults. There are institutions specifically intended to accommodate convicted minors.

Adults and minors incarcerated together in Colombia

There are three prisons in Colombia where adults and minors are often incarcerated together: (1) Carcel Distrital, a large jail in Bogota; (2) the Carcel Modelo, the largest prison in Colombia; (3) the Buen Pastor, the jail for women.

The Carcel Distrital prison was built in 1936 and is essentially for the use of adult prisoners. During this researcher's visit, however, there were sixty minors at the prison. The minors spend the day in the yard together. The authorities attempt to keep the minors separated from the adults, but many of the minors are assigned errands inside the prison which result in contact with adult prisoners. The minor ward houses males from sixteen to twenty years of age. Occasionally, minors younger than sixteen are also incarcerated in the minors' ward. There is no attempt to separate age groups within the minor wards.

In addition, the minors' ward serves as a protective custody area for older, weaker prisoners. Whenever an adult cannot survive the adult prison without being harmed, he is often placed in the minors' ward. In many instances, such an adult prisoner becomes the aggressor. It is not uncommon for an adult to have been raped in the adult prison, then be removed to the minors' ward for protective custody and subsequently to be found attempting to rape a youngster.

The Carcel Distrital is old and in a terrible state of ill-repair. The diet is barely adequate, though three meals per day are served. This researcher reported that on the day of his visit, lunch consisted of rice soup, potatoes, rice and peas. There is no dental care. There is a medical physician, although he complains that his prescriptions are rarely filled.

There is a female ward at the Carcel Distrital. The researcher did not visit this ward, but an officer of the ward affirmed that minor female prisoners are not separated in any way from their adult counterparts. Many of the adult prisoners in the female ward are lesbians. There are rumours that minor females are routinely raped by the adult women upon arrival at the prison. Rape is also rumoured to be frequent in the men's ward.

The Carcel Modelo, Colombia's largest prison, offers tremendous opportunity for adult and minor prisoners to intermingle. There is a separate ward for minors, but upon reception, minors may spend as much as two days housed with older men, while authorities decide where the minors are to be assigned. During this two-day period, minors may actually sleep in a cell with adult prisoners, and there are reports of frequent rapes in such cases.

Minors sent to Carcel Modelo may choose either work or study. In either case there is daily contact with adults. If they choose to study, adult inmates will be their teachers. If they choose work, they will spend their day with adult inmates at the shop or at the bakery.

There are no specific statistics relating to drug trafficking, but one official admitted that it is a severe problem in Carcel Modelo.

In conclusion, the segregation of adult and children prisoners in principle does not result in their separation in practice. In the prisons surveyed, there is extensive personal contact between adults and minors, especially at the Carcel Modelo. Very often, the separation provided for by the Prison Code is not implemented. Contact between the minors and adults frequently results in rape and other forms of abuse and exploitation.

Costa Rica

Scope of the report

The age of criminal responsibility in Costa Rica is set at seventeen years. Minors are therefore youths aged sixteen and younger. The terms 'minor' and 'juvenile' are used interchangeably throughout this report.

The researcher examined nine police offices in the cities of San José, Alajuela, Cartaga, Heredia, Liberia, Limón, Puntarenas and San Carlos. No minors were detained in any of these offices at the time they were visited. The practice described by police officers was identical: when minors are taken into custody Monday through

Friday during working hours, they are immediately brought before a judge. If the minor is taken into custody after working hours, or during the week-end, the police officer in charge uses his discretion as to whether to detain the minor at the police station or to release the youth to his parents until the minor can see a judge. The detention of minors in police stations most often arises because of week-end and after-hour arrests. Many other minors are detained as a consequence of arrests made in remote areas, where conditions of transportation, weather or shortage of vehicles make it impossible or impractical to transport minors to a juvenile judge immediately.

The police station in San José is the only facility which has separate areas provided for minors. The other eight facilities surveyed attempt to house minors in administrative areas, courtyards or unoccupied jail cells. This approach of separating minors from adults, though becoming more widespread, is not yet universally employed. In addition, some problems have arisen relating to the security of female minors, especially prostitutes, during the night.

The rural police reported that there were approximately 281 minors arrested between January and October 1983. Some of the juveniles interviewed asserted that they had been detained in cells with adults up to the time they were transferred; others stated that they had been released to their parents pending transfer; in some cases, since rural police stations have no cells for either adults or minors, the minors were sent to the nearest penal admission unit, pending adjudication of their cases. Those minors who were housed in cells were either by themselves or with other minors. However, the cells were dirty and inadequate. Some of the prisoners arrested by the rural police indicated that they often received no food except that which they purchased or which was brought in by their parents.

The City of San José has separate facilities for minors in police custody. Some persons familiar with the operation of the facility state that in practice minors and adults are often mixed. This may occur in many cases due to difficulty in distinguishing between adults and minors, as many minors lie about their age.

The detention of minors with adults in regional admission (penal) units

Penal institutions are under the control of the Department of Social Rehabilitation, a division of the Ministry of Justice. The Department has three basic types of facilities: the central institutions, which house the bulk of the prison population; decentralized minimum security facilities, which are mostly agricultural farms, and the multi-use regional admission units. There is never total separation of adults and minors in the major central institutions and the minimum security facility. There are cases where minors are housed with adults in the admission units as well.

The admission units house both men and women, convicted prisoners and persons awaiting trial, and, as mentioned above, minors as well as adults. Minors, in contrast to adults, may not serve sentences in the admission unit. Those minors who are detained in these units are usually there because of the difficulty in transporting them to juvenile facilities.

There are approximately seventy to one hundred minors per year at the nine units visited. Most of the units originally attempted some form of separation, but limited space or transportation rendered this impossible. The units at Liberia and San Carlos appeared to be the most inadequate of the nine visited. At these locations, prisoners slept twenty to thirty per room, on mattresses on the floor in close proximity to each other. Toilet and shower facilities — dirty, foul-smelling and uncovered — were at the end of a long corridor near the guard post. In making some effort to separate the minors, the officials often assign minors to the *calabazo* (dungeon), which are basically single cells. In Liberia and San Carlos, these are usually one meter by two meters in size, and are dirty and unlit. These cells have no opening, other than a small barred opening in the door, and contain no toilet or running water. Aware of the inhuman nature of these cells for juveniles, the officials usually permit the minors only to sleep there. During the day, the minors stay in a recreational-like area.

Surprisingly, the food at San Carlos and Liberia is relatively good. Breakfast consists of bread, coffee and milk. Rice, beans and pasta are served for lunch and dinner. Beef is served on the average of twice weekly, cooked in a soup or stew. There are indications, however, that many inmates never receive meat. Fruit and drinks are served daily.

There are no educational, cultural or other rehabilitative programmes offered at the units. Theoretically, the minors would benefit little from such programmes for their stay at the unit is supposed to be of a 'transitory' nature.

There are several modern facilities: Perez Zeledon, Union and Puntarenas. The minors housed in these institutions have a separate building of their own. Paradoxically, though the facilities in these units are superior to those found in the other prisons, the overall conditions under which minors are detained are worse. For example, although the cells are larger, with lights, running water and toilets, the minors are rarely permitted to leave their cells for exercise. Unlike Liberia and San Carlos, minors at Perez Zeledon, Union and Puntarenas remain locked in their cells day and night. The diet at these more modern facilities is also less adequate than at the older units. At the modern units, minors complained that proteins such as meat, fish, poultry and dairy products are never served. Eggs are served once a week, and fresh vegetables are served when the monthly supply arrives from San José.

The practice of housing dangerous or hard-to-control juvenile males with adult prisoners was discontinued in 1980. Such juveniles are now detained in a separate unit, which resembles an ordinary jail. Physical conditions resemble some of the older admission units, but there is no contact with adult prisoners.

Detaining difficult-to-control female minors with adult females still occurs. This is normally done on a temporary basis, until such time as the female minor can be rehabilitated and returned to the detention centre for minor females. Only two such cases occurred during 1983.

Although the recidivism rate among juvenile offenders is 40 per cent, there is no evidence of separate detention because of recidivism, nor is there separate detention based on race, language, ethnic group or socio-economic status.

Pregnant adolescents and the presence of mothers with children

There are no statistics in this report on women who had infants while incarcerated. Women are required to surrender their children to the staff social worker by the time the infant is five years old. Pregnant adolescent offenders are rarely assigned to the adult female prisons. This can only be done upon the recommendation of a social worker, and approval of a judge. There was only one such transfer in 1982, and none during the first ten months of 1983. In general, pregnant adolescents are released to their parents.

Denmark

Scope of this report

This report includes a review of Danish legislation pertaining to juvenile offenders. In addition, one section examines information on the detention of minors, while another is concerned with the physical conditions in state prisons.

The age of civil majority in Denmark is eighteen. However, the age of criminal responsibility is set at fifteen. Throughout this report, the terms 'minors' and 'juveniles' are used interchangeably, and refer to youths who are fifteen, sixteen and seventeen years of age.

Local prisons are essentially pre-trial detention jails, while state prisons serve to house persons who have been convicted of a crime. Children who are fourteen years old or younger, because they have not attained the age of criminal responsibility, cannot be detained in either state or local prisons, whether for pre-trial detention or as a penal measure. Minors in the fifteen to seventeen-year-old age-group may be placed in youth institutions, either because of social misbehaviour or criminal activity. The youth institutions are administered by the social welfare authorities, and are not penal in nature. Juvenile offenders over fifteen can be subject to incarceration in these establishments, in combination with probation.

No special juvenile courts or penal institutions exist in Denmark for minor offenders. Fifteen to seventeen-year-old offenders are not separated from their adult counterparts, and are subject to the same formal rules, with a few exceptions. The maximum sentence for a person under eighteen is eight years of imprisonment, no matter what the penalty would have been otherwise. For example, the crime of homicide carries a maximum sentence of life imprisonment for adults, but a fifteen to seventeen-year-old offender can be sentenced to eight years imprisonment at most.

The detention of minors (fifteen to seventeen-year-olds)

A 1983 report published by the Ministry of Justice, covering the period January to September 1981, indicated that 2,574 minors in this age group were detained for some length of time during this nine-month period. These juveniles were detained in either local prisons or police cells; forty two per cent of them were detained for up to twenty-four hours by police decision (the maximum time limit for police detention is twenty-four hours); three per cent were held for an additional three days by a judge's decree; and nearly four per cent were remanded in custody for a longer period.

The time people awaiting trial spend in local prisons is decided by the court, and can be extended several times. Although offenders placed in local jails, whether juvenile or adult, are in 'transit' status, all of the confining elements of prison life exist. A minor can be placed in solitary confinement almost as easily as his adult counterpart. The Administration of Justice Act regulates the rights of detainees. This act provides that before a person can be detained in a local jail, a judge must have determined that there is a high probability that he or she has committed a serious crime. The judge must also feel that if the suspect is not detained, then he is likely to avoid prosecution, make police investigations difficult by tampering with evidence, or even commit another similar crime. The provisions of the Administration of Justice Act are identical for juvenile and adult offenders. However, judges may, at their discretion, place juveniles in non-penal youth institutions as an alternative to pre-trial detention in jail, if this type of custody is deemed more appropriate.

Conditions in state prisons

Because the incarceration of juveniles in local prisons is always of a temporary nature, this report focuses upon the physical conditions of state prisons. The state prisons ultimately accommodate all adult prisoners and most fifteen to seventeen-year-olds who are sentenced to imprisonment.

The law allows for convicted juveniles to be confined in any prison in the state system. There are two types of prison — 'closed' and 'open'. Closed institutions have perimeter walls, locked doors, barred windows and television screening of outdoor areas. These prisons are used for inmates serving long-term sentences and for those considered to be escape-prone. Most closed establishments date from the nineteenth century, but have undergone a certain modernization process. Open prisons have a wire fence surrounding them, but there is no closed gate and the windows can be opened in the normal fashion. The guards at the open prisons are unarmed.

Although no juvenile prisoners were interviewed by the investigator of this report, permission to do so would be granted if requested. In addition, interviews were not conducted with mothers who have been incarcerated with their children, and no pregnant adolescents were interviewed. None of the prisons in Denmark have special facilities for mothers with babies. However, mothers who are sentenced to imprisonment do have the right to bring their babies into the prison and remain together until the infant reaches its first birthday. The prison authorities can extend this age limit. Nevertheless, available information indicates that mothers rarely choose to bring their babies into prison with them.

England and Wales

Scope of the report

The penal system in England and Wales considers 'adults' to be those persons twenty-one years of age and over. Those between fourteen and twenty who are found guilty of a crime are referred to as 'young offenders'. However, the researcher of this report defined 'children' as those persons below the age of eighteen.

In theory, current legislation discourages the use of custody for young offenders. Section One of the 1982 Criminal Justice Act states that a young offender should not be placed in custody unless the offence committed is serious enough to warrant such a measure. Section 12 of this Act provides that young offenders sentenced to youth custody should not be detained in adult prisons, except 'for any temporary purpose'.

However, there are a number of instances where offenders under eighteen can be and are held in custody with those over eighteen. Some of these 'exceptions' include:

(1) the mixing of different age groups in female establishments (existing legislation explicitly encourages this);
(2) youth custody centres are designed to accommodate fifteen to twenty-year-olds;
     although fourteen to sixteen-year-olds usually go to junior detention centres and seventeen to twenty-year-olds attend senior detention centres, some flexiblity nevertheless exists;
(4) a number of legal provisions allow for children sentenced to youth custody or those sentenced for murder or other grave offences to be held in adult prisons;
(5) babies can be imprisoned with their mothers in certain cases.

Children in adult prisons

At the time the research for this report was undertaken, there were a large number of young offenders being held in adult prisons in England and Wales. Many were young offenders on remand and unconvicted prisoners awaiting transfer to young offenders' wings.

The general problems of overcrowding within the penal system have led to some young people spending the whole of their sentence in an adult local prison.

There are also many children detained with adults under the Immigration Act of 1971 upon entry to the United Kingdom from their country of origin. These children can be held for many months while going through the formal procedures. In 1982, there were 102 such children at one particular prison (Harmondsworth).

Living conditions in prisons

As mentioned above, prisons are grossly overcrowded. Few attain the goal of one person per cell and most have two or three prisoners occupying cells designed for one. This problem of overcrowding is exacerbated when the only place to eat is in the cells. The worst overcrowding was found at the Ashford Remand Centre. This centre holds young men who have been remanded in custody by the courts, those who have been convicted but not sentenced, as well as a number of men (including adults) who are awaiting deportation to their country of origin.

Most prisons are old and ill-equipped by modern standards. Lavatory and washing facilities are totally inadequate. In one prison, forty inmates share one lavatory, while sixty to seventy prisoners in another institution share one lavatory, slop sink, wash handbasin and a water tap.

In the establishments for young offenders, food standards are reportedly good, in terms of cleanliness and taste, although little or no choice is given. Young people in these detention centres and borstals are kept occupied most of the time by either education, vocational training or work, or a combination of these. Inmates of compulsory school age are supposed to participate in education or vocational training courses for at least fifteen hours per week, although this regulation is not always adhered to. Educational facilities and programmes in prisons are poor, even in prisons where children are incarcerated.

Federal Republic of Germany

Scope of the report

The first section of this report is a review of legal and judicial standards relating to the trial and punishment of minors in the Federal Republic of Germany. The second contains a detailed description of the facilities in one juvenile prison (opened in 1980 and located in the town of Hameln). Interviews conducted with three juvenile prisoners and one voluntary staff member form an integral part of this section. In the third and final part, the positive and negative aspects of mother–child penal institutions are discussed from a practical, sociological and psychological perspective. Mother–child departments which have been opened in several women's prisons are examined, and detailed assessments of their features and implications are based on interviews with prisoners, staff members and researchers.

According to the Juvenile Court Law of 1923, a child may be charged with a criminal offence when he or she reaches the age of fourteen. The law distinguishes between fourteen to eighteen year olds (youths) and eighteen to twenty-on year olds (growing-up youths). The maximum sentence that can be legally imposed on a convicted juvenile is ten years' imprisonment. Although eighteen to twenty-one year olds are considered to have reached the age of majority under civil law, in some cases persons in this age group may be subjected to juvenile punishment, when such action is deemed appropriate. In the special situation of juvenile delinquents being placed on remand, the law stipulates that such youths are to be confined apart from adults, in a separate section of the prison. This provision is not always implemented in practice, however.

With regard to women prisoners with young children, the 'law of imprisonment' allows for children under the age of six to be placed with their mothers, and also provides for the establishment of special mother–child departments in women's prisons. The law focuses on promoting the 'well-being' of these children. However, the report points out that the question of how best to define 'well-being', and determine what measures are most likely to ensure it, has been the subject of much study and debate.

Juvenile prisons in the FRG

For the most part, the law stipulating that children and adults be imprisoned separately is strictly adhered to. However, children and adults are usually confined in separate sections of the same prison, rather than in separate institutions. In one establishment examined, youths aged fourteen were housed together with young adults who had reached the age of twenty-five.

Between the years 1972 and 1981, a total of 605 youths (twenty-four girls and 581 boys) aged fourteen to fifteen were sentenced to juvenile punishment. A random survey of 207 of these children showed that the large majority (71 per cent) received prison sentences from one to four years. Most of the crimes for which these punishments were administered involved theft (52 per cent) and robbery/blackmail (25 per cent).

Detention in the juvenile prison in Hameln is of a group nature, with seven to eight youths forming a group. The average duration of incarceration is one year. In 1983, there were 3,746 minors in Hameln prison, of whom 750 were new admissions. Living conditions are felt to be adequate by the staff and inmates, especially when compared to existing standards in other prisons.

A medical examination is performed when a juvenile is first admitted to the prison. A physician visits the institution each day for one hour, at which time the prisoners have the possibility of seeing him or her. Psychological consultations are also available, on a voluntary basis. There is a main kitchen where food is cooked, and the youths are entitled to participate in the arrangement of the menu. The hygienic conditions of the kitchen are controlled by the house physician, and are also inspected once or twice a year during unannounced visits by the Public Health Office.

Each communal area has two showers, and toilet and washing facilities are in every individual cell. Either an educationalist, tutor, psychologist or prison official with specialized training works within each group of seven to eight juveniles. Educational instruction is offered up to the 'General Certificate of Education', and numerous vocational training courses are also available. Contacts between prisoners of various ages are not restricted in any way, as separation of the younger detainees from the older ones was not considered useful. Unsupervised visits by persons outside the prison are permitted during free time periods, except for those youths on remand or in the drug section.

Mother–child establishments

There are six prisons in the FRG with mother–child establishments. One such institution exists as an independent building on the grounds of a general prison. The other five are sub-divisions within a regular prison building. Even though the law allows for children up to the age of six to be kept together with their mothers, only one establishment admits children up to this age. In the other prisons the age limit is theoretically set at three years. In fact, the average age of mothers imprisoned in these institutions is 27.3 years; that of their children is 1.1 years. In June 1983, there were forty-one mothers and forty-two children living together in mother–child establishments.

France

Scope of the report

There are no penal institutions specifically for minors in France. As a general rule, the principal objective of the Board of Supervised Education (éducation surveillée) is to attain the integration or re-integration of delinquent minors into society. Included in the report was a description of a prison in the Paris region, where a considerable number of minors (thirteen to eighteen) and young adults (twenty-one to twenty-three years of age) are held. The fact that this prison contains a disproportionate number of immigrants posed special problems for both the prison staff and the detainees.

The age of penal responsibility in France is thirteen. This means that minors (those under eighteen) can be placed in prison following criminal proceedings. Those under thirteen can be temporarily detained until such time as an educational measure can be taken concerning them. Under no circumstances can a minor below the age of thirteen be the object of a penal conviction.

Minors between thirteen and sixteen years of age can be placed in preventive detention until they are judged by a juvenile court. If found guilty, they can be sentenced to a penalty which is more severe than the period they served in temporary detention. Minors between the ages of sixteen and eighteen can be placed in temporary detention until the criminal court for minors passes judgement.

According to French law, minors below the age of thirteen cannot be imprisoned. Those between thirteen and sixteen cannot be detained in a prison for more than ten days. Minors from sixteen to eighteen can be temporarily detained in prison until judgement is pronounced by a Juvenile Court. Sentences can be passed calling for such minors to be imprisoned until they have reached the age of majority. In case of either educational measures or penal sanctions, the minor can be entrusted to an education, a permanent delegate of the probation board (Délégué Permanent à la Liberté Surveillée).

Minors imprisoned with adults

The report concludes that minors share prison cells with adults in nearly all French penal institutions. Only minors under sixteen are separated from adults, but this occurs within each penitentiary, rather than provision being made for separate prisons for children.

Although the Penal Code calls for imprisoned minors to be isolated at night, the presently over-populated prisons prevent the prison administrators from implementing this provision. The most frequent practice is to set aside a section of the prison for minors and young adults, called the Centre for Young Detainees (Centre de Jeunes Détenus). Such practice inevitably has harmful consequences — both physical and psychological — for the youngest and most fragile personalities. These minors are often the victims of various forms of physical harassment, including sodomy. The prison authorities are usually unable to prevent such occurrences, or even to intervene in an efficient or effective manner.

Living conditions in prisons where minors and adults are incarcerated together

Each prison cell is supposed to contain only one person. Obviously, if from time to time one cell holds two minors, there may be negative consequences. However, in reality the cells are shared by three or four prisoners, making life very difficult for them in a short period of time. This is especially true in those institutions where minors are kept in their cells twenty-four hours per day. In addition, there is no doubt that prison staff members do not insist that inmates go for walks since such activity is optional in most institutions. In a large number of prisons, educational, athletic or cultural activities for detained minors are practically non-existent. It is also rare that prisoners are able to take showers twice a week. There is no air-conditioning, and during the summer the cells are unbearably hot. In winter, the cells are not warm enough, and the air is very bad since windows are never opened. The medical and psychiatric services are entirely insufficient.

India

Scope of the report

The Indian Penal law refers to minors up to the age of seven years as being in a state of innocence. Such minors are therefore not criminally responsible, and may never be incarcerated. Youths between the ages of seven and twelve are also presumably in a state of innocence, but the burden of proof is on offenders in this age group to demonstrate their lack of criminal responsibility. Thus, a youth between the ages of seven and twelve may in fact be convicted of a crime, and can be subject to incarceration. According to the Children Act and the Code of Criminal Procedure, any minor under sixteen so convicted should be detained in a house intended for youths. Any convicted youth aged sixteen to twenty-one should be housed in a Borstal Institution intended for young persons. However, in actual practice, because of economic or pragmatic administrative reasons, sixteen and seventeen-year-old youths are normally housed with adults in prisons intended for adults. There are even cases where children under sixteen have been incarcerated in adult prisons, although this is reportedly a rare situation.

India, the world's second most populated country, has twenty-two states and nine territories. Each of the states and territories has a number of large and small cities, as well as its own historical, geographical, economic and cultural uniqueness. This report, however, focuses on only three of the states: one was chosen for its affluence (which is rather recent); another because it is one of the most populous states and has a long tradition of education and political awareness; the third because of its post-independence development and progress.

Minors and adults at prisons visited

No female juvenile prisoners were found in any of the thirteen prisons visited during the course of this study. However, juvenile girls in all prisons are normally housed in the area of the prison intended for adult women prisoners.

Although these girls are separated from male prisoners, the research indicated that female minor prisoners are in no way separated from female adults. A woman warden is in charge of the women's section of the prison. In one of the thirteen prisons visited, there were no juvenile males in custody on the day visited. In the remaining twelve prisons visited, there was a total of approximately 235 minors (males), between ten and twenty years of age, in institutions intended for adult men. There is some attempt to separate younger prisoners from older ones, but there are numerous situations where the minors in these institutions come in contact with adult prisoners.

Conditions of the juvenile wards in the adult prisons surveyed

The juvenile wards are generally overcrowded and, as with the adult section of the prison, woefully inadequate for any form or semblance of rehabilitation of youth. Nearly every prison visited is more than a hundred years old. The ventilation is poor. During the summer, the cells are unbearably hot; during the winter, they are unbearably cold. In some of the northernmost states, the cold can be severe. In only two of the thirteen prisons visited was there running tap water in the cells, and the water at these two facilities runs only infrequently. The other eleven facilities only had running water taps outside the barracks. In these institutions, prisoners are given earthen jugs in which water may be stored for the purpose of drinking, washing the body and clothes, and flushing the toilet. Many of the minors destroy the earthen pots in order to intimidate the authorities. Often, latrines are not flushed, and are filled with earth or bricks.

Minors at the prisons must in most cases bathe in the open, sometimes on a meagre portion of water. In some prisons there is no official supply of soap, and in others the supply is inadequate. Occasionally, a relative will supply soap. Female prisoners, however, are provided a small portion of soap.

The minors are usually locked in their cells from sunset to sunrise. At most prisons, juveniles may leave their cells during the day. There are reports, however, that in some institutions minors are kept in their cells during the day, from 12 p.m. to 3 p.m. There are also reports that some minors are forced to work from seven to eight hours per day. Minors awaiting trial are not obliged to work, but there is evidence that minors awaiting trial have been required to work as much as seven to eight hours per day.

There are no educational programmes for minors at the prisons visited. Some of the facilities had teachers, but they tended to help the administration with paperwork, rather than engage in teaching activities. When the teachers do teach, they tend to teach the adults, not the minors.

Medical attention is generally available at all facilities, but is nevertheless inadequate. There were no particular complaints made with regard to the dietary plan at any of the institutions surveyed.

Jamaica

Scope of the report

The terms 'children', 'juveniles' and 'young persons' as used in the context of the Jamaican legal system, merit definition. The term 'children' applies to persons under fourteen years of age; 'juveniles' refers to persons between the ages of fourteen and seventeen; persons between seventeen and twenty-one are referred to as 'young persons'. Though there is some overlapping in the age groups relative to the data supplied for this report, the researcher chose 'young persons' as the targeted group for this study, because it is this group which most frequently encounters adults in penal situations.

The Jamaican Prison Act of 1947 is the statutory authority which governs judicial activity over young persons. This Act provides in pertinent part that: young persons shall not be detained in the same part of any prison with adult inmates, and that juveniles and young persons awaiting trial or remanded in custody shall, whenever possible, be separated from the adult population.

The detention of young persons with adults

In reality, the principle that young persons accused or convicted of a criminal offence should be separated from adults in penal situations is regularly violated. In Jamaica, the convicted young person in an adult penal institution shares the same provisions as his adult counterpart. Similarly, the young person in police custody is treated no differently than detained adults. This is also true of those young persons remanded in custody at remand centres.

The remand centres house persons awaiting trial, whereas prisons accommodate young persons and adults who are convicted. Sixteen-year-old 'juveniles' are often found housed with adults at police 'in custody' stations, as well as at remand centres. Female prisoners are also not usually separated at the remand centres, although they are kept in different cells according to age.

At the remand centres, there is no attempt made to separate detainees by age groups. Convicted persons and those awaiting trial are not only kept in sight and hearing of each other, they also communicate and intermingle quite openly. As a result, young persons come into contact not only with hardened adult criminals, but also with other young persons who may have committed serious crimes. Furthermore, young persons who are found guilty of a crime are almost without exception sent to adult penal institutions. Young persons may be sent to an adult institution for any misdemeanour or felony. A capital offence will normally ensure a young person's being incarcerated in an adult prison. A person convicted of murder is given a mandatory death sentence, unless he is under eighteen. Hence, fourteen to seventeen year olds found guilty of murder are placed in an adult institution. In addition young persons convicted of the following crimes may be incarcerated in an adult prison: manslaughter, treason, infanticide, illegal possession of ammunition and/or firearms, robbery, demanding money with menace, conspiracy, soliciting a crime, attempted murder, writing letters threatening murder, acts causing danger to life, bodily harm, sexual abuse, abduction or kidnapping.

The Governor General has statutory authority to impose sentences, and his discretion is unquestioned and unchallenged. Theoretically, however, he is guided by the Prison Act of 1947. The Prison Act provides that every three years the Governor General must review the status of a confined young person to determine his potential for rehabilitation. The Governor General may grant a licence of release if he finds: (1) there is a reasonable probability that the young person will abstain from crime and lead a useful, productive life; (2) that he is no longer capable of engaging in crime; or (3) that for other reasons it is desirable to release him from confinement in prison. This release should take place five years from the start of the young person's initial sentence.

The Governor General is not required to release the young person, even when there is conclusive evidence that the person has been rehabilitated. There is no appeal process, and the Governor General is accountable only to the Privy Council, to whom he makes a written report. The report is confidential, and the Council cannot overrule the Governor General's decision.

Unlike his adult counterpart, when the young person is sentenced to an adult prison, he is not eligible for parole. The young person must serve his entire sentence, unless, as noted above, he is expressly granted a licence of release by the Governor General or reduced time for good behaviour. Most young persons, as well as their parents, are relatively uninformed about the process of applying for a licence of release from the Governor General. Many attorneys are also not aware of the procedural requirements, and young persons are rarely granted a licence of release. Adult prisoners are usually released upon serving the requisite two-thirds of the term fixed by the sentencing judge, provided none of the time has been forfeited by misconduct.

Japan

Scope of the report

This report is confined to an analysis of some of the legal instruments in Japan pertaining to the prevention and correction of juvenile delinquency. Conclusions are presented with regard to features and issues associated with child and family law.

Juvenile delinquency and the law

There are two legal instruments dealing specifically with juvenile offenders in Japan. One is the Juvenile Law, which is part of the criminal law system; the other is the Child Welfare Law, which falls under the social welfare system. Children who are thirteen years of age or younger, as well as juveniles between fourteen and twenty, are all subject to the Juvenile Law. This law provides for educational measures to be applied in cases of proven delinquency. No penal sanctions are to be applied, and complete separation from adults is mandatory.

Under the Juvenile Law, trials take place in Family Courts and if educational measures are decided upon, the youth concerned can be sent to a juvenile training school. Those who are over the age of sixteen can be prosecuted under criminal procedure, if this is deemed appropriate. In fact, this rarely occurs (only in about 2 per cent of the cases).

Under the Child Welfare Law, juvenile delinquents under the age of eighteen who are not subject to the Juvenile Law are dealt with by local government bodies called Child Guidance Centres. These institutions are established to implement educational, supportive measures. In cases where more severe measures appear necessary, the Child Guidance Centres must refer the children concerned to a Family Court.

Specific findings and observations

The report concludes that the legislative system of juvenile protection in Japan, particularly regarding the separation of children from adults works very successfully. In the relevant laws, adults and juveniles are treated separately as to each phase of the criminal proceedings. Within the juvenile training schools, children are treated differently, according to their age and the seriousness of the infraction committed.

There are, however, problems associated with the system of juvenile protection, and these have been the subject of much study and debate. The discussion centres around the most appropriate and useful interpretation of 'protection', including how to best achieve the most effective balance between corrective, punitive and educational measures. In 1984, the Ministry of Justice began revising the Juvenile Law. The Ministry is aiming to alter trial proceedings, especially for adolescent juveniles (eighteen to nineteen year olds) by making them more similar to those of adults. The Japanese Association of Lawyers is opposed to such a change.

The present system in Japan is based on a type of 'pluralism'. Rather than distinguishing solely between 'adults' and 'juvenile', distinctions are made between children, juveniles, adolescents and adults. Thus, the question is not one of deciding how to treat juvenile delinquents differently from adult criminals. The issue to be addressed is whether the corrective treatment of children, juveniles and adolescents who have broken the law should be purely educational in nature, or whether measures taken should vary according to age.

Morocco

Scope of the report

This comprehensive study is divided into three basic sections. The first comprises a general description of the demographic, economic and social situation in Morocco, including the problem of juvenile delinquency and attitudes among the youth. In the second part, the legal framework and existing infrastructure with regard to judicial and correctional facilities for minors are examined. Finally, two centres for the observation and correction of minors are described, and conclusions are made regarding the living conditions in them.

Information is based on visits to the two centres concerned, as well as conversations with educators, magistrates, lawyers, Presidents of Regional Courts and representatives of the Royal Attorney dealing with children. Permission to visit the juvenile sections of detention centres and prisons was not granted by the Ministry of Justice. However, data on the type of offences committed by boys and girls of different age groups was obtained for one year (1978) from the Protection of Children organization (Sauvegarde de l'Enfance).

The report offers a detailed summary of the legislation pertaining to the legal procedures to be followed in the trial and detention of children. Articles 514 to 567 of Book III of the Code of Penal Procedure relate to child delinquency. Article 514 sets the age of penal majority at sixteen years. Article 517 allows for minors above the age of twelve to be fined or imprisoned, in exceptional cases.

A Juvenile Court, composed of the Juvenile Judge, the President and two Assessors, is attached to every Regional Court and Regional Tribunal. A Minors' Chamber is attached to every Court of Appeal. These institutions are specifically established to deal with offences allegedly committed by minors. Juvenile Judges are authorized to give instructions for medical and psychological examinations or to place minors in hostels, observation centres or provisional custody. The parents or guardians of all minors must be informed of any action taken. Responsibility for juvenile delinquents is entrusted to the Ministry of Youth and Sports. Minors under twelve years of age cannot be placed in a penal institution. Those between twelve and sixteen may be sent to a penitentiary, although in such cases they are to be housed in a special section. Measures taken to incarcerate juvenile delinquents must be pronounced for a fixed period, and are not to allow for institutionalization beyond the age of eighteen.

Institutions for juvenile delinquents and salient features of offences committed

There are twenty institutions for child offenders in Morocco. These include: four social service centres, which can accommodate an average of thirty children each. Fifteen centres, with room for ninety children each, are divided into two sections: one for observation, the other for correction. Finally, one centre is allocated for female delinquents, and can hold 120 persons. Its three sections are for observation, correction and social action.

The purpose of observation centres is to accommodate minors during judicial proceedings and to ascertain the causes of their delinquency. Only juveniles between the ages of nine and sixteen are admitted to these centres. The correctional centres are for minors who cannot be entrusted to their families for some reason. They aim to rehabilitate, provide occupational training and then re-integration of the minors into society. The social action centres are 'open' hostels which usually serve as a transitional phase for juveniles coming out of correctional centres, but who are not quite ready for complete reintegration into society.

According to magistrates who were interviewed, the application of procedures to minors is below standard, and measures for juvenile offenders are inadequate, due to the insufficient number of centres for guidance and correction.

Although official statistics are not available, there are believed to be between 2,000 and 4,000 minors presently held in the juvenile sections of adult prisons. Lawyers have indicated that the prisons fall short of respecting the minimum regulations — the juvenile sections are often overcrowded, and hygienic conditions are poor.

In 1978, two-thirds of the offences committed by minors were misdemeanours aimed at fulfilling basic needs (stealing of food, etc.). However, among girls the largest number of infractions involved 'moral offences', especially by those in the fifteen to seventeen year age-group. Boys between the ages of fourteen and sixteen were found to commit more offences than any other age group. Furthermore, available statistics indicate that nearly two-thirds (63 per cent) of the offences committed by minors were accounted for by those living in urban centres, pointing to the inherently urban character of juvenile delinquency in Morocco.

Findings regarding living conditions in two centres for observation and correction

The inadequate budget provided for food means that children do not receive a balanced diet or proper nutrition. The seriousness of this is compounded by the fact that most children are already under-nourished when they arrive at the centres. Visits by doctors do occur, but health care and medicine are lacking due to budgetary constraints. Hygienic equipment is in poor condition and promiscuous behaviour occurs in the lavatories. The dormitories are unsanitary and overcrowded, although hygienic conditions were found to be less deplorable in one centre than in the other.

Many children are illiterate, and only a small proportion had ever had any schooling. Teaching materials and curriculum are inadequate. Workshops do exist, for activities such as ironwork, carpentry, handicrafts and sewing. These are intended mainly for the minors in the corrective sections.

Netherlands

Scope of the report

The Netherlands has had special civil and criminal laws for minors since 1905. To enforce these laws, there are special police departments and juvenile judges. 'Minors' are defined as persons up to the age of eighteen. There are situations, however, when 'minors' aged sixteen to seventeen are treated as adults and housed in adult facilities. Although some 'minors' as young as twelve have committed serious offences, these youths cannot be prosecuted in a criminal court. Such youths are often subject to civil measures, but in no case is there incarceration.

For the purposes of this report, minors are considered detained with adults when they are kept overnight in facilities holding adult inmates. No distinction is made regarding the nature of the juvenile offence necessitating detention. For example, minors may be detained because a parent is an inmate, the minor was destitute, abandoned or a 'status ofender' (a minor who breaks a law applicable to delinquent youths, e.g. truancy). The minor is a ward of the state with nowhere to go; or, more typically, there has been a charge or conviction for some criminal offence.

Institutions for the detention of minors

Ideally, minors who are incarcerated should be housed in state institutions designed for this purpose. There are five different kinds of institutions:

(1) reception homes: the homes are intended for minors who are in preventive custody, or minors who must be detained temporarily in a home pending transfer to a more permanent location. Usually, these minors are psychological or social wards of the government;

(2) correctional schools: these schools house minors who are to undergo a correctional school term, a remand sentence or placement in an institution for prolonged supervision;

(3) treatment institutions: these are for minors who cannot be

maintained by private treatment institutions or who are wards of the government or in need of special counselling or supervision;
(4) girls: there is one state institution for girls. This institution serves as a reception home, a correctional school and as an institution for special treatment;
(5) juvenile prisons: since juvenile prisons in the Netherlands house persons aged eighteen to twenty-three, these persons are considered as adults and are not included in this report.

In May 1983, there were a total of thirty-six adults detained in institutions designed for minors. This number was representative of the total number detained in such institutions throughout the year. The adults in these institutions had in most cases begun their sentences at the age of sixteen or seventeen years. Due to the length of their sentences, they remained at the prison into adulthood. There is no mechanism within the prison system to transfer such minors to an adult prison upon reaching the age of legal majority.

Most of the adults in institutions designed for minors are eighteen years old, and none have been found who passed the age of twenty-three. The difference in age however, has apparently created no particular problem of discipline. In addition, there is no indication that minors in daily contact with young adults are abused, neglected or otherwise exploited. Since all cells at these units are one-person cells, it is unlikely that adults ever sleep in a cell with minors. This obviously decreases the chances of sexual abuse of minors.

The living conditions in these institutions are adequate. Each cell is furnished with a bed, a desk, a chair, a wardrobe and curtains. There are two toilets with two showers for every eight to ten boys. The minors are served three nutritional meals daily. There is an ongoing medical programme administered to all youth. The discipline is firm, based on rules of the individual institutions, but not abusive. Although most of these institutions are eighty years old, the physical facilities and overall state of repair seem to be adequate.

Minors in police stations, remand houses and other institutions for adults

Adults and minors are brought to the same police station upon arrest. In principle, any minor who must remain at the station longer than four days for investigation and interrogation is to be taken to a youth facility. This rule exists because any suspect must be brought before an investigating judge. Theoretically, the judge should have a minor transferred to a youth facility if the youth is to be detained. In actuality, the minor is housed with adults during the initial four days, as there are no separate facilities at these stations for minors. This practice is often continued beyond the four days, because investigating judges are often late in interviewing the minor. Also, it is often not deemed practical to transfer minors.

There were approximately fifteen minors housed at police stations for more than four days during a typical day in 1983. However, though the minors were housed with the adult population, they were all kept in individual cells. They did have daily contact with the adults when they were not locked in their cells. But because there are always guards walking in the corridors, as well as cameras placed throughout the institutions, incidents of abuse resulting from the mixing of the age groups are rare. Unlike the institutions for youth, where the educational opportunities for minors are good, there are no educational facilities at police stations due to their intended transitory nature.

In the Netherlands, there are also remand houses, designed for adults as a crime prevention measure or for adults who are serving short sentences. Often, minors are sent to these houses, because none exist that are specifically established for minors. Minors sent to remand houses usually display disruptive behavioural traits and would, in the opinion of the judge, be a negative influence on minors in a juvenile institution. The average number of minors in remand houses in 1983 was seven. These minors mix with the general population, but all inmates sleep in individual cells. There are no reported incidents of minors being abused. The general conditions and facilities of the remand houses are good. The minors here are given the opportunity to continue their education. Most of the remand houses are over a hundred years old, but all have been kept in good condition.

There are also cases of minors who are placed in institutions for adults under the care of the government. These institutions are for adults and children who are considered not to be completely responsible for their criminal activity. Minors, according to the law, should go to a treatment institution for minors. Minors who have some psychological or social aberration are however, usually transferred to treatment centres for adults with similar problems. There were four such children in these institutions in 1983 and no cases of abuse were reported.

Finally, it should be noted that there are instances when children under the age of three are permitted to stay with their mothers in prison. This normally occurs when there is no other family member or friend able to take care of the child during the period of the mother's incarceration. In general, when such children reach the age of three they are placed under the care of a social worker. In 1983, there was one child in each prison with its mother, on average.

Nigeria

Scope of the report

The age of criminal responsibility in Nigeria is sixteen. It was generally deemed by this researcher that there were no minors under the age of eighteen in any adult prison in Nigeria. The one instance where minors (under eighteen) may find themselves in contact with adult prisoners is at the Borstal Institution. There are two Borstal Institutions in Nigeria, intended solely for the use of minors.

Mixing of adult prisoners and minors in the Borstal Institutions

The major Borstal unit is an attached wing of Kakuri Prison. Originally, young boys were housed in the prison totally unseparated from adult men. Since the addition of the Borstal wing in 1961, in theory sixteen to seventeen-year-old minors are separated from adults. In practice, however, the Borstal unit typically houses young men between the ages of sixteen and twenty-two. There are even situations where minors under the age of sixteen have been found at the Borstal unit, unseparated from the older population. Nevertheless, this researcher did report that a serious attempt was made to separate youths under the age of sixteen from the older population, at least in the cells. Particularly incorrigible minors under the age of sixteen may find themselves in a Borstal unit where they are in contact with older prisoners (adults of eighteen to twenty-two). The contact of minors and young adult prisoners at the Borstal unit is virtually assured due to the nature of the cells. The cells are large enough to accommodate up to sixty prisoners (who are mostly sentenced for gambling, loitering, stealing or unlawful possession of drugs). The younger inmates (under seventeen) are often accommodated in the adult wing of the Borstal unit. Furthermore, all those who are incarcerated, no matter what their age, shower and eat together.

There is another Borstal unit attached as a wing of the Ikoyi Prison, near Lagos. The situation at Ikoyi is similar to that of the Borstal wing attached to Kakuri Prison. In Nigeria in 1980, there were 30,281 inmates aged nineteen to twenty-one in the two Borstal units. These figures, however, pertain to prisoners who are considered as adults. There are no specific statistics reported for minors under the age of eighteen who are housed with adults at the Borstal units. There are indications of unusual circumstances where a particularly incorrigible minor charged with a serious offence may find himself in the adult section of Kakuri or Ikoyi Prison. This situation is reportedly rare and exceptional, though there are no statistics available.

Conditions of minors incarcerated with adults

Whenever young prisoners are imprisoned, they are in continuous communication with the adult prisoners. There is a recognized system of hierarchy, and the young prisoners are at the lowest rung of the ladder. They are, therefore, subject to maltreatment both from older inmates as well as the wardens. When, as sometimes happens, they are beaten up by adult prisoners, they are usually afraid to report the beating to authorities. They are also exposed to other criminal activities, e.g. robbery and smoking of Indian hemp (similar to marijuana), as well as being subjected to homosexual practices.

The adult prisoners force the young prisoners to do all the dirty work, such as cleaning out toilet pails and washing clothes and blankets. Sometimes, a young prisoner's clothes are seized by an adult. Often, the young prisoners are forced, by threats of physical violence, to carry out instructions by the adult prisoners, which may be violating prison regulations. Indeed, observation and interviews revealed that the young prisoners are more anxious to abide by rules and regulations set up in their cells by their peers than those of the prison authorities. There are reported incidents of sexual attacks on young prisoners. Although homosexual activity occurs, it is not rampant and is reportedly never forced on young prisoners. Apparently, young prisoners are often lured into such sexual activity by adult prisoners who offer them gifts.

Minor females in prison with adult women and infants in prison with their mothers

There is one female prison in Nigeria. Female minors and adults are housed together at this unit. No statistics were obtained on the number of female minor inmates, nor was any information available on conditions under which these minor females live.

There were nine infants at the Kirikiri prison during this researcher's visit. It is reported that there are some 240 infants at other female prison annexes throughout Nigeria.

Pakistan

Scope of the report

This survey focuses upon the relevant legislation in force, as well as the conditions of child prisoners in the one adult prison visited, in Lahore (Punjab). Also included in the report are findings regarding the Borstal Institution and Juvenile Jail in Bahawalpur (Punjab), one of the two juvenile jails in Pakistan, although no field survey of this institution was conducted. Information was provided by the Punjab Prisons Department and the Superintendent of the Juvenile Jail pertaining to the 263 inmates, most of whom (225) are serving sentences of 'rigorous imprisonment', for crimes ranging from pick-pocketing to murder.

Conclusions are based on the condition of child prisoners in one adult prison in the Punjab Province. Data were collected during the visit to the prison, and include figures provided by the Punjab Prisons Department.

The detention of children

According to the law, 'young persons' convicted of a crime and sentenced to confinement for a period of three months or more, are to be sent either to a Borstal Institution or a reformatory school. While all 'juveniles' (males who are under eighteen years of age at the time of conviction) can be committed to Borstal, only offenders below the age of fifteen are eligible for confinement in a reformatory school. In 'extreme' cases, however, a child who is more than ten years old can be ordered to be incarcerated in the juvenile ward of an adult prison. There is no provision for the detention of female juveniles in Borstal or reformatory institutions. All convicted girls are incarcerated in the women's jail in Multan, where they are kept with other female adult offenders.

In December 1983, the Punjab Youthful Offenders Ordinance was enacted, which was the first legislation to provide for a separate system of criminal justice for children in Pakistan. 'Child' is defined by the 1983 Ordinance as a person of either sex below the age of fifteen years. The words 'conviction' and 'sentence' are not to be used in reference to children, and juvenile offenders cannot be sentenced to death or imprisonment.

The Ordinance calls for the establishment of separate juvenile courts for the trial of 'youthful offenders' (defined as males under fifteen years of age), as well as separate facilities for the confinement of those juveniles who are under trial or convicted. However, since this is a provincial statute, its application is limited to only one Province — the Punjab. Furthermore, none of the provisions of this Ordinance have yet come into force, and no steps have been taken to set up separate courts or confinement facilities for juveniles.

Thus, under the Code of Criminal Procedure in force in Pakistan, children above the age of seven are tried by ordinary criminal courts for all offences, and are subject to the same penal sanctions as adults.

The Jail Manual containing rules for the management of prisons was last revised in 1977. Most of the regulations regarding juvenile prisoners were incorporated at that time. Provision was made for setting up separate juvenile wards in most district jails. However, no rules have been formulated to restrict confinement of juveniles to independent institutions.

Findings and conclusions of the field survey report

The District Jail in Lahore (Punjab) contains two juvenile wards. These wards house a total of 118 prisoners, ranging in age from ten to twenty-one years. At the time of the survey, all inmates were under trial prisoners. In addition to inspecting the facilities, twenty prisoners of various ages and the superintendent of the jail were interviewed.

The minimum duration of imprisonment in the Lahore Jail was six months. Some juvenile inmates had been awaiting trial for nearly two years. Others, whose cases had reached the trial stage, were being held jointly with adult defendants. Lack of legal assistance had resulted in a serious deprivation of rights for many prisoners.

Rules pertaining to segregation were found to be broken, as it was learned that a ten-year-old child accused of pick-pocketing was sharing a cell with a fifteen-year-old boy accused of sodomy. No toilet facilities were available to the inmates after lock-up at sundown, or between 12.00 noon and 2.00 p.m. The prisoners were not provided with any formal education, despite an expressed desire by many of them to receive educational instruction. No recreational facilities or opportunities for physical exercise were available.

No regular schedule for medical check-ups existed, although medical care was provided by two doctors when necessary. There were dental care facilities inside the jail. No welfare officer, social worker or psychiatrist ever visited the prisoners.

In Pakistan, most juvenile offenders are presently imprisoned in separate wards of adult jails, despite legislation and regulations expressly forbidding this. In the Punjab Province, there are twenty-eight prisons, with an average of thirty juvenile prisoners in each of them. Thus, only 25 per cent of the juvenile offenders in this province are provided with the separate facilities and reformatory treatment that are called for by the law.

Romania

Scope of this report

The researcher claims that minors (persons under the age of eighteen) are not incarcerated with adults in Romania. Imprisoned minors and adults are strictly separated, in accordance with Article 57, Paragraph 3 of the Romanian Penal Code, adopted in 1968. This provision is reportedly strictly enforced. Furthermore, Romania has taken radical steps to change its criminal justice system in the last several years. During May–June 1977, the Romanian Communist Party adopted a set of principles which acts as a guideline for the punishment of minors who violate the law. These principles can be stated as follows:

(1) persuasion should be used as opposed to constraint;
(2) legitimate determinants should be used as the rationale for punishing criminal acts;
(3) humanism should be combined with firmness;
(4) the power of state organizations should be used to deter and punish anti-social actions.

The change in the handling of criminals in Romania is intended to ensure a shift from imprisonment to punishment that does not deprive the criminal of his freedom. Particularly with regard to minors, there is an emphasis on re-education, with the assistance of the family, school or the working collective. An attempt is made to rehabilitate minors without incarceration even when they are convicted of a particularly serious offence.

Categories of criminal responsibility with respect to minors in Romania

Minors between the ages of fourteen to sixteen are considered to have 'relative' criminal responsibility, and are almost never incarcerated. The emphasis is clearly on rehabilitation for this age group, and they are generally allowed to remain with their families. However, during the court-imposed period or rehabilitation, the state, the public organization and the work collective all play a vital role.

The second category, the age group from sixteen to eighteen is said to have 'absolute' criminal responsibility. It must be stressed, however, that this age group is still handled differently from adult persons convicted of an offence. In cases of particularly serious crimes, a minor (sixteen to eighteen) may be incarcerated. The tendency, however, is towards rehabilitation without incarceration, even if this involves attendance at a special work and re-education school.

The fourteen to sixteen-year-old minor who is found guilty of committing a criminal act, is sent either to a working or to a learning collective. The judge, upon sending him to the collective, will set strict rules of discipline and behaviour. In addition, the family is called on to ensure that the rules stipulated by the judge are observed.

Convicted minors aged sixteen to eighteen must attend special schools, and are obliged to work, to learn a trade and to complete compulsory education. Minors in this age group may spend from two to five years at the special school, depending on the gravity of the offence.

Minors receive 50 per cent remuneration for any work they perform in the collective. This sum is put into a savings account and kept for the minor until release from the programme. The remaining 50 per cent is used for the maintenance of the Special School for Work and Re-education. Minors who are sent to special schools may receive mail, food, visits or anything judged not to be detrimental to their rehabilitation. There were no reports of unfair or abusive treatment at the Special School for Work and Re-education.

Scotland

Scope of the report

According to the latest legislative change courts in Scotland should not in principle order a person under the age of twenty-one to be imprisoned. Convicted young persons under that age are to be sent to a detention centre for a period of 'short, sharp shock' kind of treatment. There are only two such centres in Scotland, housing a total of 250 persons. There are usually youths aged fifteen to twenty-one at these centres, serving sentences of approximately four months.

A juvenile whose offence is relatively severe may be sent to one of several Youth Offenders' Institutions located throughout Scotland. The duration of sentence imposed on youths at these centres must not exceed a sentence that would be imposed on an adult for a like offence. Through an extremely disciplined regime and communal living, the young offender is expected to acquire social skills, to develop talents, to overcome feelings of inadequacy and to prepare for employment upon release. There are six Younger Offenders' Institutions in Scotland, accommodating approximately 954 males and sixty females. Youths at these institutions are usually twenty years old and under. There is also a remand centre for offenders under twenty-one years of age. This institution accommodates 285 males. There is no distinction or separation according to age at either the Youth Offenders' Institutions or the remand centre. Since the age of criminal responsibility in most Scottish jurisdictions is fourteen years, youths between the ages of fourteen and twenty mix freely with one another.

Minors incarcerated with adults

The majority of minors in adult penal institutions are there as a result of what is commonly termed the 'unruly certificate'. They are usually housed with adults while on remand awaiting trial or they have already been tried and are awaiting sentencing. Youths between the ages of fourteen and sixteen can be detained on an unruly certificate if, in the judgement of a sheriff, they are particularly unruly and should be kept in a more adult centre for twenty-four to forty-eight hours, until such time as they can be transported to a youth detention centre or institution. There were approximately 139 youths certified as 'unruly', housed in such tentative accommodations with adults in

1982. The alleged offences for these youths included housebreaking and theft (46 per cent); assault, murder and attempted murder (16 per cent); and traffic offences (23 per cent). It must be emphasized that youths who are detained with adults are usually in transit to detention centres or Youths Offenders' Institutions, and therefore remain in contact with adult offenders for not more than forty-eight hours.

Conditions of minors in the Youth Offenders' Institutions

As stated above, all age groups mix freely, although youths under the age of sixteen are separated during the hours of compulsory education. (These institutions for the most part house juveniles between fourteen and twenty years of age.) There have been reports that bullying is widespread. The younger inmates tend to be more aggressive than the older ones. The younger the inmate, the more likely he is to present an air of toughness. Threats and extortions are common: many youths run up gambling debts in which tobacco is the standard currency. The problem does not necessarily appear to be one of the older youths dominating the younger ones, but of the aggressive, psychopathic personalities manipulating and dominating those who are more timid and insecure. There has recently been an increase in suicide.

All offenders are accommodated in single rooms, and each room is sufficiently furnished. All young offenders (up to the age of sixteen) are required to attend educational classes. The medical and nutritional programmes appear to be adequate.

South Africa

Scope of the report

This report deals with children who are under the age of eighteen, even though a person is not considered an adult in South Africa until he reaches the age of twenty-one years. Paradoxically, however, the age of criminal responsibility in South Africa is seven. Any minor who has reached his seventh birthday at the time an offence occurs may be imprisoned. Nevertheless, in practice seven to fifteen-year-old minors are rarely incarcerated. Such convicted minors are usually placed with their parents or in institutions designed specifically for minors. There are, however, exceptional cases where a

minor has been a repeat offender, or the seriousness of the crime is
such that he is imprisoned as early as the age of seven.

Juvenile delinquency and relevant legislation

With the advent of the majority white National Party Government in
1948, racial segregation and the oppression of the majority black
population evolved. Apartheid regulates and controls every aspect of
black life in South Africa. This control and its effect on the arrest and
detention of black children and adults was clearly demonstrated with
the implementation of the 'Pass Laws and Influx Control'. At birth,
each child is classified as either white, coloured or black. The 'Pass
Laws' require each black minor, upon reaching his sixteenth
birthday, to obtain and be in possession of a pass. Any black found
not to be in possession of his pass can be accused of having
committed a felonious offence.

It has been argued that apartheid with its negative effects such as
unemployment, poverty, insufficient education, emotional deprivation and family problems, encourages people to disrespect the legal
institutions and turn to a life of crime. Many of those who turn to
crime are minors. A survey of juvenile cases in 1981 showed that 70.6
per cent of juvenile convictions were for theft. Most of the children
were from socially disrupted families and 94 per cent were black.

Mixing of juvenile and adult prisoners

As stated above, a person in South Africa is a juvenile until the age of
twenty-one, so cells may house any juvenile aged seven to twenty-one.
As far as possible, juveniles sentenced to imprisonment are to be kept
from hardened prisoners. This is not always possible, and hardened
criminals and gang members in the eighteen to twenty-one-year-old
age-group often constitute as great a danger to young offenders as an
adult criminal would.

The following surveys indicate the general status of minors in
prisons in South Africa. Although the chart deals with minors up to
eighteen years old, in reality eighteen to twenty-one-year-olds are
housed in the same institutions.

Number of children in prisons

Replying to questions from the white official opposition party in

Table 17 Unsentenced juveniles in prison 17 July 1983*

Age in years	Offence	No.	Total for age group	White M	White F	Coloured M	Coloured F	Asian M	Asian F	African M	African F
10 to under 11	Economic	1	1							1	
	Violent										
	Other										
11 to under 12	Economic	4	7			3					1
	Violent	2				2					
	Other	1									1
12 to under 13	Economic	6	12			5				1	
	Violent	4				2				2	
	Other	2				2					
13 to under 14	Economic	14	20			9				5	
	Violent	2				2					
	Other	4								2	2
14 to under 15	Economic	35	51			20				15	
	Violent	11				7				4	
	Other	5		1		2				2	
15 to under 16	Economic	60	106			34	1			24	1
	Violent	37		2	23	1				11	
	Other	9				3	2			4	

Table 17 (*continued*)

16 to under 17	Economic	102		5		44	2	50	1
	Violent	70	191	2		35	1	32	1
	Other	19				9	1	7	
Other					1		1		
17 to under 18	Economic	168		9		62	1	73	23
	Violent	130	355	3		79	3	45	
	Other	57		3		10	9	34	3
							1		
Under 18 (totals)	Economic	389				353	21	312	33
	Violent	257							
	Other	97							
			743	23		374	1		1
Grand totals			743	23		374	1	345	33

Summary: 743 unsentenced juveniles were in prison; 96.9 per cent were black and of these: 51.9 per cent were coloureds and 47.97 per cent African; 92.6 per cent were males and 7.4 per cent females; 52.4 per cent were economic crimes. 34.6 per cent violent crimes and 13 per cent other.

* These figures do not include children held in police cells.

Table 18   Sentenced juveniles in prison 17 July 1983

Age in years	Offence	No.	Total for age group	White M	White F	Coloured M	Coloured F	Asian M	Asian F	African M	African F
14 to under 15	Economic	1								1	
	Violent	2								2	
	Other	2	5			1				1	
15 to under 16	Economic	9				3				6	
	Violent	11				5				6	
	Other	7	27			1				4	
16 to under 17	Economic	85			2	28	1	1		52	1
	Violent	67			2	27	1			37	
	Other	14	166			3				11	
17 to under 18	Economic	526		8		248	1	2		247	20
	Violent	416		7		145	3	3		255	3
	Other	87	1,029			19	2			41	25
Under 18 (totals)	Economic	621		19	0	480	8	6	0	663	51
	Violent	496									
	Other	110	1,227								
Grand totals			1,227	19		488		6		714	

Summary: 40.9 per cent were coloured and 59.1 per cent Africans; 95.2 were male and 4.8 per cent female; 50.6 per cent were for economic crimes, 40.4 per cent violent crimes and 9 per cent other.

Table 19   Children admitted to prison with their mothers

	Males	*Females*	*Total*
		(1 July 1982–30 June 1983)	
White	6	6	12
Coloured	109	152	261
Asian	0	0	0
African	1,254	1,403	2,657
Total	1,369	1,561	2,930
		30 June 1983	
White	1	0	1
Coloured	13	19	32
Asian	0	0	0
African	90	115	205
Total	104	134	238

Parliament, the Minister of Justice supplied information on children (under the age of eighteen years) in South African prisons, for September 1983, shown in Tables 17, 18 and 19.

Conditions in prisons

Cells comply with minimal standards relating to space, ventilation and general health requirements. Single cells should accommodate one person only, but often as many as three people are placed in a cell. Exercise is usually from thirty minutes to one hour daily. There is a dietary programme established by the government, although ex-prisoners state that in actuality the race of the prisoner determines his dietary intake.

A prisoner may consult with his lawyer, but the conditions for lawyer visitation are often regulated by the prison warden. A prisoner may be tried and punished for an infraction of any of the prison rules and regulations. Punishment is at the discretion of the prison warden, and may entail deprivation of one or more meals per day, corporal punishment, solitary confinement or a combination of all of these.

Spain

Scope of this report

According to Spanish law, the age of majority is twenty-one. Adolescents between the ages of sixteen and twenty-one are held to be criminally responsible, although such minors must never be incarcerated with inmates over twenty-one years old. Minors aged sixteen to twenty-one are usually sent to a juvenile facility, though on occasion they are sent to an adult institution.

Situations where minors and adults are detained together

Since the Spanish Penal Code classifies sixteen and seventeen-year-olds as criminally responsible, minors in this category always find themselves unseparated from eighteen, nineteen and twenty-year-olds. This does not cause any apparent problems, although the mixing of sixteen and twenty-year-olds could conceivably create a situation for physical and psychological abuse and exploitation of the younger prisoners. In 1984, there were approximately 290 minors aged sixteen to seventeen housed with older inmates of eighteen, nineteen and twenty in Spanish prisons. Of these 290 minors, 81 per cent were incarcerated for heroin addiction; seventy were serving sentences for theft, in addition to heroin convictions. Fifteen per cent of the minors interviewed indicated that they would prefer to be incarcerated with adults. Most of this group indicated they had other (adult) family members in the prison. More than 50 per cent had prior arrests; and some 20 per cent had previously served time in prison.

   Minors under the age of sixteen are rarely detained in adult prisons. They are usually placed in protective custody with their parents. Particularly recalcitrant minors under sixteen are often sent to reformatories designed specifically to reform and rehabilitate them.

Conditions in prisons where minors are incarcerated

The facilities in the institutions which house sixteen to twenty-one-year olds were found to be adequate. There are several inmates per cell. Each inmate, however, has a separate bed. There are common bathrooms, as well as the shared use of a cooker and refrigerator. Meals are served daily, although parents often bring food for the minors to prepare.

There are educational programmes through the third grade. Upon completion of the third grade, a minor may be allowed to attend classes outside the prison compound. There are no provisions for vocational training in the adolescent units. Psychological, medical and dental programmes are reportedly sufficient.

Minor females in prison with adult females; infants born in prison

There are three women's prisons in Spain, located in Madrid, Barcelona and Valencia. There are also separate facilities for women and adolescent girls attached to some of the men's prisons. There is no indication that adolescent females are separated in any way from their adult counterparts, although women and girls are separated from men in every case. At the time this researcher visited Spanish prisons (during 1984), there were forty-eight infants under the age of five residing in prisons with their mothers.

Many mothers opt to turn their young infants over to guardians or foster parents because dietary plans in the prisons are not designed to afford an infant proper nutrition. The sanitary conditions are also not conducive to child-rearing. There is a shortage of medical and dental facilities, and pre-school programmes are woefully inadequate.

Switzerland

Scope of the report

The data included in this report is inconclusive due to the different reporting systems in the various cantons of Switzerland. However, the Federal Statistics Office is planning to compile statistics on the detention of minors, in collaboration with the Swiss Society for Penal Law.

According to Swiss penal law, no person under the age of eighteen is ever to be imprisoned with adults. This law is based on the assumption that rehabilitation is more effective when minors are separated from adult prisoners. The New Swiss Penal Reform for minors instituted in 1971, states that there are four distinct kinds of institutions: institutions for vocational training; educational institutions; therapeutic institutions and reformatories. Throughout most of Switzerland, the educational institution is the basic form of rehabilitative treatment for minors under the age of eighteen.

A minor who has reached seventeen and who is particularly recalcitrant may be placed in an institution for vocational training or a therapeutic institution. If a minor proves to be intolerable at the educational, vocational and therapeutic institutions, he may be transferred to a reformatory or an adult prison. In actuality, however, there are no reformatories in Switzerland established specifically for minors. Swiss penal law allows for minors to be temporarily transferred to a penal facility, pending construction of the reformatories. It is for this reason that minors under the age of eighteen are sometimes incarcerated with adults.

Minors incarcerated with adults

A 1983 statistical study prepared by the Federal Department of Justice indicated that five adolescent boys were incarcerated in prison with adults in Switzerland. These adolescents were between the ages of fifteen and eighteen. There were no female prisoners under the age of eighteen housed in adult female facilities during the 1981–3 period. These statistics, however, only pertain to those minors in prison on whom sentences have been imposed. They do not include minors who may be housed with adults for preventive detention or minors held in custody as a result of administrative decisions based on civil law.

When the New Penal Reform for minors was enacted in 1971, it provided that the reformatories and all other specialized facilities for minors were to be completed by 1 January 1984. However, many of the reforms mandated by the Act (including the building of reformatories) have not been implemented. A number of Juvenile Judges believe that it was unrealistic for the legislature to call for highly specialized institutions intended for different categories of minors (such as those labelled exceptionally difficult or intolerable). These judges expressed the wish for a revised Penal Code to be drawn up that is better adapted to modern concepts of the judicial protection of youth. Such concepts are defined by the Congresses of the International Association of Magistrates dealing with Youth and the Family (l'Association internationale des magistrats de la jeunesse et de la famille).

Thailand

Scope of the report

In Thailand, the law provides for separate judicial procedures and sentencing for children and adults. Because of this, the possiblity of minors being incarcerated with adults is limited. There are, however, occasions where the separation of minors from adults is not possible.

The Thai law makes a distinction between 'children' and 'youth'. A person betwee the ages of seven and fourteen is considered a 'child'; a person between the ages of seven and fourteen is considered a 'child'; a Persons in this latter age group are more likely to be incarcerated with adults.

Children and youth incarcerated with adults

Although Thai law stipulates that children are never to be jailed with adults, there are several ways in which this frequently happens:

(1) police custody: during an investigating process, normally held at a public station house, minors are routinely put in the same cells as adults, even though such mixing is expressly forbidden by law. In areas where there are no juvenile courts, there is little pretext of separating minors and adults in the station house. In Bangkok, however, because of the availability of juvenile centres, minors and adults are separated in the station houses;

(2) in prisons: both at the provincial prisons and central prisons minors are often kept in the same cell with adult inmates. In cases where they do not share a cell with an adult, they are nevertheless often in contact with adults throughout the day. No attempt is made at the provincial prisons to separate sixteen and seventeen-year-olds from the adult population. Such minors are routinely found at the central prisons. Usually they have been convicted of committing felonious offences, and are treated no differently than their adult counterparts. There are also cases where minors under sixteen are housed in cells with adults.

According to the statistics of the Central Juvenile Court, in 1982, a total of 324 juveniles between the ages of seven and fourteen were found guilty of committing an offence. Among the fourteen to eighteen year olds, 1,005 were convicted. Of this total of 2,329 juveniles, 193 were girls and 2,136 were boys. More than half of these offences were theft and drug-related infractions.

Children incarcerated with their mothers

Children are often kept in jail because their mothers are inmates. Legally, a minor may remain in prison with its mother until the age of six, and both mother and child must stay in the same cell. According to the data available to this researcher, in 1982 there were 124 children (mostly infants) incarcerated with their mothers in jails and prisons throughout the country., The majority of these children were in the Bangkok Detention Centre for females. Some were born in prison.

Living conditions in prisons

Police detention centres, provincial prisons and central prisons in Thailand are extremely substandard. At the typical police station, one toilet (located outside) is provided for as many as eighty prisoners. The toilet is usually unsanitary and foul-smelling. There are two meals served daily. Parents often bring food to their imprisoned children.

According to the survey carried out by *The Nation* in May 1984, life in Thai jails and prisons is substantially lower than the standard required by the United Nations. Prisoners are packed in jails 20 per cent above their capacity. Financial constraints have also caused problems of inadequacy in medical care.

United States

Scope of the report

Most of the information provided and conclusions drawn in this report are based on statistical studies which have been conducted in the United States. There was some difficulty collecting data, due to the different reporting systems that exist in various states, as well as some requirements of confidentiality. In addition, the definition with regard to what constitutes a 'juvenile' varies from state to state.

The Juvenile Justice and Delinquency Prevention Act, adopted in 1974, calls for each state to develop plans to 'remove all non-offenders (dependent and neglected youth), and all status offenders (youth who have committed non-criminal offences) from secure detention or correctional facilities.' This act also required that juveniles and adults may not be detained together, and that any juveniles presently (1974) incarcerated in adult prisons be removed immediately. Any state found not to be in compliance with the Act was to be held ineligible to receive juvenile justice funds. The act was amended in 1980 to provide that any state receiving such funds was to keep juvenile and adult inmates separated by 'sight and sound'. Several states have subsequently adopted legislation going beyond this amendment prohibiting the placing of juveniles and adults in the same prison. However, despite the legal provisions requiring the separation of imprisoned adults and juveniles, there are still many juveniles confined in jails with adults throughout the United States.

Juveniles in adult prisons

A study conducted by the Law Enforcement Assistance Administration in 1970 concluded that prisons throughout the country were in a deplorable condition. Particular attention was paid to the detention of juveniles, both in adult prisons and in facilities established only for youth. A total of 449 prisons in nine different states were visited, and many cases were found of either juveniles in adult prisons or adult inmates in the juvenile section of the jail (usually trustees performing staff functions). This usually occurred as a result of understaffing in the prisons, but the negative impact on juveniles incarcerated together with adult criminals cannot be overlooked. A survey conducted in 1976 estimated that 500,000 juveniles were held in adult prisons in the United States in 1975. Of that number, the survey indicated that:

(1) 9 per cent were charged with committing crimes against persons;
(2) 18 per cent were status offenders;
(3) 4 per cent had committed no crime;
(5) 9 per cent were thirteen years of age or younger;
(5) 83 per cent were male; 17 per cent were female; and
(6) 81 per cent were white; 19 per cent were non-white.

A separate survey was recently undertaken by the National Centre on Institutions and Alternatives, to which ten states responded. In these states, a total of 94,173 juveniles were found to be incarcerated in adult jails and lock-ups over a twelve-month period between 1982 and 1983. Although this data pertains to only ten of the fifty states, the National Center of Institutions and Alternatives considers these figures to be representative of the country as a whole. It must nevertheless be borne in mind that, as pointed out above, the age definition of 'juvenile' differs between states. Each of the ten states that reported provided statistics according to what is considered to be a 'juvenile' in that particular sense.

Finally, it is important to note that these statistics are especially alarming in view of the fact that the suicide rate of juveniles who are incarcerated in prisons has been found to be seven times higher than the corresponding rate of children who are placed in juvenile facilities.

West Bank

Scope of the report

This report concerns only those minors living in the area of the West Bank which was occupied by Israel in 1967. This area has a total population of approximately 750,000 Palestinian Arabs. The report does not cover the additional 450,000 Palestinian Arabs living in the Gaza Strip, which has also been under Israeli administration since 1967.

The researcher noted that the incarceration of minors in the West Bank and Gaza Strip is unique, quite different from that faced by children anywhere else in the world. This is due to the unusual and extremely volatile political situation in this region. There is a widespread feeling of frustration and intimidation as a result of the Israeli authorities' actions aimed at crushing the Palestinian armed resistance to occupation. The children thus often find themselves in violation of the restrictive military laws, which prohibit nearly every form of expression of Palestinian patriotism or nationalism. It is fair to state, therefore, that most minor offenders in adult facilities in the West Bank are political prisoners. There is a distinction made between political prisoners and those criminals incarcerated for committing common law crimes. In East Jerusalem, common law criminals who are minors are subject to the provisions of Israeli law concerning juvenile delinquents. In the West Bank, the military regulations instituted after 1967 are applicable, although Jordanian laws pertaining to common law crimes hold concurrent jurisdiction with the Israeli military courts.

The information in this report is gathered from secondary sources, including interviews with lawyers and ex-prisoners. In addition, thirty-four responses to a questionnaire circulated in the West Bank provide further data. Statistics from Israel (and particularly the occupied territories) on the status of prisoners are confidential. A request to visit penal institutions on the West Bank was not granted by the Israeli authorities.

At the six penal facilities surveyed in the West Bank, minors constitute well over one-third of the roughly 2,400 prisoners. This number does not include the female minors who are incarcerated with adult women in the West Bank's female prison (El Maskobia). Of the minors sampled in this study, 85 per cent were being detained without charges. Minors can be held without charges for eighteen days. However, to intimidate a minor and to stifle his political activism, the authorities often arrest him, then release him on the eighteenth day, and re-arrest him if his political activism continues.

Minors in contact with adult prisoners

Of the minors sampled, 79 per cent slept in rooms with adults; 41 per cent stated that they were in contact with adults at all times. There are occasionally incidents between minors and adults, but these incidents are less common that those typically found in prisons. The explanation for this is attributed to the high proportion of political prisoners, who feel that they are in prison for a worthy cause and live up to a different moral standard. This is especially true of the adult prisoners, who feel a moral reponsibility to educate and guide the minors.

Living conditions in West Bank prisons

Many reports have highlighted the overcrowding that exists in the prisons. Minors are not provided with beds, but are given a sponge mat and blankets and sleep on the floor. Only one of the six prisons had sinks in the cells. In all prisons, inmates use either a pail or an uncovered toilet. All personal items of prisoners are confiscated by the authorities.

Israeli military orders relating to prisoners in the West Bank state that there should be adequate health care, sufficient dietary intake and sanitary living conditions. However, inmates complain that health care is woefully inadequate and that the food is insufficient in quantity and lacks variety. Anemia, ulcers and other dietary-related illnesses are reportedly common among prisoners.

There are no specific educational or recreational programmes. The entire day, except for two exercise periods of one hour each, is spent in the cell. Prisoners are allowed to read three newspapers, as well as books which are approved by the prison commander. Adult inmates often teach the minors during free-time periods allotted to educational activities.

Yugoslavia

Scope of the report

In Yugoslavia, children under the age of fourteen are considered too young to be criminally responsible and are never imprisoned. There are two groups of youth who are criminally responsible: 'Minors' (those aged sixteen to eighteen) and 'younger minors' (those aged fourteen to sixteen). Those can be incarcerated in the same institution with adults, according to the law. However, the Criminal Code specifically states that minors are to be incarcerated as a last resort. When minors are incarcerated, they must be separated from adults, and this measure should be taken essentially as an educational, rehabilitative measure. The 1981 Yugoslav Penal Code states that:

> Within the framework of the general purpose of penal sanctions, the purpose of educational measures and juvenile imprisonment is to ensure the education, re-education and correct development of minors, by securing protection and assistance to juvenile criminal offenders, by supervision over them, by their vocational training and by the development of their sense of responsibility . . .

In practice, however, minors are often incarcerated with adults throughout Yugoslavia. This is particularly true for minors held in detention while awaiting trial, and for minors held for less serious offences.

The mixing of minors and adults in Yugoslav prisons or in preventive custody

Adolescent girls between the ages of fourteen and eighteen are always imprisoned with adult women, as there is no specialized institution for them. Moreover, there are no facilities at the women's prisons providing for the separation of the adolescent girls from the adults. There are two specialized institutions for minor boys (fourteen to eighteen), but both of these institutions house adult men as well, and there is no separation according to age.

At the time of the survey, between 300 and 500 minors were detained in jail during the criminal process; in 60 per cent of the cases, they were detained for less than two months and 5 per cent of these minors were kept for longer than six months. Though the legislation states that detained minors are to be separated from adults, there is no separation of minors from adults in practice. Several proposals that courts ensure the separation of minors from the adult population have not yielded fruitful results.

Some 20 per cent of minors arrested are detained in pre-trial custody for approximately three to ten months. These minors are detained in the same jails as adults, and are generally not separated from the adult population.

There exist two juvenile institutions, KPD Celje and KPD Valjevo, although minors are likely to be confined with adults even there. Both of these institutions were built for juveniles (fourteen to eighteen), but 50 per cent of the population is comprised of young adult men, aged eighteen to thirty. There are even some inmates who are more than thirty years of age.

Conditions of the prisons

Almost without exception, the prisons where minors and adults are incarcerated are old and ill-suited for the educational and recreational needs of young inmates. There is a lack of qualified personnel and opportunities for implementing educational programmes are limited. All inmates, including minors, must work in Yugoslav prisons, making education virtually impossible. The educational programme is industrial in nature, qualifying minors for semi-qualified manual labour, at best, upon release.

Zaïre

Scope of the report

The age of criminal responsibility in Zaïre is sixteen. However, the researcher of this report included those persons under the age of eighteen in the analysis. Although there are many prisons throughout Zaïre, four specific prisons were chosen as representative samples. The prisons surveyed and visited were: the Central Prison of Kisangani at Kisangani; the prison of the sub-region of Ituri at Bunia; the prison of the sub-region of Lower Uele at Buta; and the prison of the sub-region of Upper Uele at Isiro.

Minors and infants incarcerated with adults

(1) The Central Prison at Kisangani   During the researcher's visit to Kisangani there was one minor, aged seventeen. He was under preventive detention for murder. He was lodged together with the adults and was in contact with them all the time. Often the adult inmates made use of him as a servant, although it could not be definitively ascertained whether he was coerced or acting voluntarily.

There is a women's ward at Kisangani, although there was no indication of any minor females being incarcerated among the women. There were two women with children. One had two children, aged three and five years. The other mother had a sixteen-month old child.

(2) The Prison at Bunia.   This prison has two sections, one for men and one for women. There are minor males and females at this prison, but no statistics are available. Minors under the age of eighteen and young men share the same sleeping cells, and the daily operation of the prison is carried out without regard to inmates' age. There are cases where minors as young as twelve are housed in the prison, although children below the age of twelve are not permitted to live at Bunia prison.

Adult inmates who attack minors for any reason are severely disciplined. Adults who attempt to squander sweets sent in for the minors by their families are also disciplined. The women's section had five infants during this researcher's visit. There were no available data regarding the number of minor females.

(3) The Prison at Upper Uele at Isiro.   There were no minor male or female prisoners at this prison, nor were there any women with infants.

(4) the Prison of the Lower Uele at Buta. There were no minor males or females at this prison. among the women prisoners, three had infants, all under one year old. The women with babies live under the same conditions as the other women at the unit. No special provisions are made for them.

Conditions in the prisons

The prisons visited were relatively clean, but all of the facilities were old and in a state of ill-repair. Health sanitation and the dietary programmes at each of the institutions were minimal, but seemed adequate to this researcher.

Index

NOTE: *passim* means that the subject so annotated is referred to in scattered passages throughout these pages of text. Page numbers in italics refer to Tables; 'n' indicats that the reference is in a note.

216   *Index*

New Zealand 89
NGO *see* non-governmental
      organizations
Nigeria 29, 33, 53, 55, 61, 73, 85, 86,
      88, 93, 97, 183–5
non-custodial sentencing 127, 128,
      149, 188
non-existence of legal
      representation of children
      103
non-governmental organizations
      (NGO)
   crucial role in investigations 141
   data collected by 39
   documentation of 40, 129
   'mobilization of shame'
      campaigns 67
   Protection of Children group 178
normative action 137–9, 146
Norway 140

Occupied Arab Territories 47
offences, children charged with 13,
      112
ombudsman 140
Ordinances
   Detention Centres 72, 186
   Execution of the Punishment of
      Whipping (1979) 45
   Prison 72
   Training Centres 72
   see also Acts

Paez Indians 40–1, 48n
Pakistan 11, 33, 45, 60, 72, 86, 97,
      112–13, 118, 120, 125, 126,
      185–7
Palestine 47
Paraguay 44–5
parasitism 65
parents
   child suffering through action
      against 37, 38, 44–5, 64, 91–
      102
   children tortured for information
      about 43
   failure to discharge their
      obligations 32

In prison with their children 91–
      3, 152
   separation of 30
   state acts in place of 32
   and welfare support 9
   see also children, Detainee
      Parents' Support
      Committee, family, mother
penal
   Code 65, 88, 119, 153, 171, 178,
      196, 198, 204
   facilities/institutions *see* prisons
   institution funding 113
   procedures 153
   sanctions 50
penal systems 32, 78, 146, 148, 166,
      167
Penal System, Advisory Council
      on 92
People's Union for Civil Liberties
      (PUCL) 42, 48n
Peru 43
planners, ignorance of 139–40
planning 137, 139–40
police
   caution by 149
   custody 47, 68, 104, 124, 199
   Commissioner 81
   detention by 46, 100, 164–5
   enforcement 65
   investigation by 68–9, 105
   can issue certifiates of
      unruliness 88
   powers of 103
   practices of 160–1
   record 149
   should have no powers to detain
      minors 139
   station 120, 182, 200
   use of force by 120, 158
policies
   on babies in prison with their
      mothers 95–7
   concerning mothers and
      children in prison 94
   economic 21
   sentencing 34
   social 21
political